KLEZMER

JOANN SFAR

KLEZMER

Book One: TALES OF THE WILD EAST

Translated by ALEXIS SIEGEL

First Second

NEW YORK & LONDON

To Arthur Haftel, born January 7, 1913, in Bolekhov, Ukraine
To Raoul Sfar, born April 3, 2003, in Paris, France

Joann Sfar, a notorious ganev, presents:

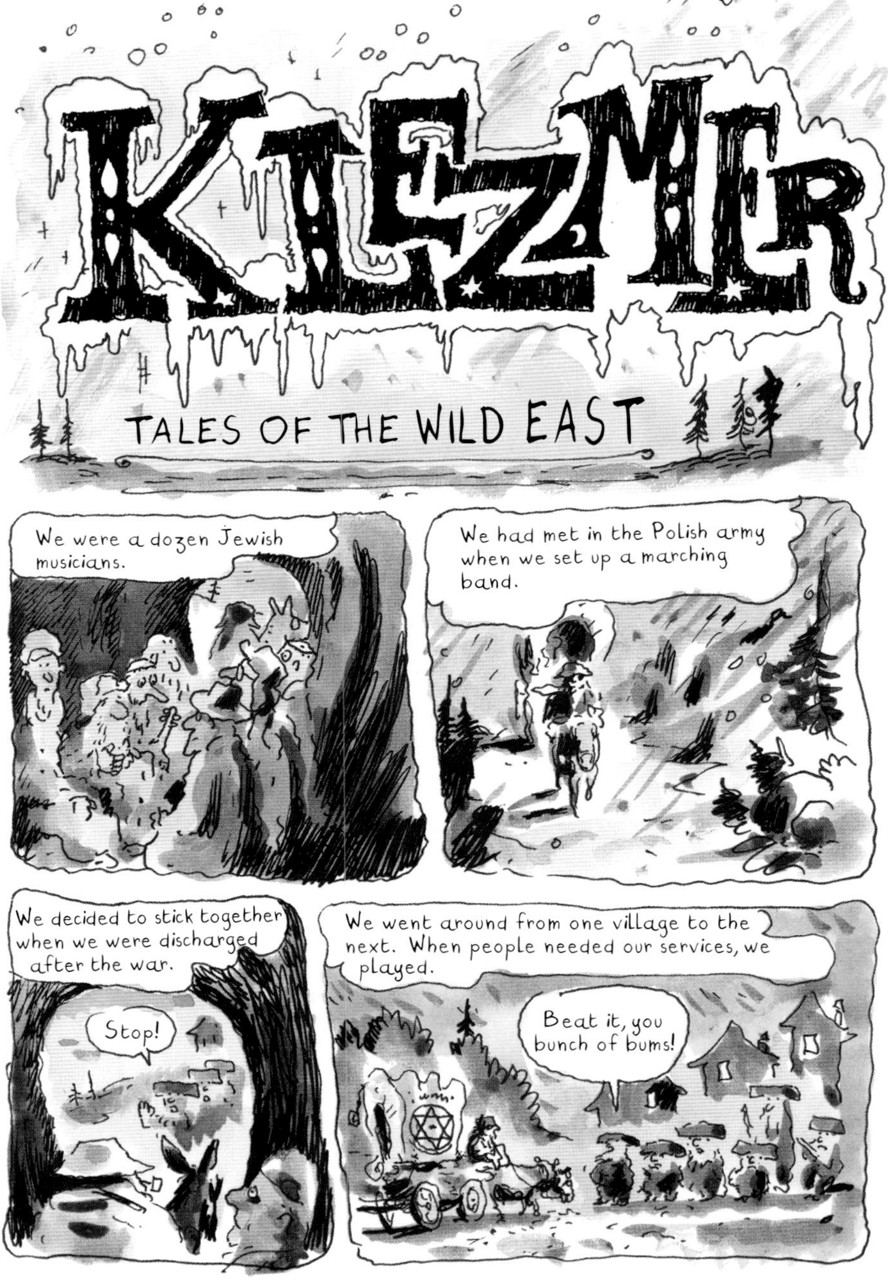
KLEZMER
TALES OF THE WILD EAST
We were a dozen Jewish musicians.
We had met in the Polish army when we set up a marching band.
We decided to stick together when we were discharged after the war.
Stop!
We went around from one village to the next. When people needed our services, we played.
Beat it, you bunch of bums!

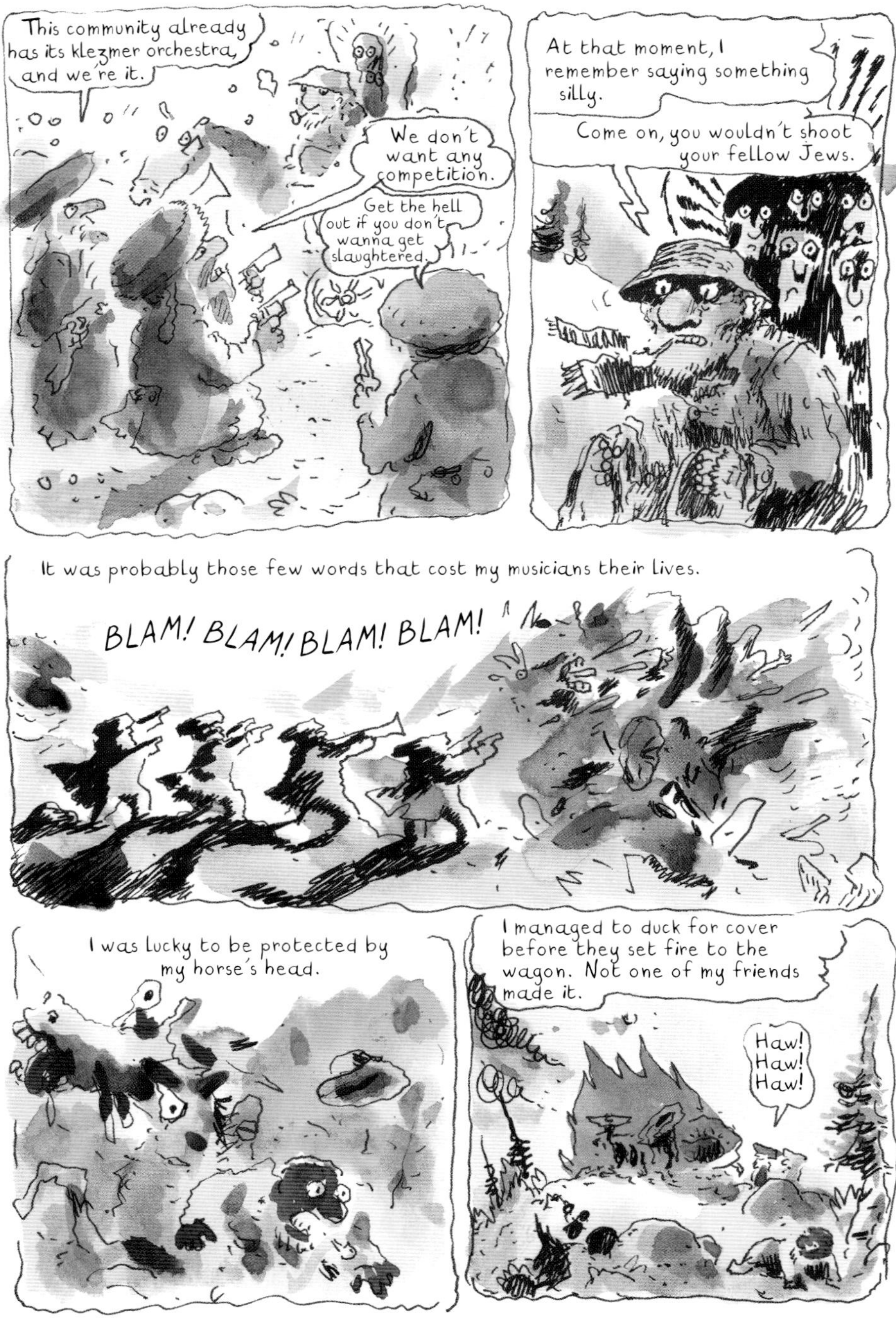
This community already has its klezmer orchestra, and we're it.
We don't want any competition.
Get the hell out if you don't wanna get slaughtered.
At that moment, I remember saying something silly.
Come on, you wouldn't shoot your fellow Jews.
It was probably those few words that cost my musicians their lives.
BLAM! BLAM! BLAM! BLAM!
I was lucky to be protected by my horse's head.
I managed to duck for cover before they set fire to the wagon. Not one of my friends made it.
Haw! Haw! Haw!

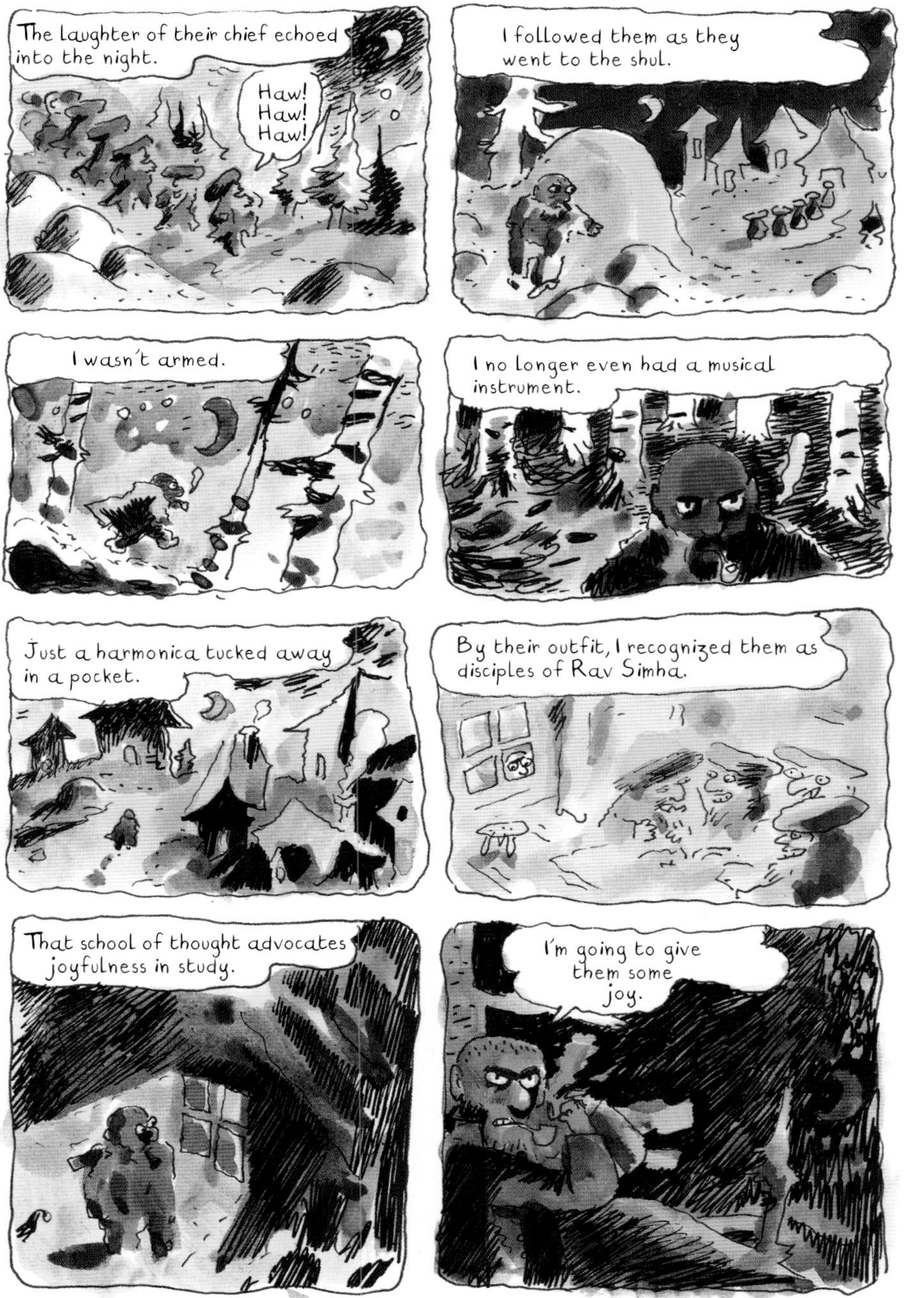
The laughter of their chief echoed into the night.
Haw! Haw! Haw!
I followed them as they went to the shul.
I wasn't armed.
I no longer even had a musical instrument.
Just a harmonica tucked away in a pocket.
By their outfit, I recognized them as disciples of Rav Simha.
That school of thought advocates joyfulness in study.
I'm going to give them some joy.

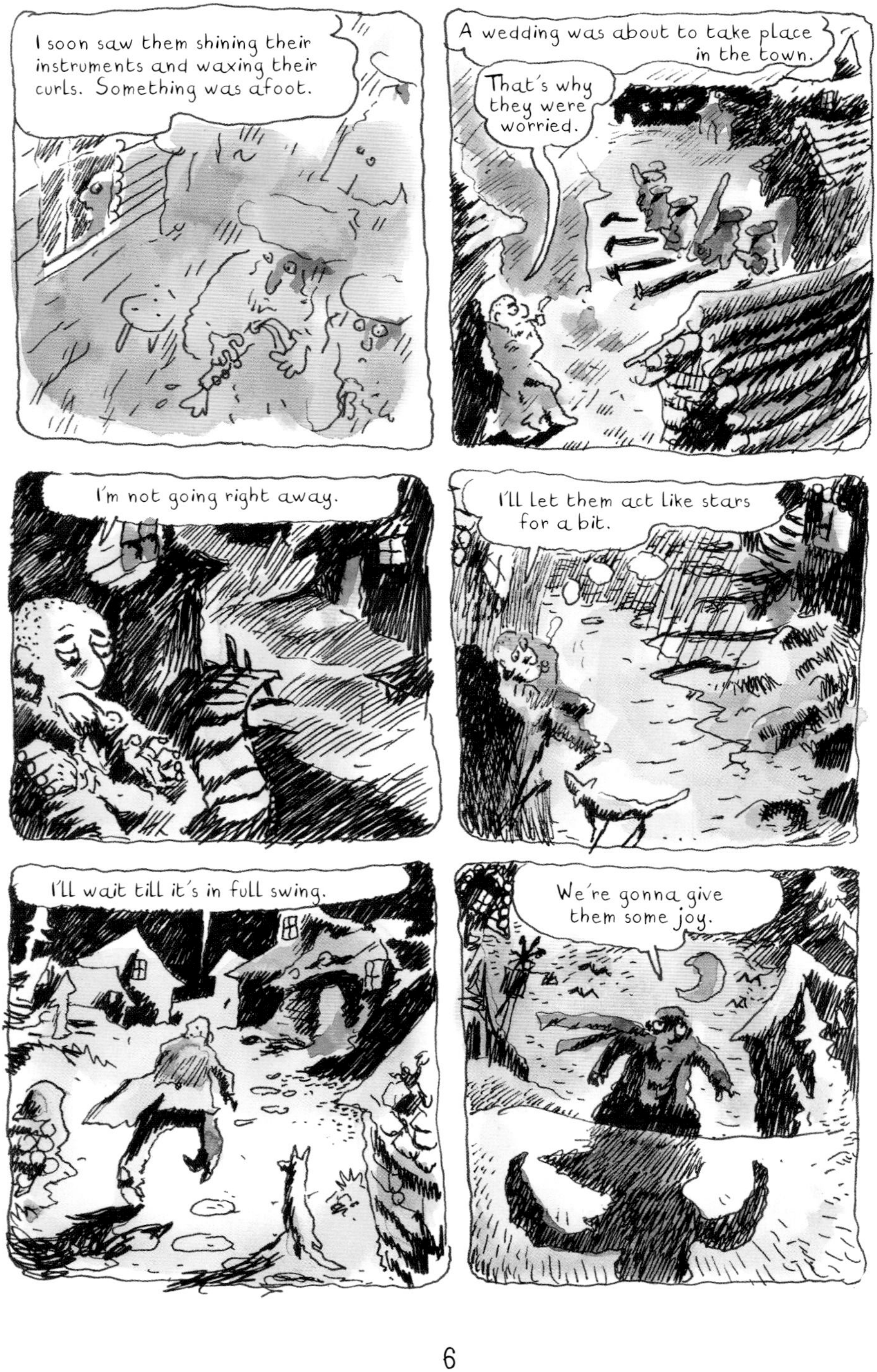
I soon saw them shining their instruments and waxing their curls. Something was afoot.
A wedding was about to take place in the town.
That's why they were worried.
I'm not going right away.
I'll let them act like stars for a bit.
I'll wait till it's in full swing.
We're gonna give them some joy.

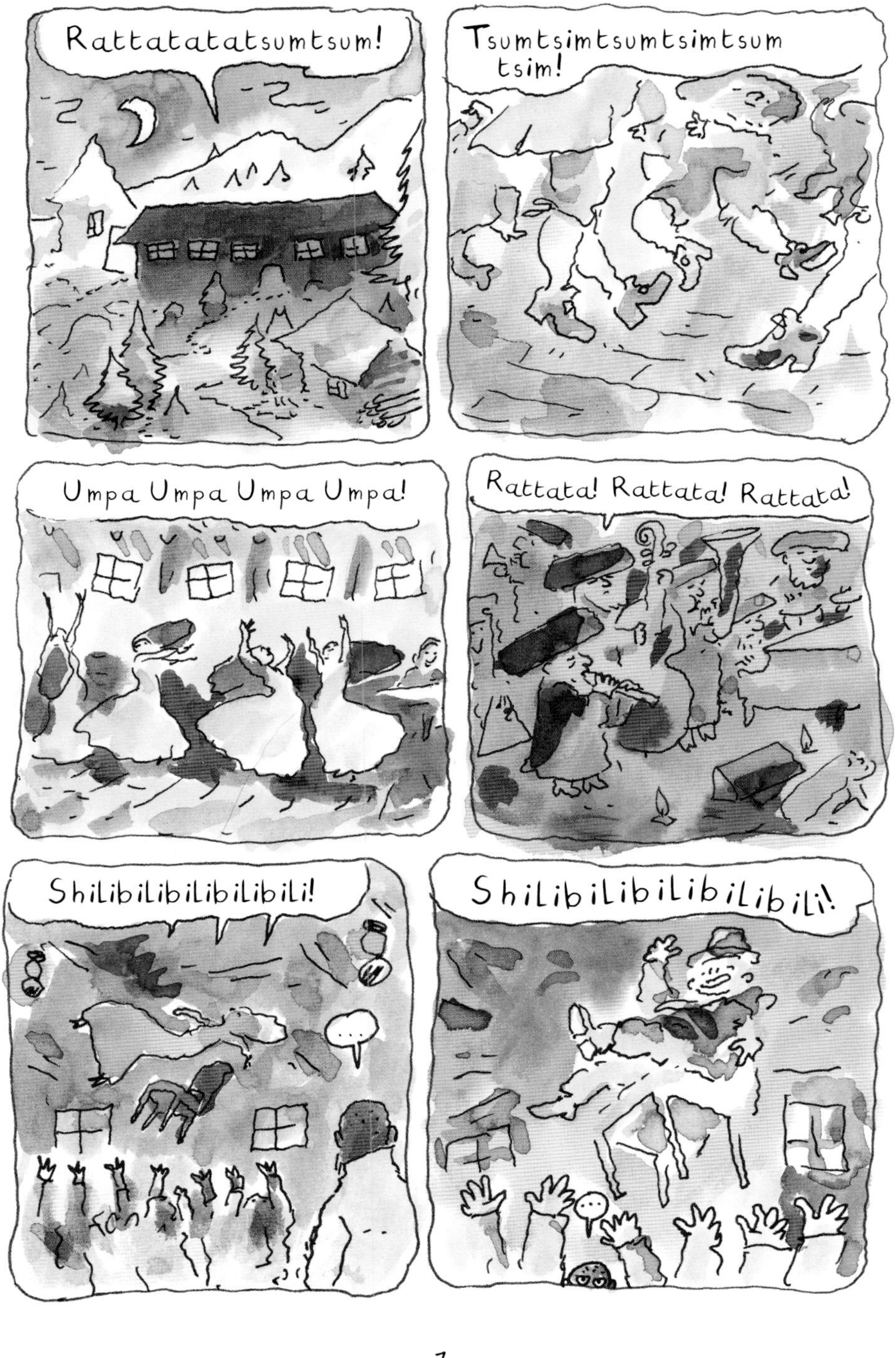
Rattatatatsumtsum!
Tsumtsimtsumtsimtsum tsim!
Umpa Umpa Umpa Umpa!
Rattata! Rattata! Rattata!
Shilibilibilibilibili!
Shilibilibilibilibili!

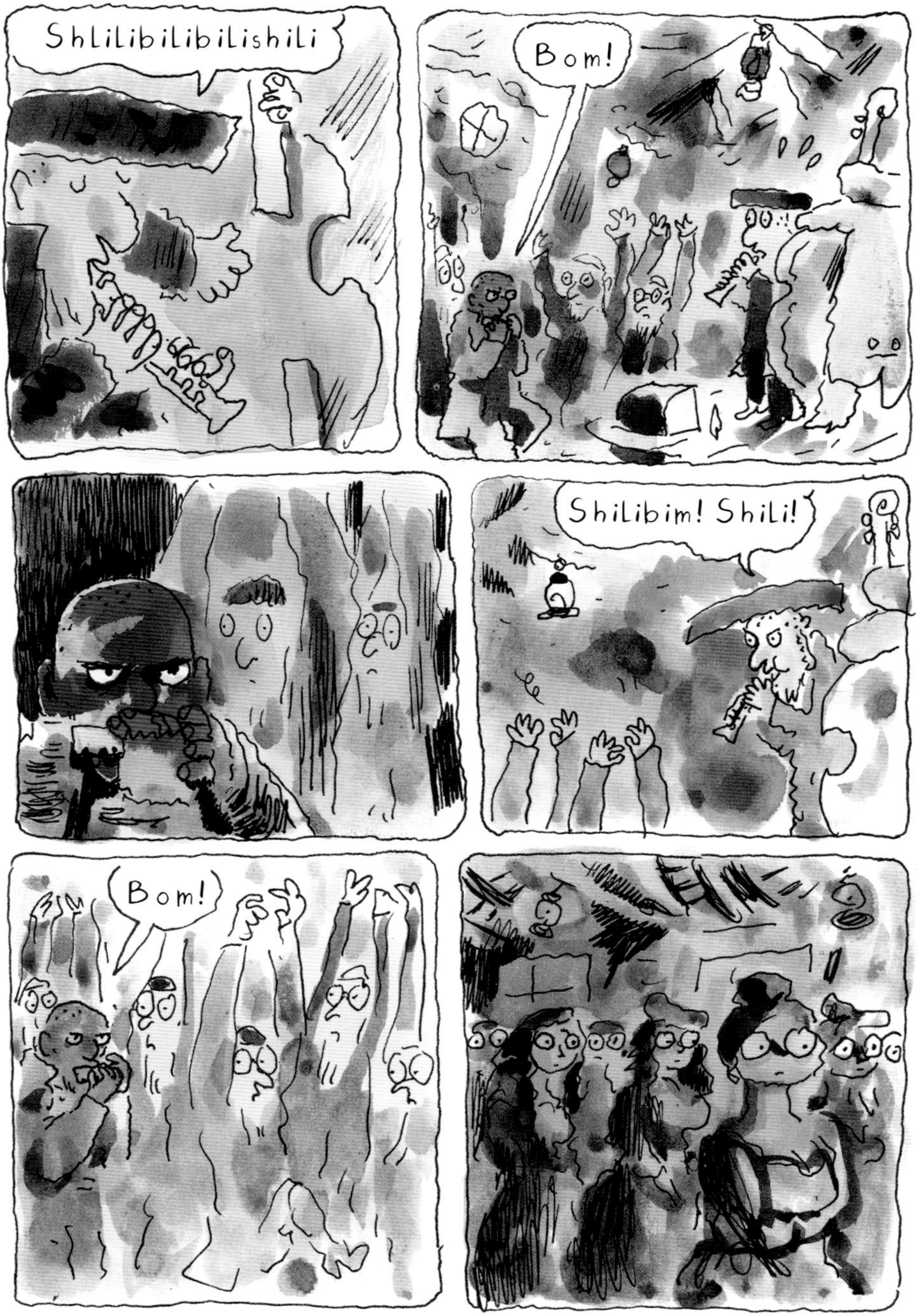
Shlilibilibilishili
Bom!
Shilibim! Shili!
Bom!

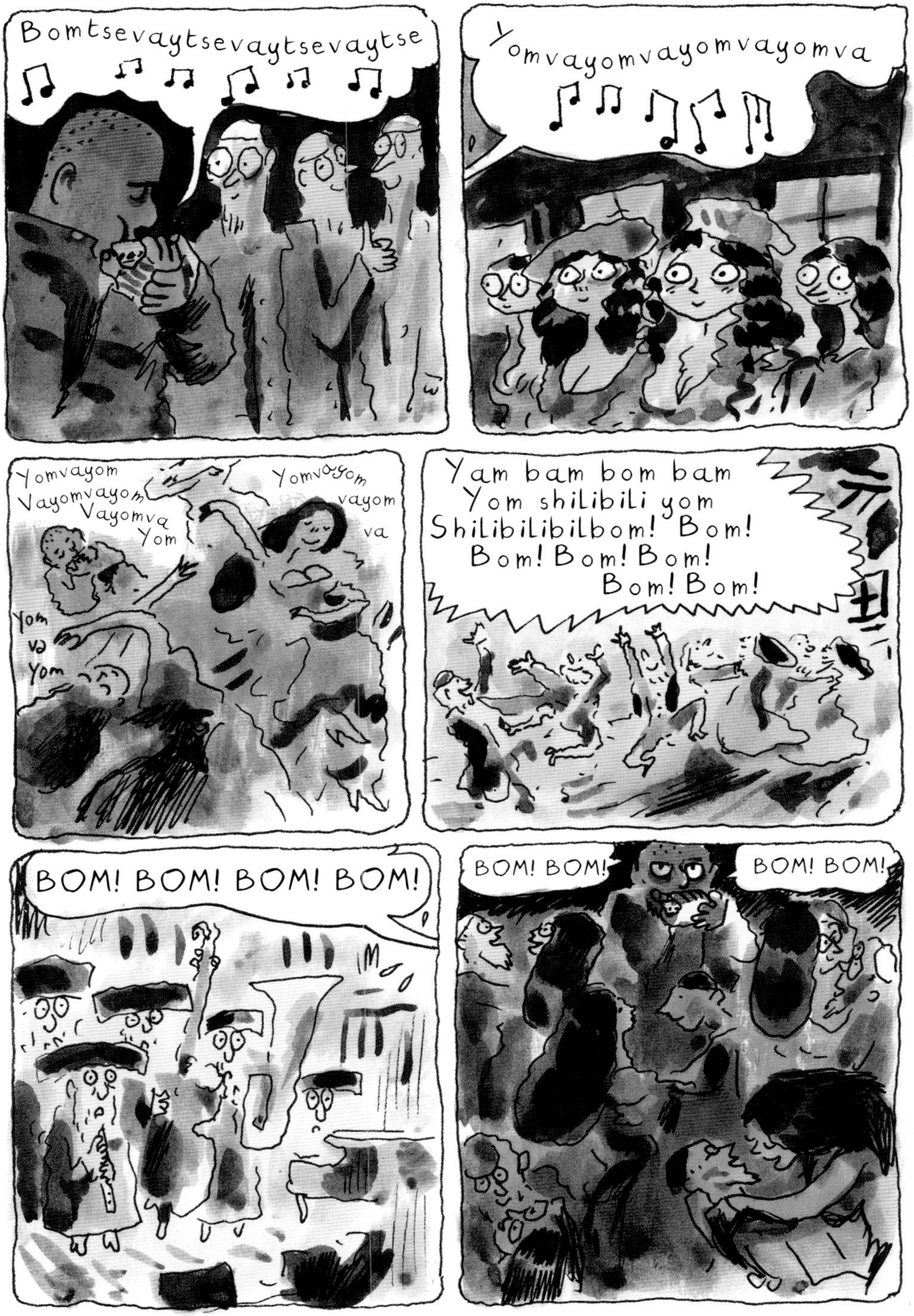
Bomtsevaytsevaytsevaytse
Yomvayomvayomvayomva
Yomvayom
Vayomvayom
Vayomva
Yom
Yomvayom
vayom
va
Yom
va
Yom
Yam bam bom bam
Yom shilibili yom
Shilibilibilbom! Bom!
Bom! Bom! Bom!
Bom! Bom!
BOM! BOM! BOM! BOM!
BOM! BOM!
BOM! BOM!

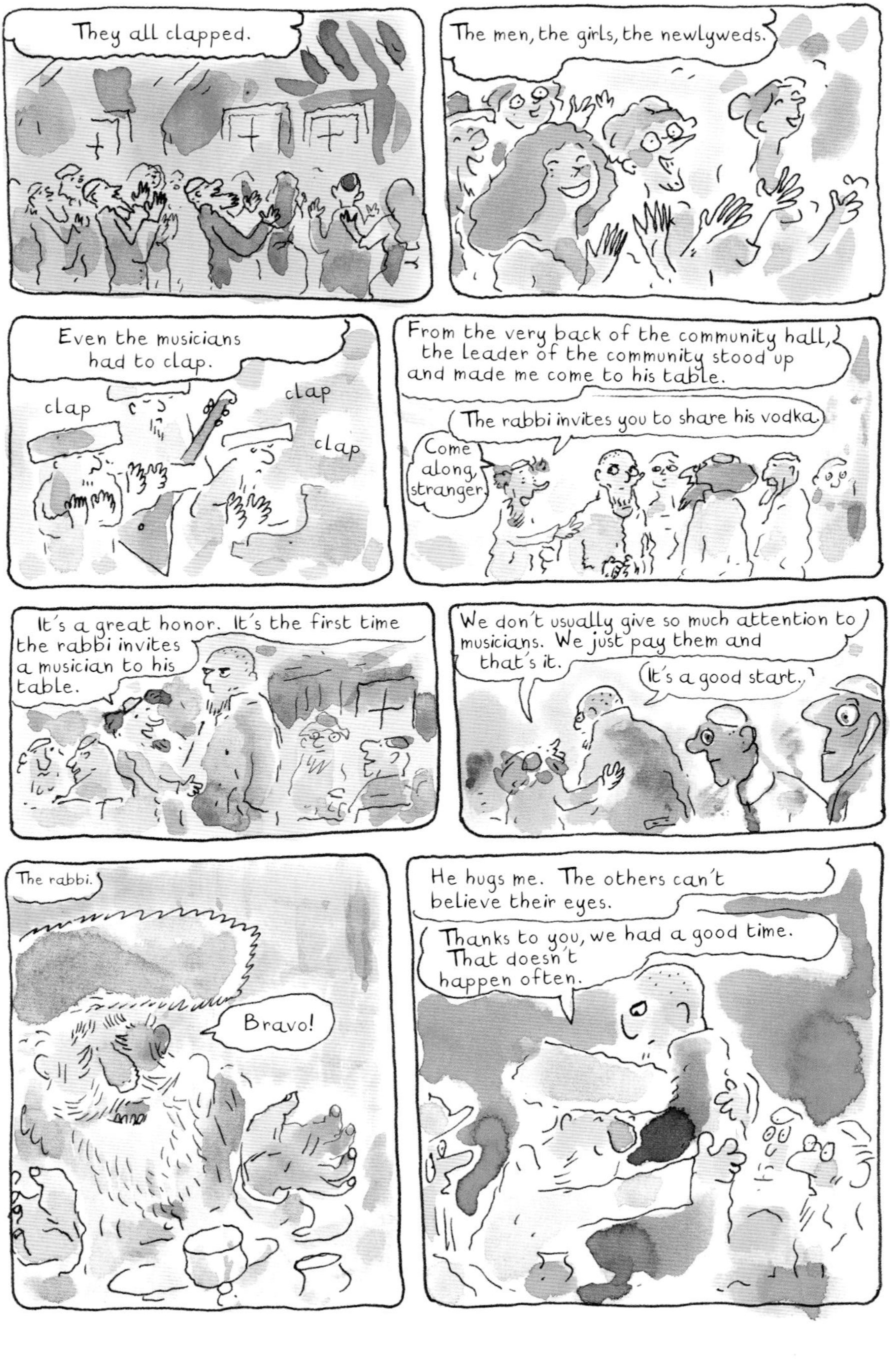
They all clapped.
The men, the girls, the newlyweds.
Even the musicians had to clap.
clap
clap
clap
From the very back of the community hall, the leader of the community stood up and made me come to his table.
The rabbi invites you to share his vodka.
Come along, stranger.
It's a great honor. It's the first time the rabbi invites a musician to his table.
We don't usually give so much attention to musicians. We just pay them and that's it.
It's a good start.
The rabbi.
Bravo!
He hugs me. The others can't believe their eyes.
Thanks to you, we had a good time. That doesn't happen often.

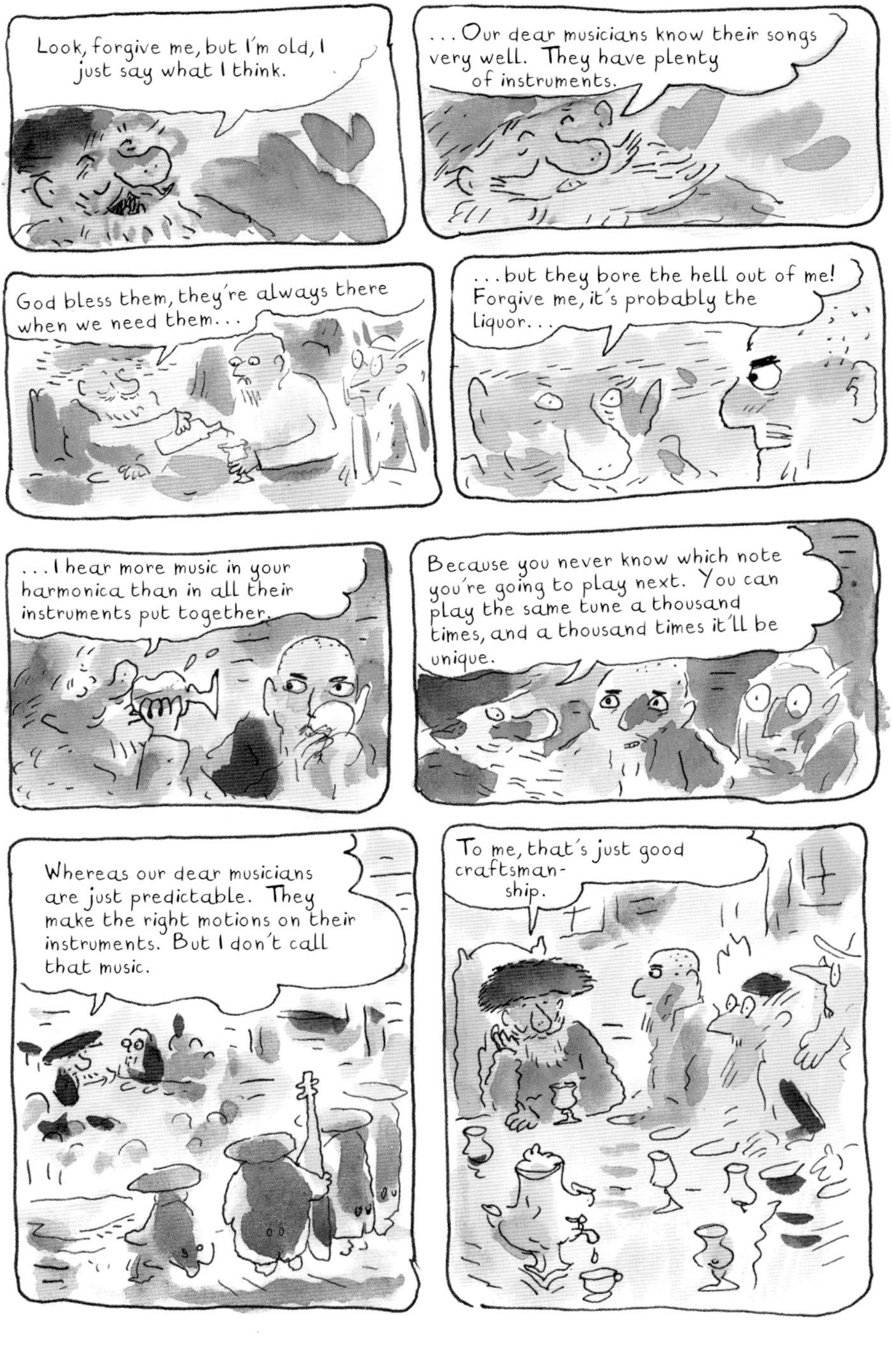
Look, forgive me, but I'm old, I just say what I think.
...Our dear musicians know their songs very well. They have plenty of instruments.
God bless them, they're always there when we need them...
...but they bore the hell out of me! Forgive me, it's probably the liquor...
...I hear more music in your harmonica than in all their instruments put together.
Because you never know which note you're going to play next. You can play the same tune a thousand times, and a thousand times it'll be unique.
Whereas our dear musicians are just predictable. They make the right motions on their instruments. But I don't call that music.
To me, that's just good craftsman-ship.

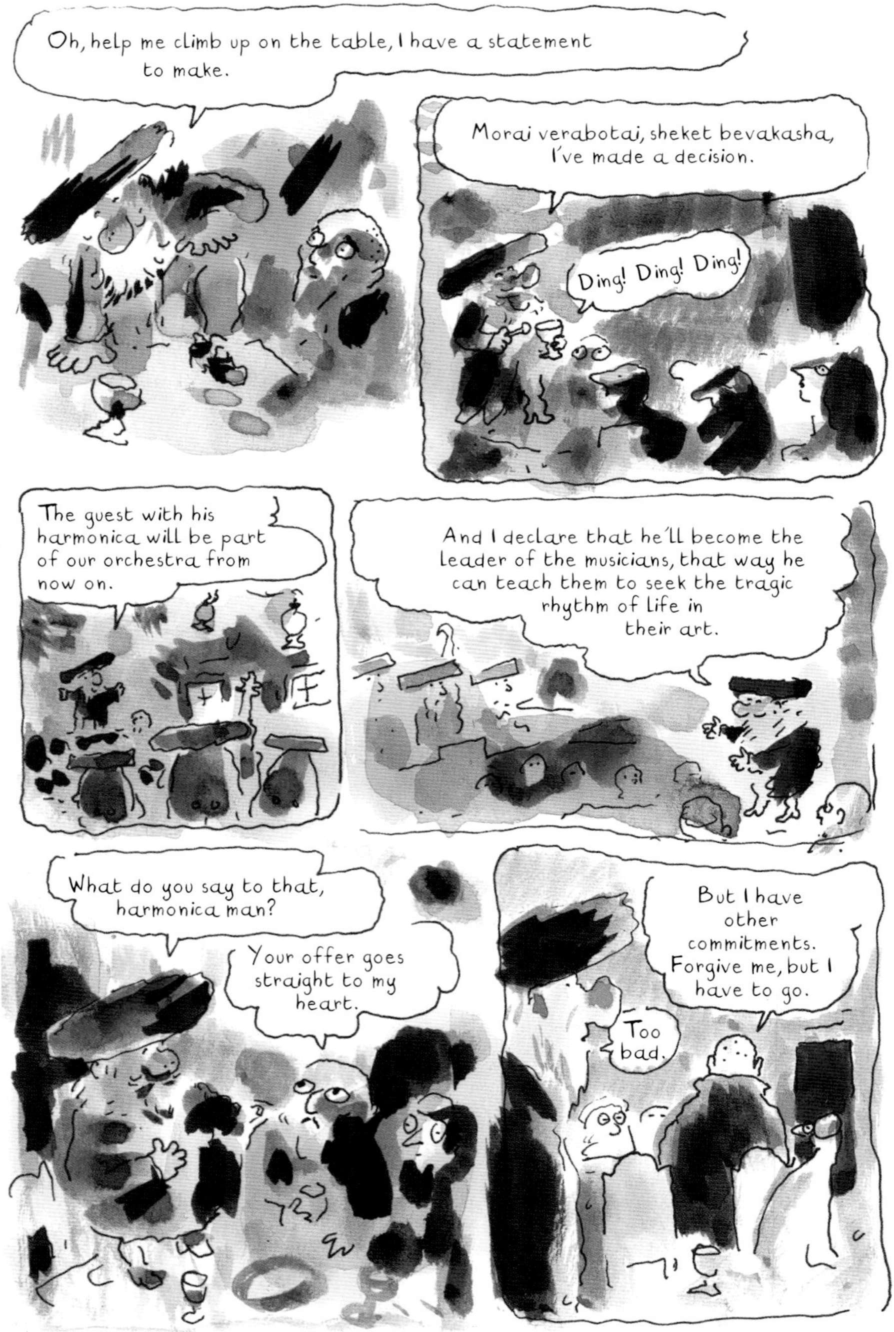
Oh, help me climb up on the table, I have a statement to make.
Morai verabotai, sheket bevakasha, I've made a decision.
Ding! Ding! Ding!
The guest with his harmonica will be part of our orchestra from now on.
And I declare that he'll become the leader of the musicians, that way he can teach them to seek the tragic rhythm of life in their art.
What do you say to that, harmonica man?
Your offer goes straight to my heart.
But I have other commitments. Forgive me, but I have to go.
Too bad.

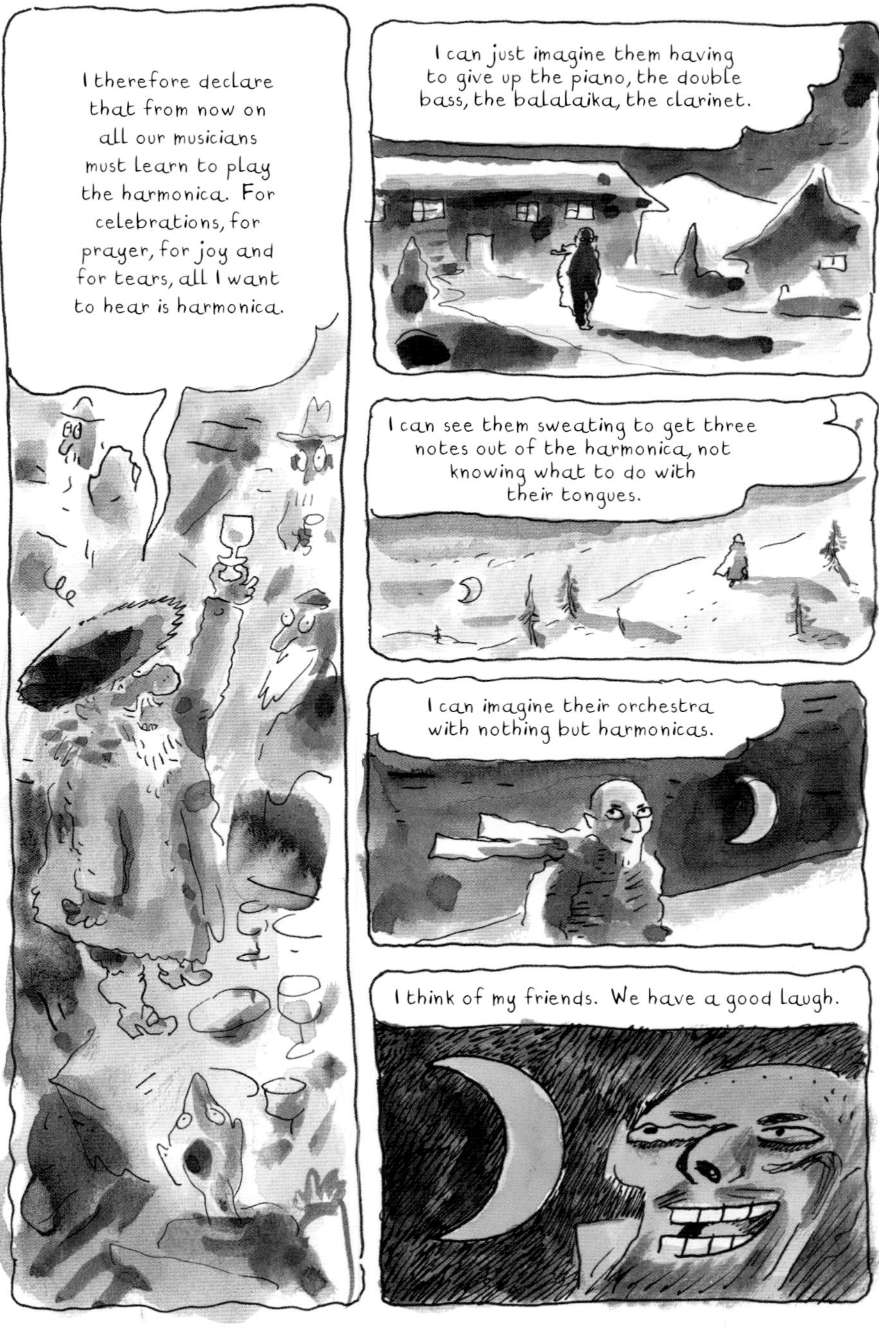

I therefore declare that from now on all our musicians must learn to play the harmonica. For celebrations, for prayer, for joy and for tears, all I want to hear is harmonica.
I can just imagine them having to give up the piano, the double bass, the balalaika, the clarinet.
I can see them sweating to get three notes out of the harmonica, not knowing what to do with their tongues.
I can imagine their orchestra with nothing but harmonicas.
I think of my friends. We have a good laugh.

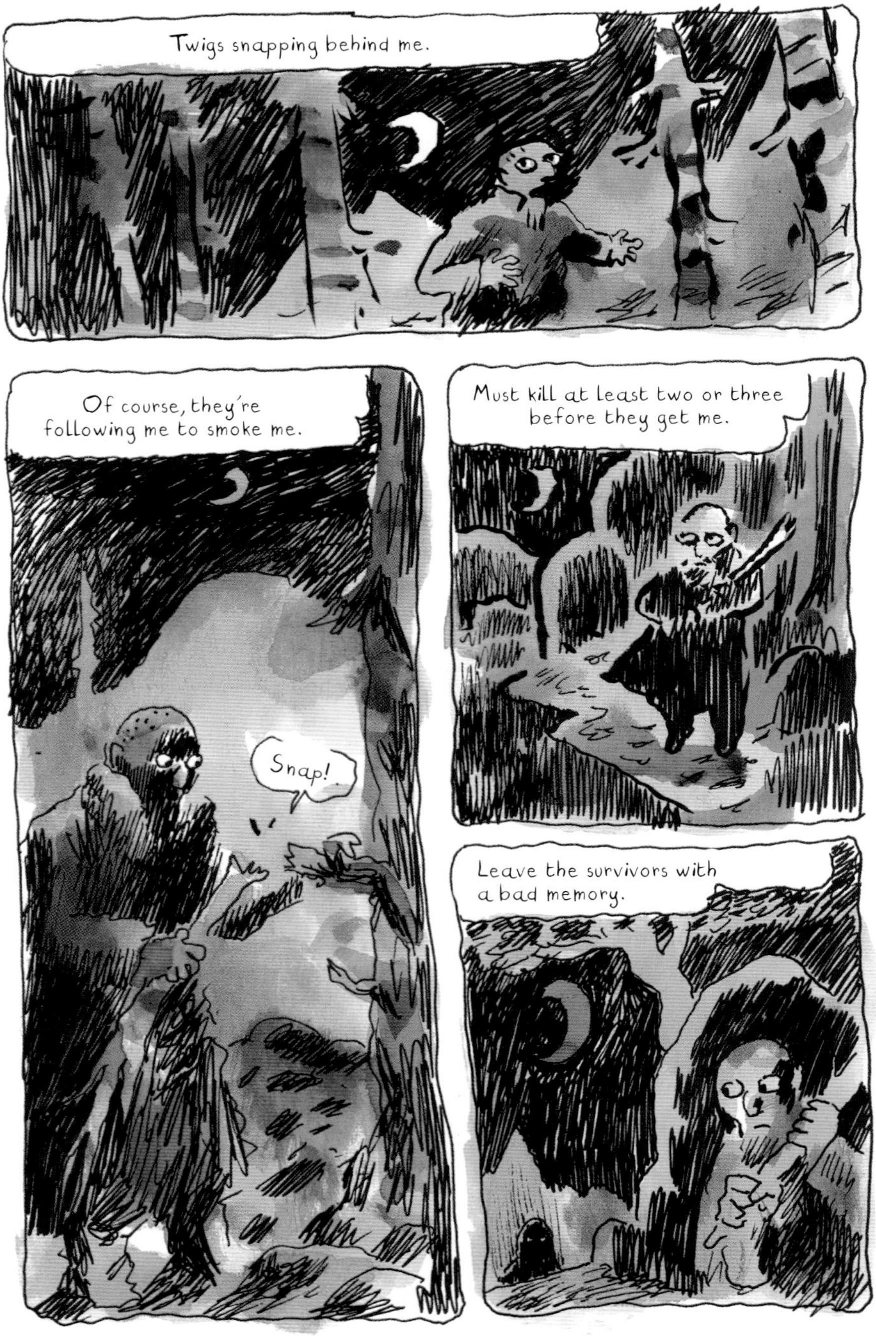
Twigs snapping behind me.
Of course, they're following me to smoke me.
Snap!
Must kill at least two or three before they get me.
Leave the survivors with a bad memory.

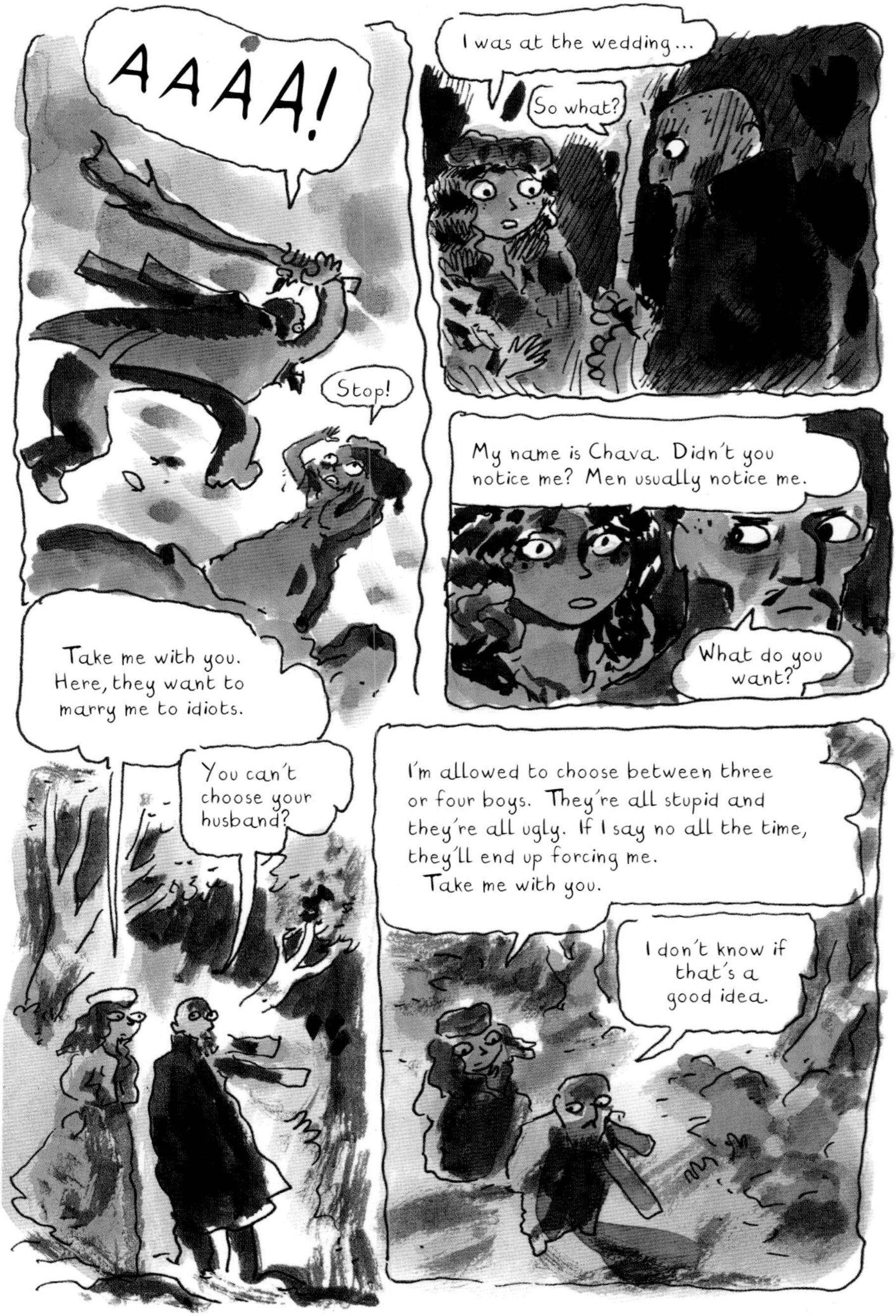
AAAA!
Stop!
I was at the wedding...
So what?
My name is Chava. Didn't you notice me? Men usually notice me.
What do you want?
Take me with you. Here, they want to marry me to idiots.
You can't choose your husband?
I'm allowed to choose between three or four boys. They're all stupid and they're all ugly. If I say no all the time, they'll end up forcing me.
Take me with you.
I don't know if that's a good idea.

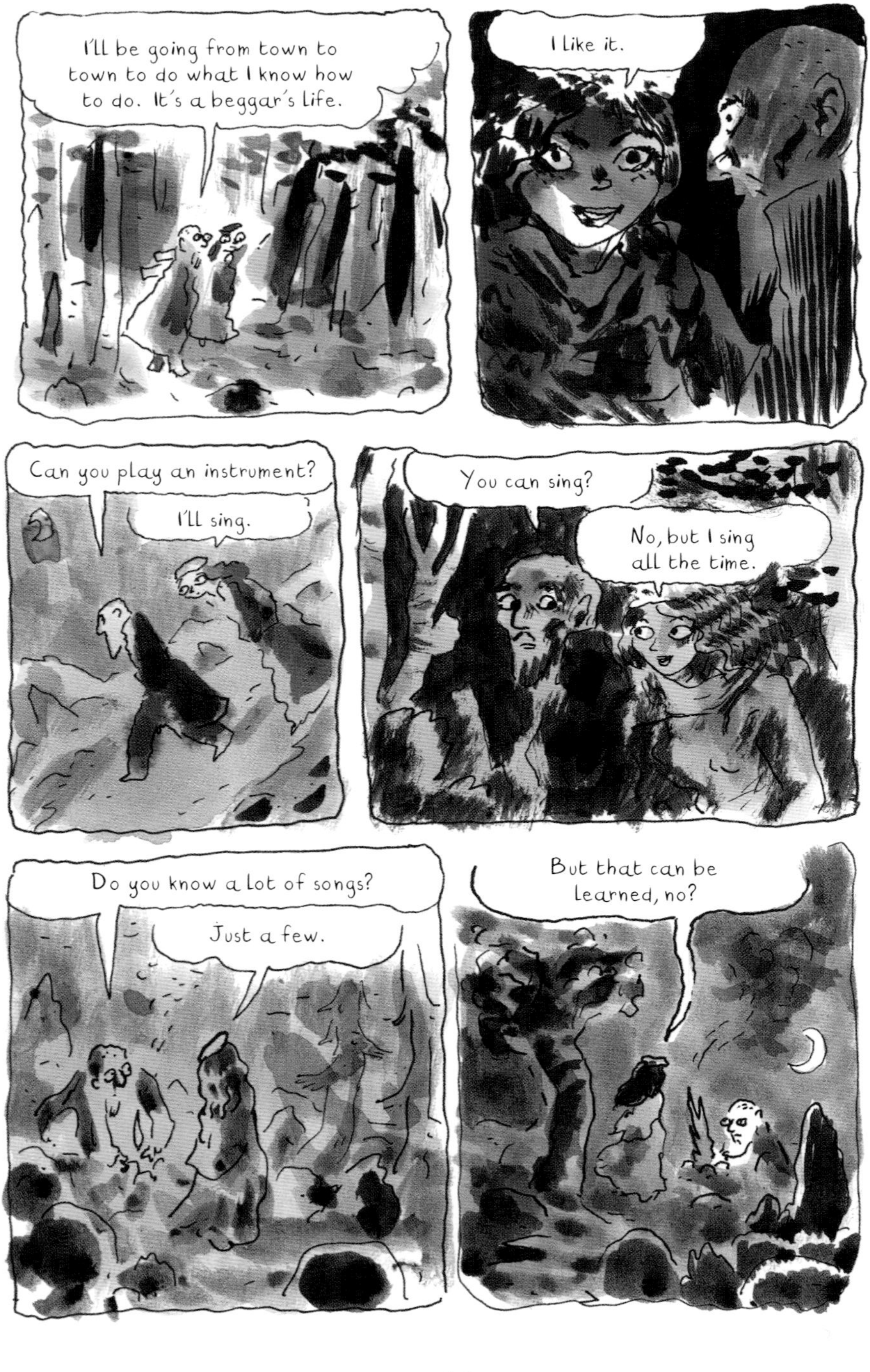
I'll be going from town to town to do what I know how to do. It's a beggar's life.
I like it.
Can you play an instrument?
I'll sing.
You can sing?
No, but I sing all the time.
Do you know a lot of songs?
Just a few.
But that can be learned, no?

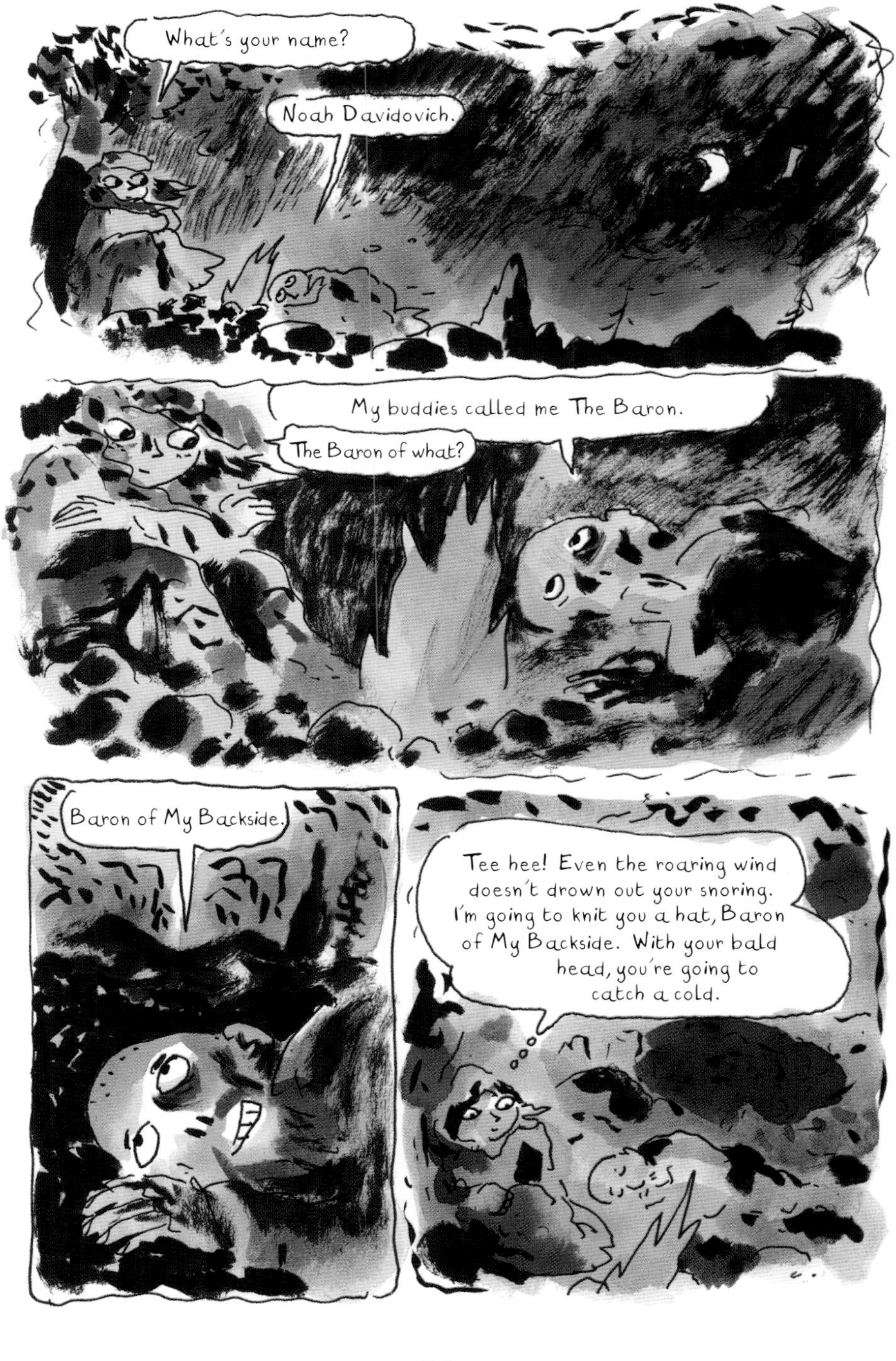
What's your name?
Noah Davidovich.
My buddies called me The Baron.
The Baron of what?
Baron of My Backside.
Tee hee! Even the roaring wind doesn't drown out your snoring. I'm going to knit you a hat, Baron of My Backside. With your bald head, you're going to catch a cold.

The Baron of My Backside's dream

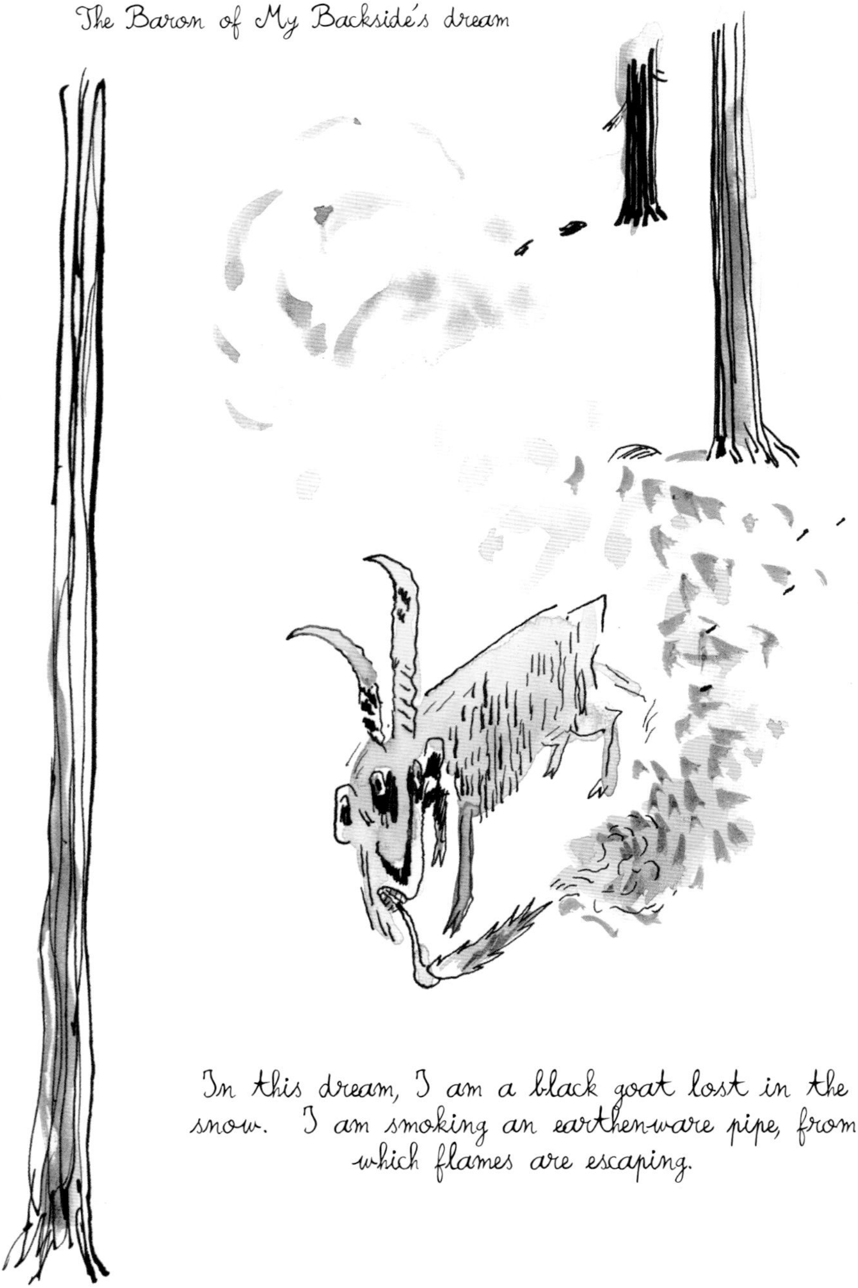

In this dream, I am a black goat lost in the snow. I am smoking an earthenware pipe, from which flames are escaping.

I see my musician buddies appear.

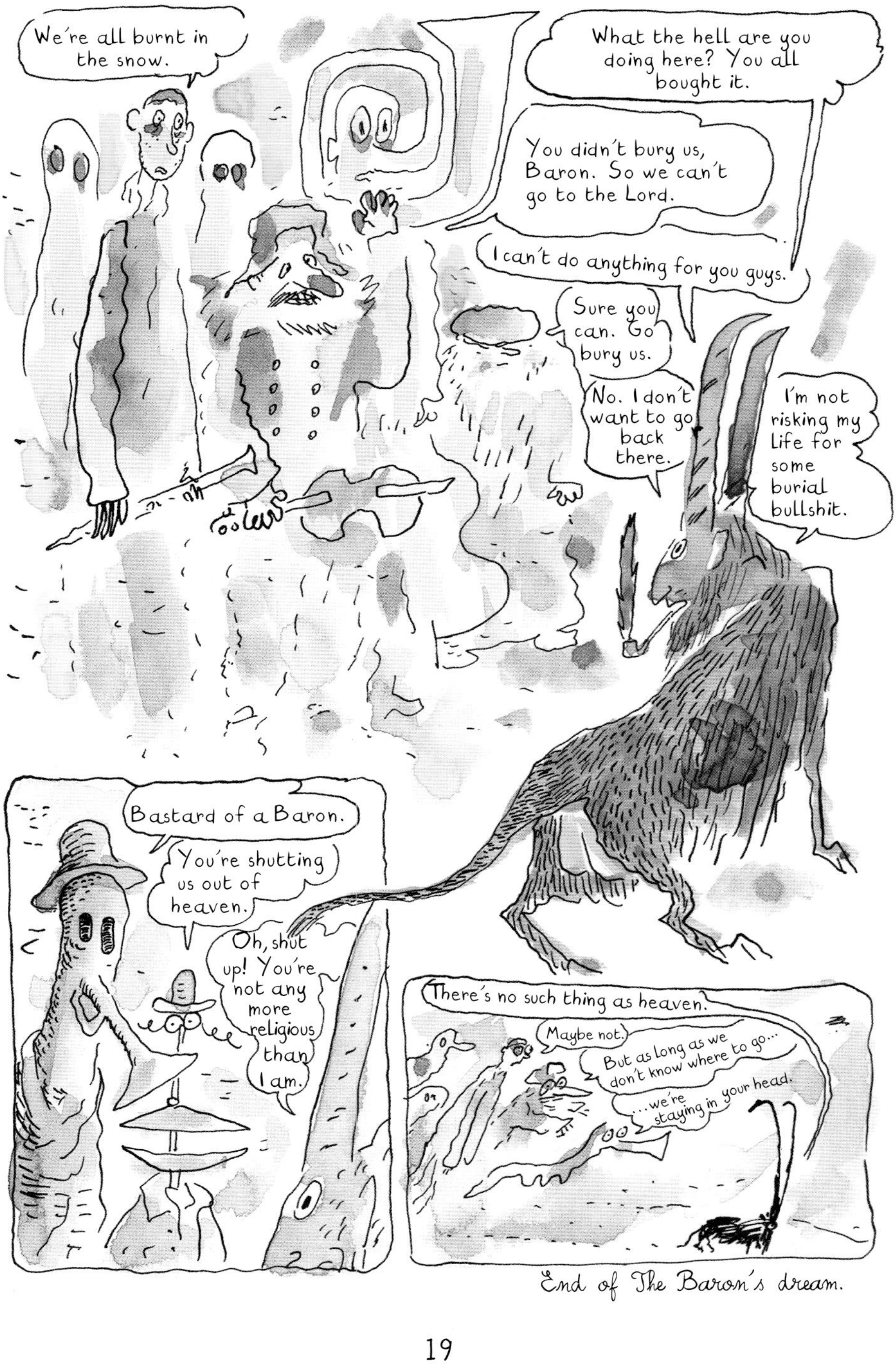
We're all burnt in the snow.
What the hell are you doing here? You all bought it.
You didn't bury us, Baron. So we can't go to the Lord.
I can't do anything for you guys.
Sure you can. Go bury us.
No. I don't want to go back there.
I'm not risking my life for some burial bullshit.
Bastard of a Baron.
You're shutting us out of heaven.
Oh, shut up! You're not any more religious than I am.
There's no such thing as heaven.
Maybe not.
But as long as we don't know where to go...
...we're staying in your head.

End of The Baron's dream.

The following morning, on a nearby mountain, a very upset rabbi summons his students.

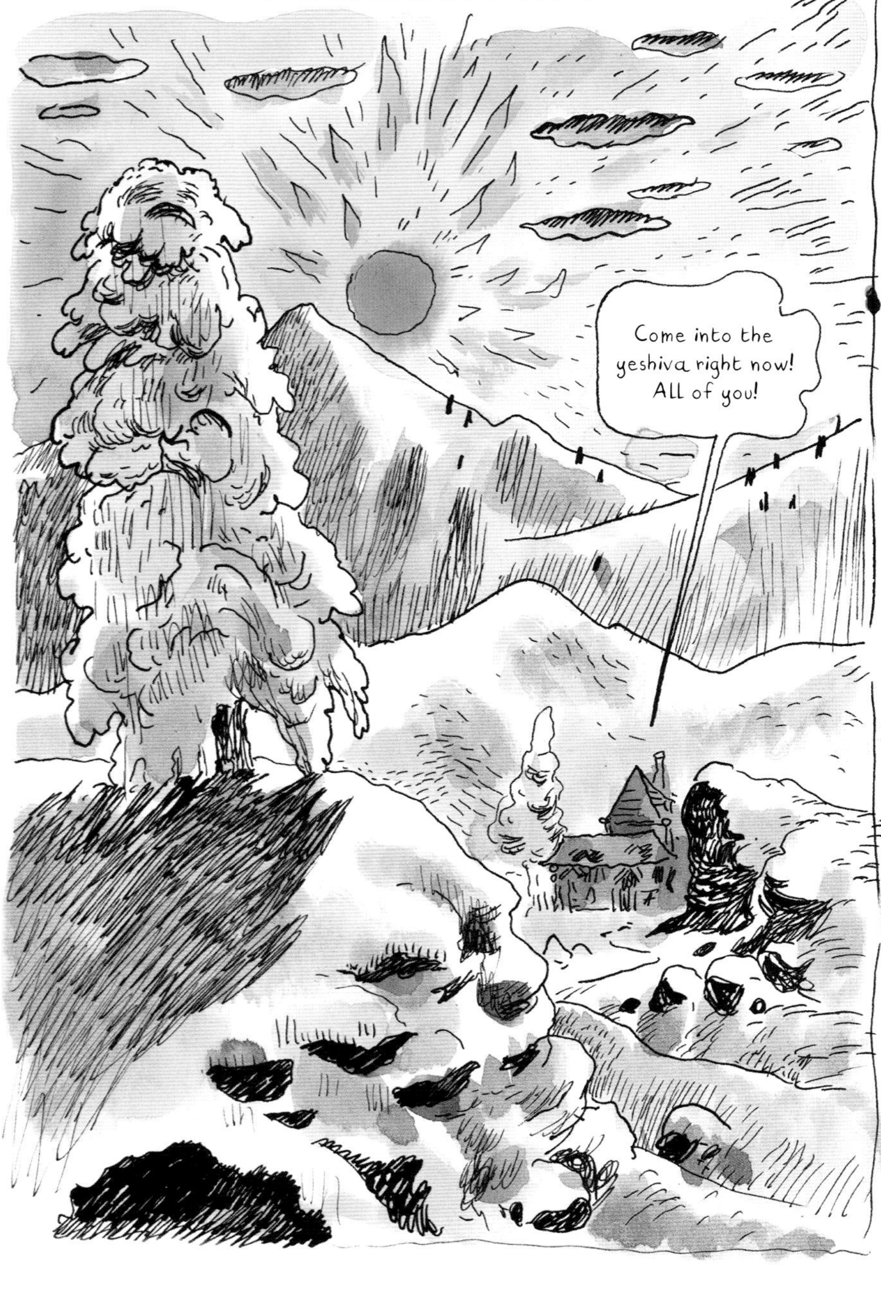
Come into the yeshiva right now! ALL of you!

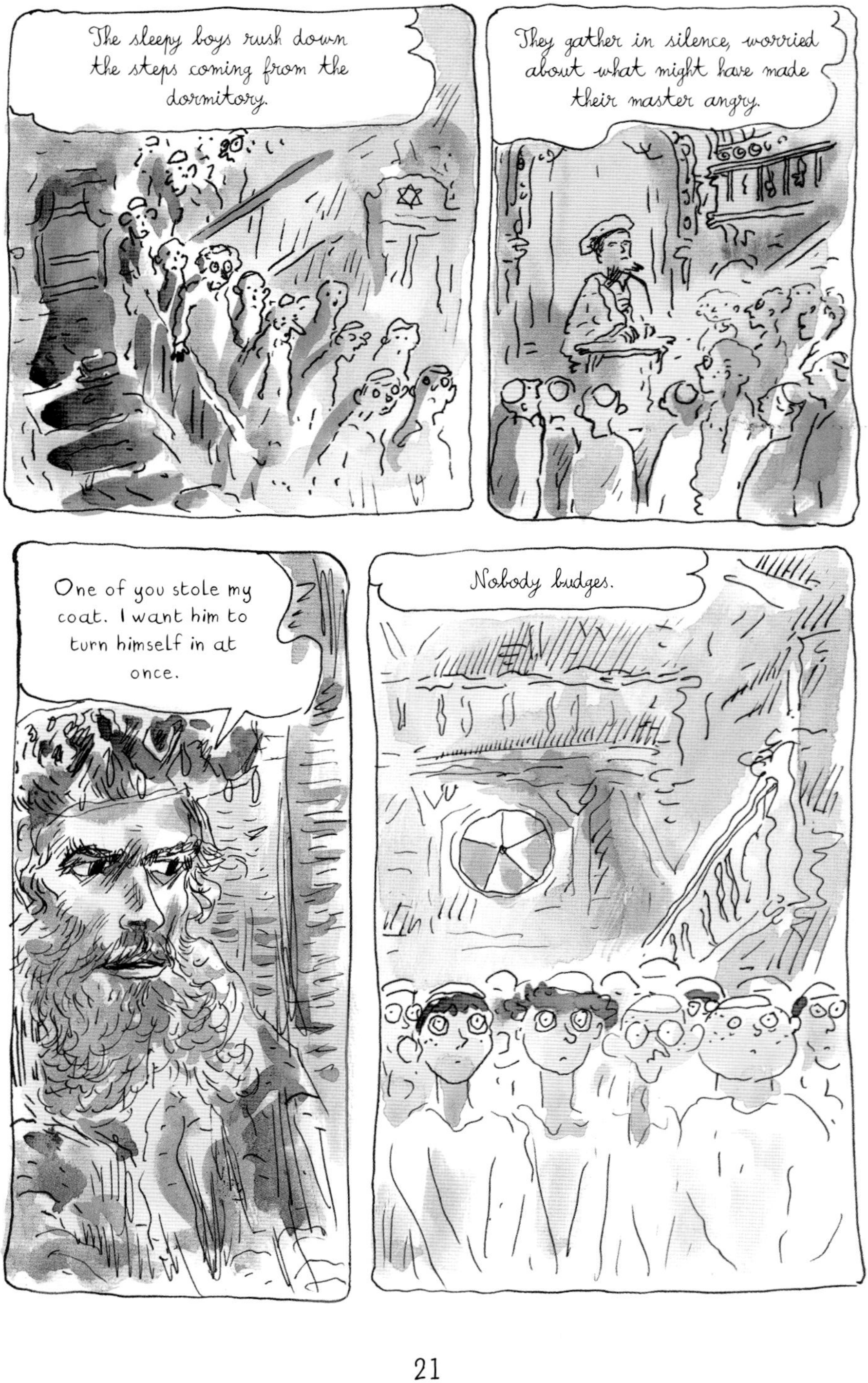
The sleepy boys rush down the steps coming from the dormitory.
They gather in silence, worried about what might have made their master angry.
One of you stole my coat. I want him to turn himself in at once.
Nobody budges.

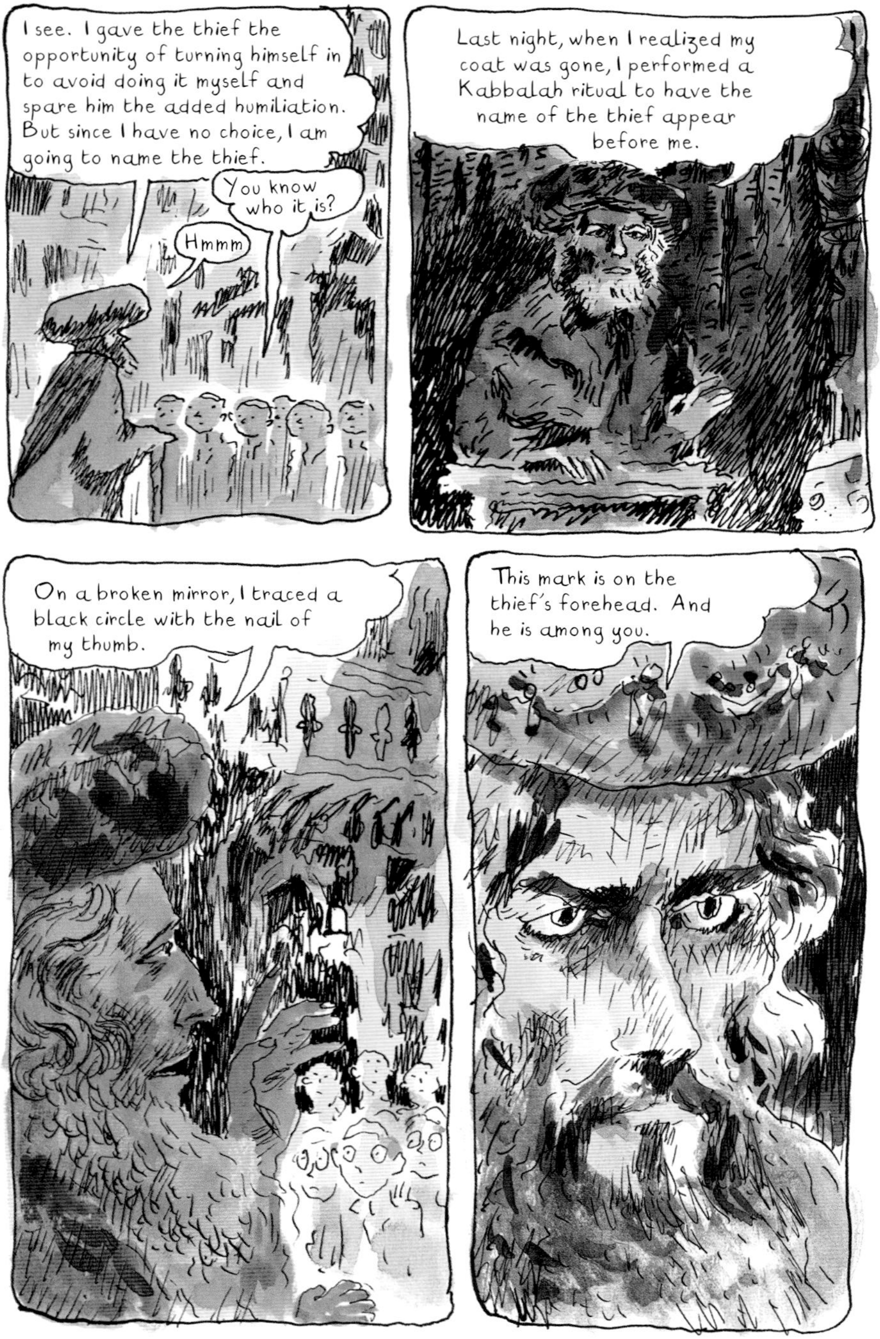
I see. I gave the thief the opportunity of turning himself in to avoid doing it myself and spare him the added humiliation. But since I have no choice, I am going to name the thief.
Hmmm
You know who it is?
Last night, when I realized my coat was gone, I performed a Kabbalah ritual to have the name of the thief appear before me.
On a broken mirror, I traced a black circle with the nail of my thumb.
This mark is on the thief's forehead. And he is among you.

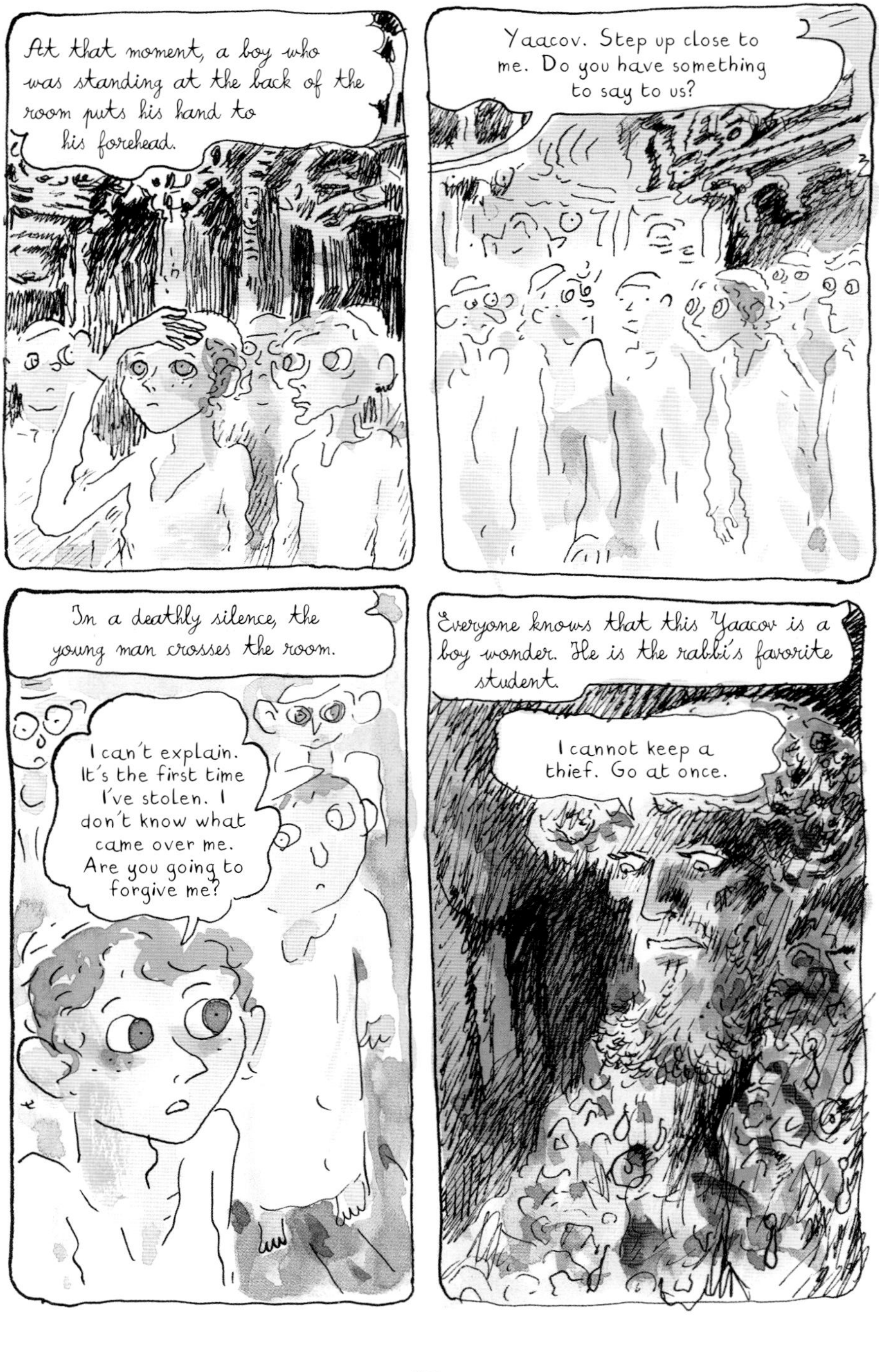
At that moment, a boy who was standing at the back of the room puts his hand to his forehead.
Yaacov. Step up close to me. Do you have something to say to us?
In a deathly silence, the young man crosses the room.
I can't explain. It's the first time I've stolen. I don't know what came over me. Are you going to forgive me?
Everyone knows that this Yaacov is a boy wonder. He is the rabbi's favorite student.
I cannot keep a thief. Go at once.

Less than an hour later, the thief has packed his belongings and leaves the school.

Less than an hour later, the thief has packed his belongings and leaves the school.

His master awaits him on the threshold.

The coat is yours.

Perhaps it'll keep you warmer than my teaching did.

Are you returning to your family?

No.

Yaacov drags his bag behind him. Over his own coat, he is wearing the master's coat, the bottom of which brushes against the freshly fallen snow.

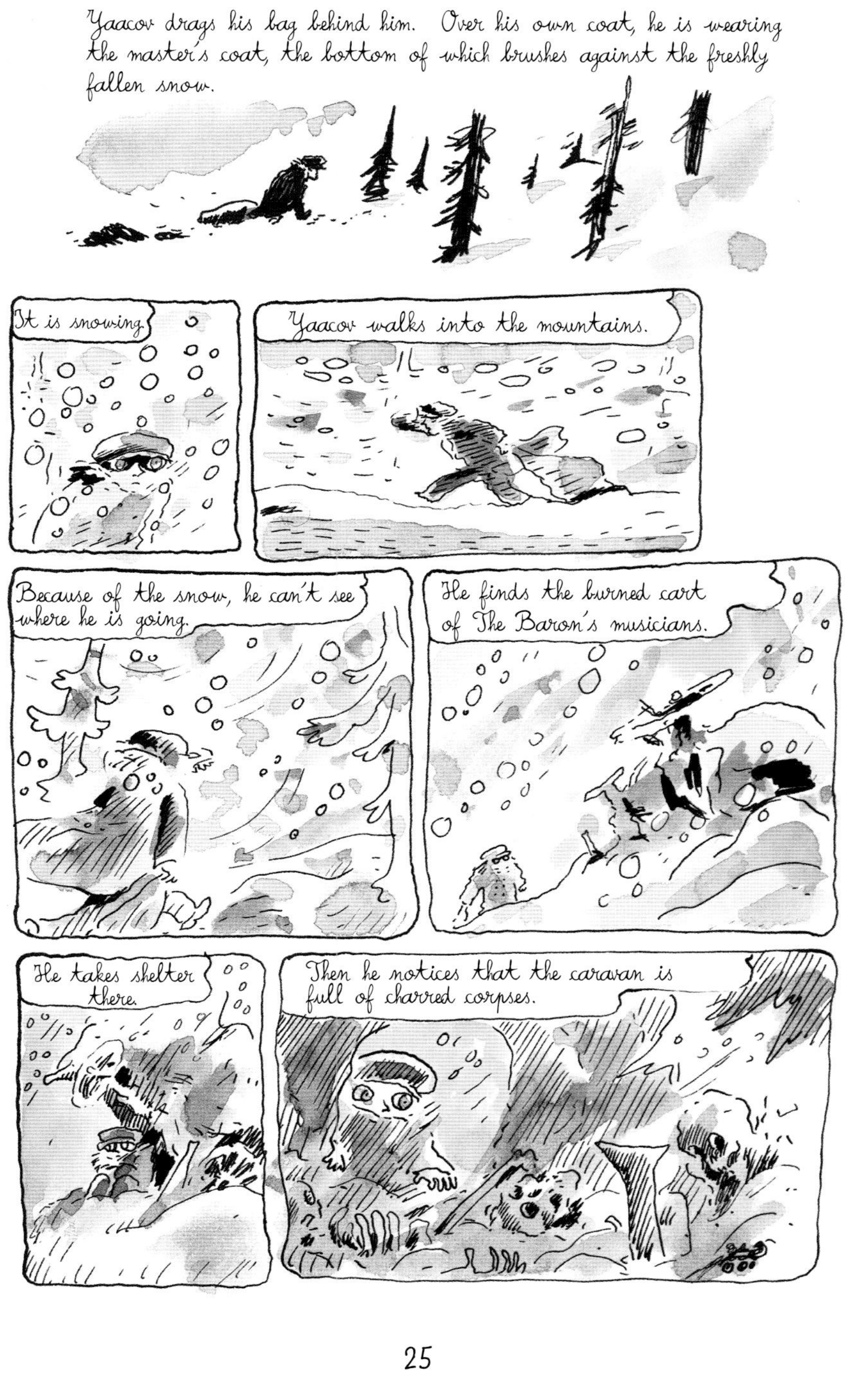
It is snowing.
Yaacov walks into the mountains.
Because of the snow, he can't see where he is going.
He finds the burned cart of The Baron's musicians.
He takes shelter there.
Then he notices that the caravan is full of charred corpses.

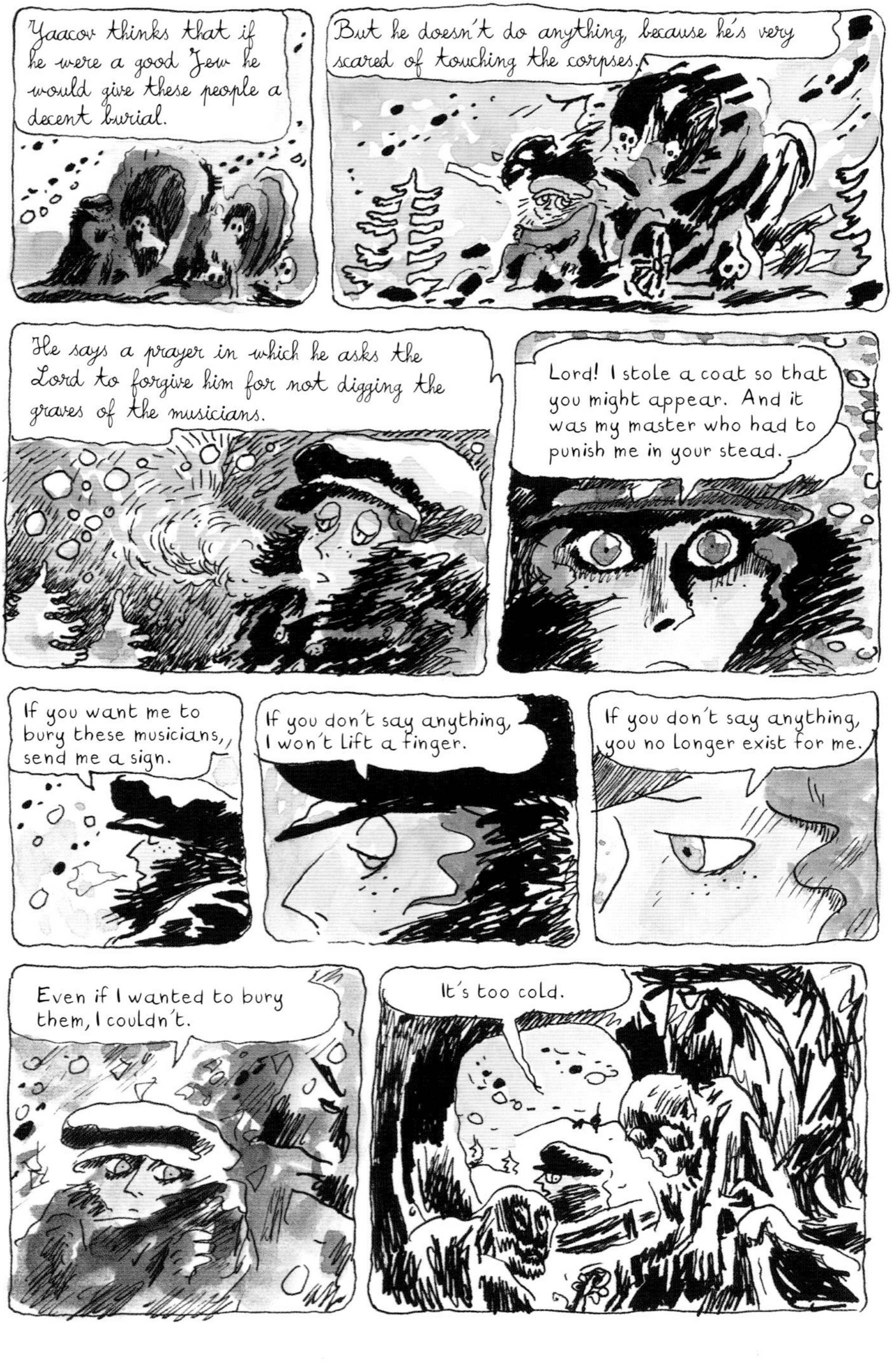
Yaacov thinks that if he were a good Jew he would give these people a decent burial.
But he doesn't do anything, because he's very scared of touching the corpses.
He says a prayer in which he asks the Lord to forgive him for not digging the graves of the musicians.
Lord! I stole a coat so that you might appear. And it was my master who had to punish me in your stead.
If you want me to bury these musicians, send me a sign.
If you don't say anything, I won't lift a finger.
If you don't say anything, you no longer exist for me.
Even if I wanted to bury them, I couldn't.
It's too cold.

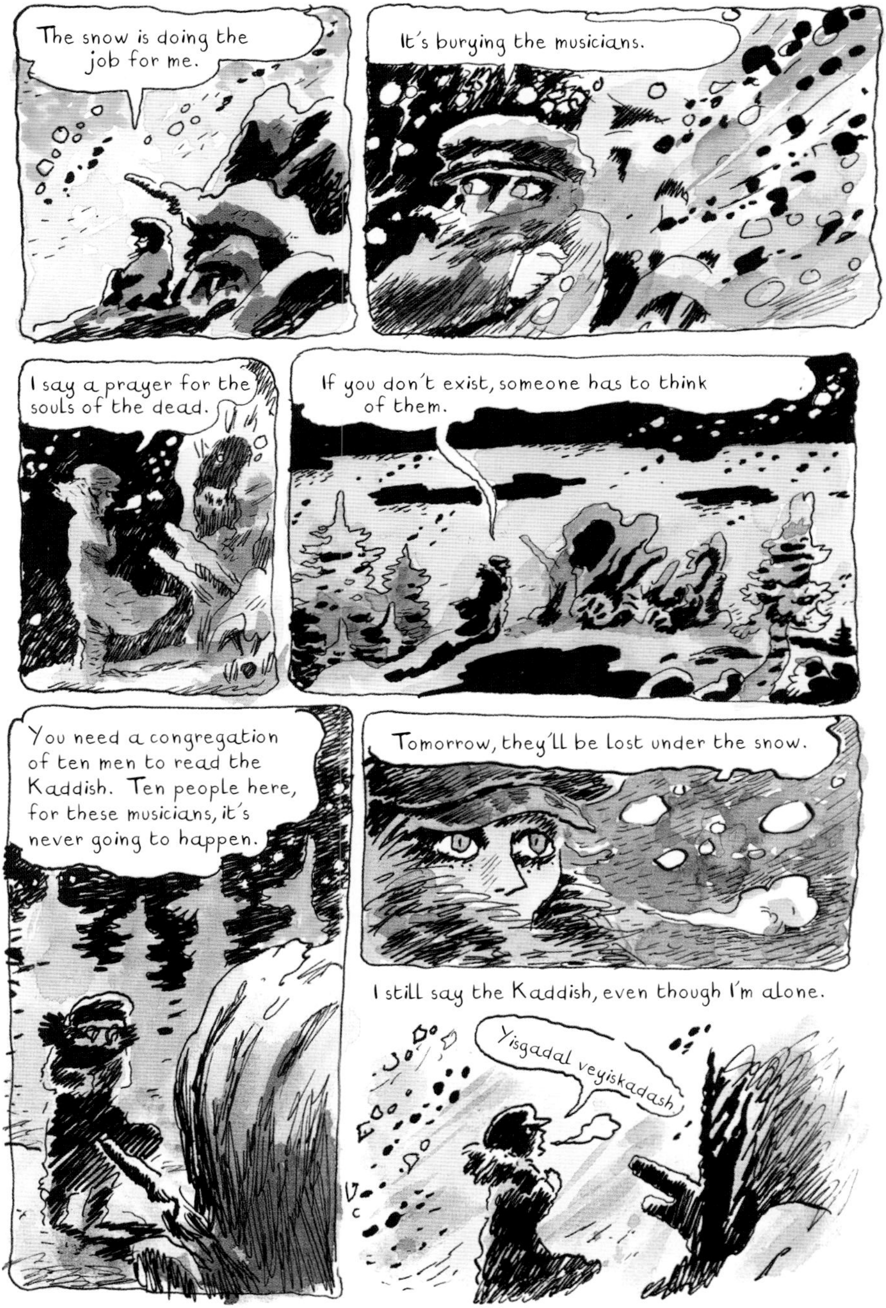
The snow is doing the job for me.
It's burying the musicians.
I say a prayer for the souls of the dead.
If you don't exist, someone has to think of them.
You need a congregation of ten men to read the Kaddish. Ten people here, for these musicians, it's never going to happen.
Tomorrow, they'll be lost under the snow.
I still say the Kaddish, even though I'm alone.
Yisgadal veyiskadash.

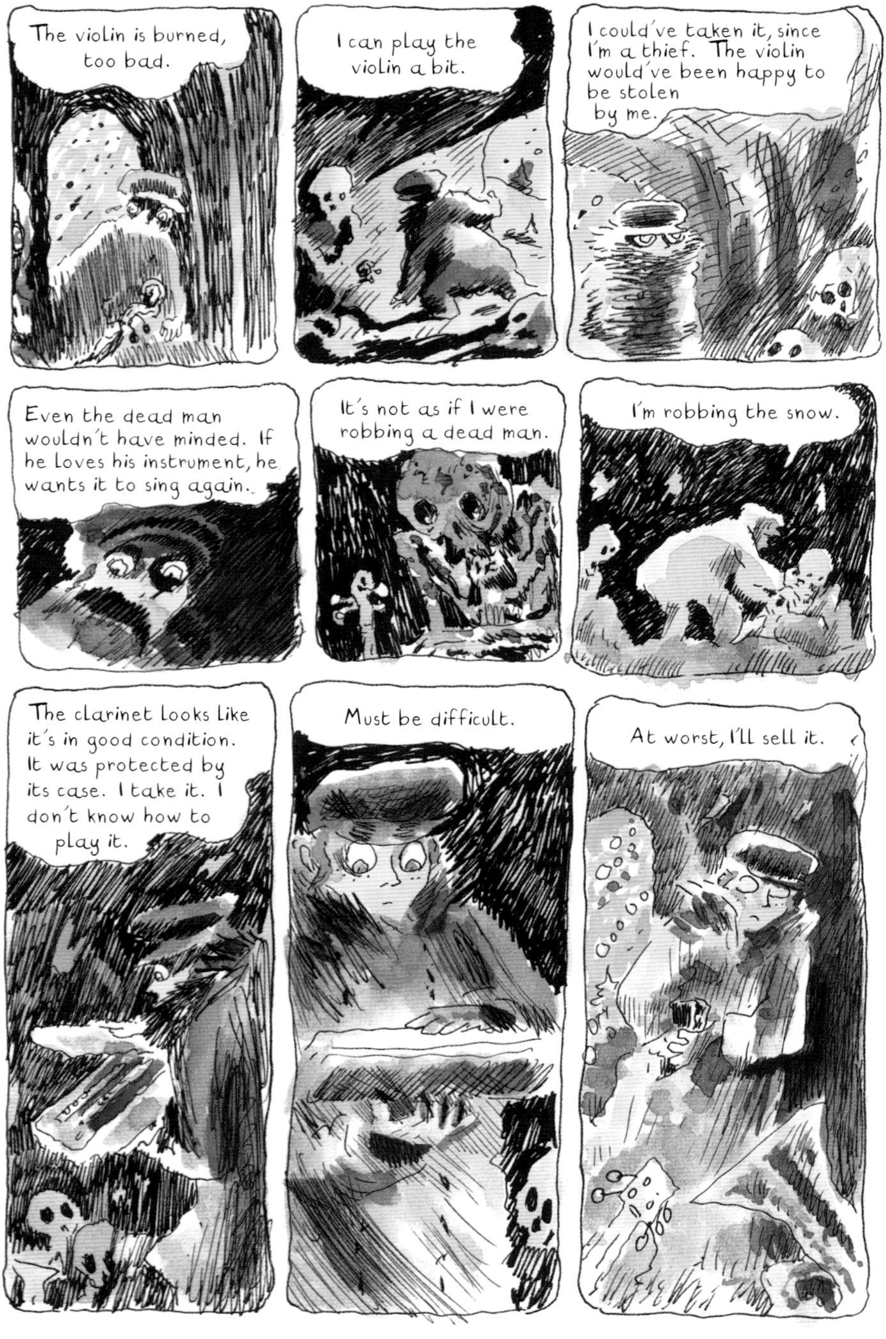

The violin is burned, too bad.
I can play the violin a bit.
I could've taken it, since I'm a thief. The violin would've been happy to be stolen by me.
Even the dead man wouldn't have minded. If he loves his instrument, he wants it to sing again.
It's not as if I were robbing a dead man.
I'm robbing the snow.
The clarinet looks like it's in good condition. It was protected by its case. I take it. I don't know how to play it.
Must be difficult.
At worst, I'll sell it.

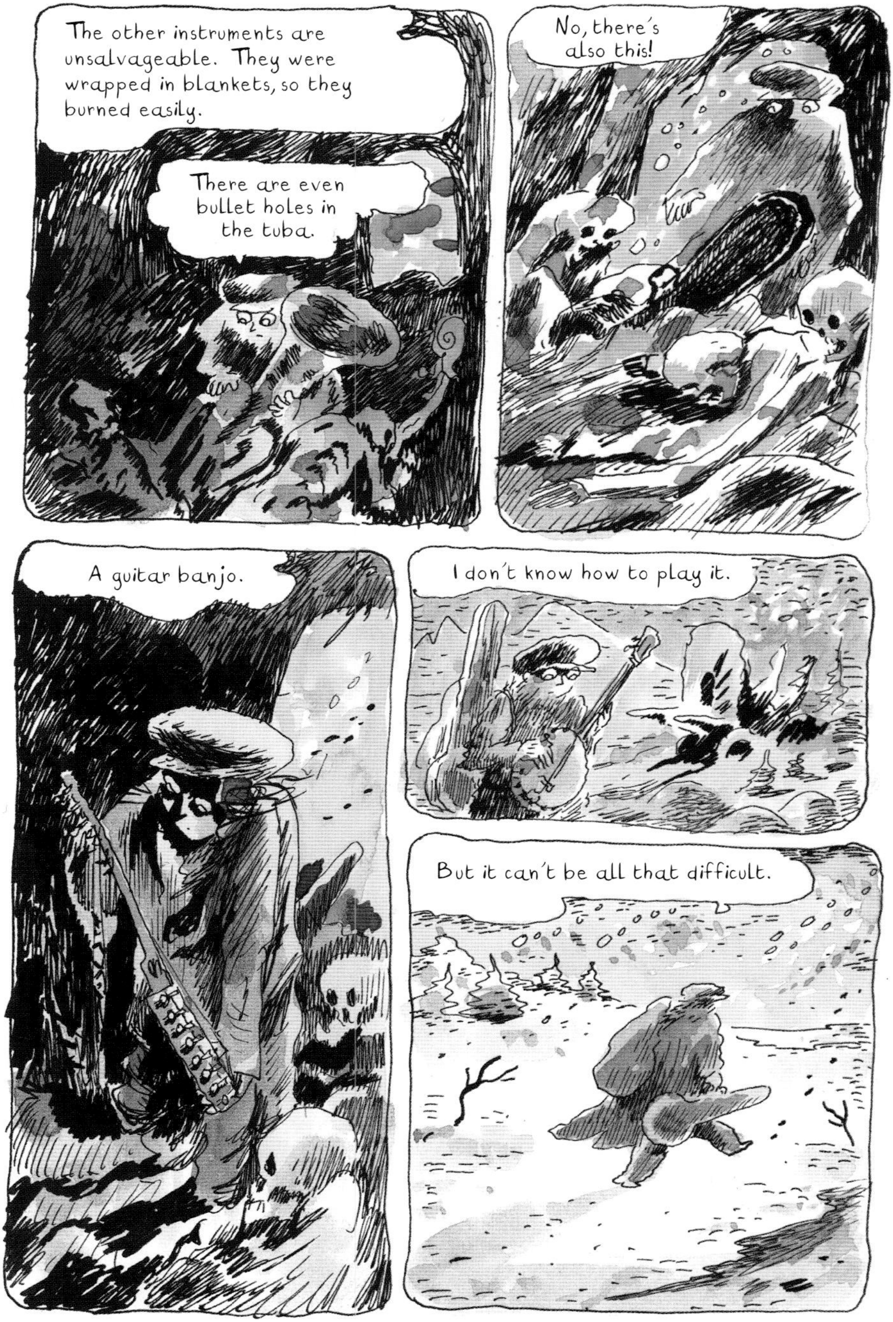
The other instruments are unsalvageable. They were wrapped in blankets, so they burned easily.
There are even bullet holes in the tuba.
No, there's also this!
A guitar banjo.
I don't know how to play it.
But it can't be all that difficult.

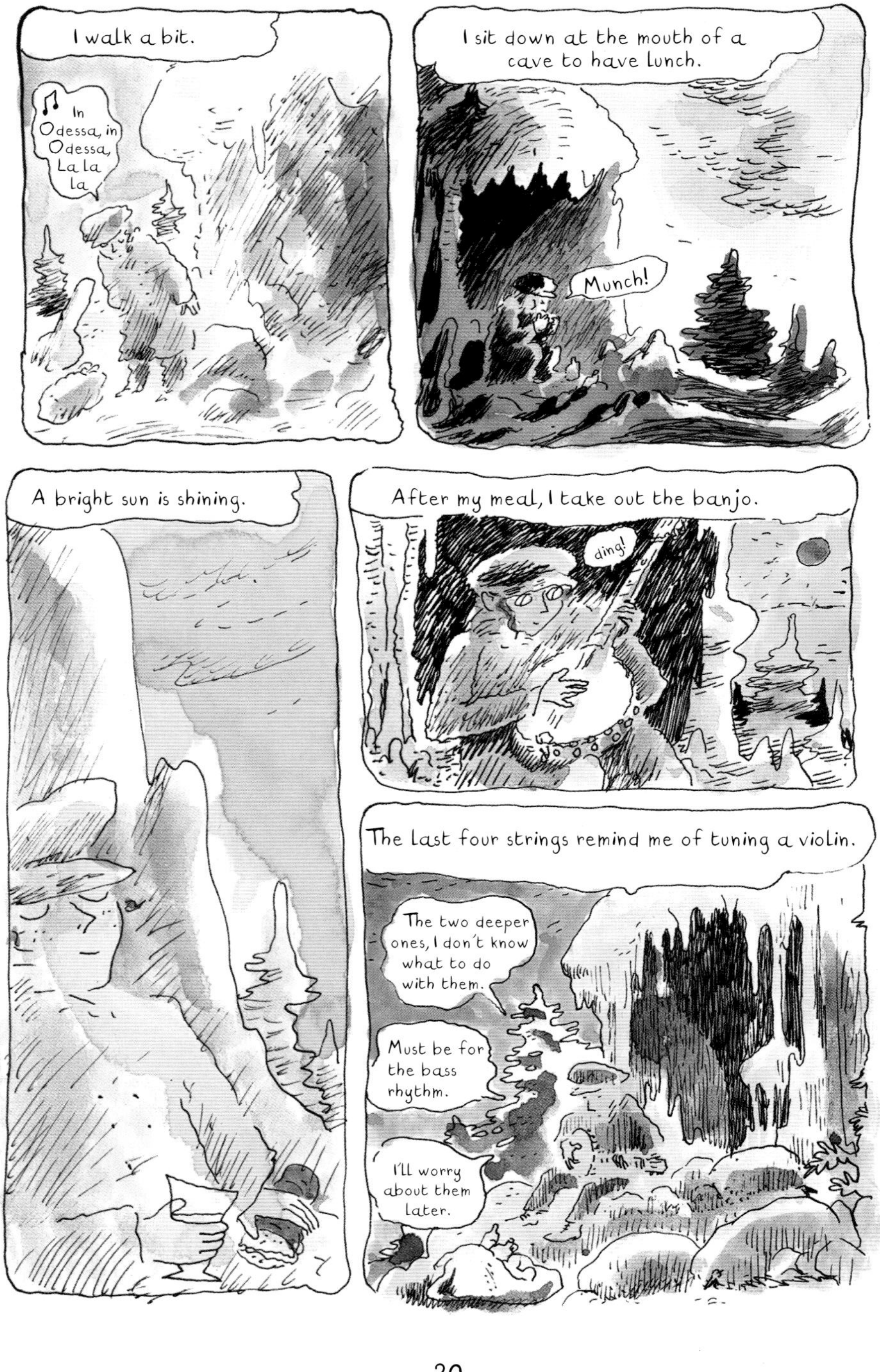
I walk a bit.
In Odessa, in Odessa, La la la
I sit down at the mouth of a cave to have lunch.
Munch!
A bright sun is shining.
After my meal, I take out the banjo.
ding!
The last four strings remind me of tuning a violin.
The two deeper ones, I don't know what to do with them.
Must be for the bass rhythm.
I'll worry about them later.

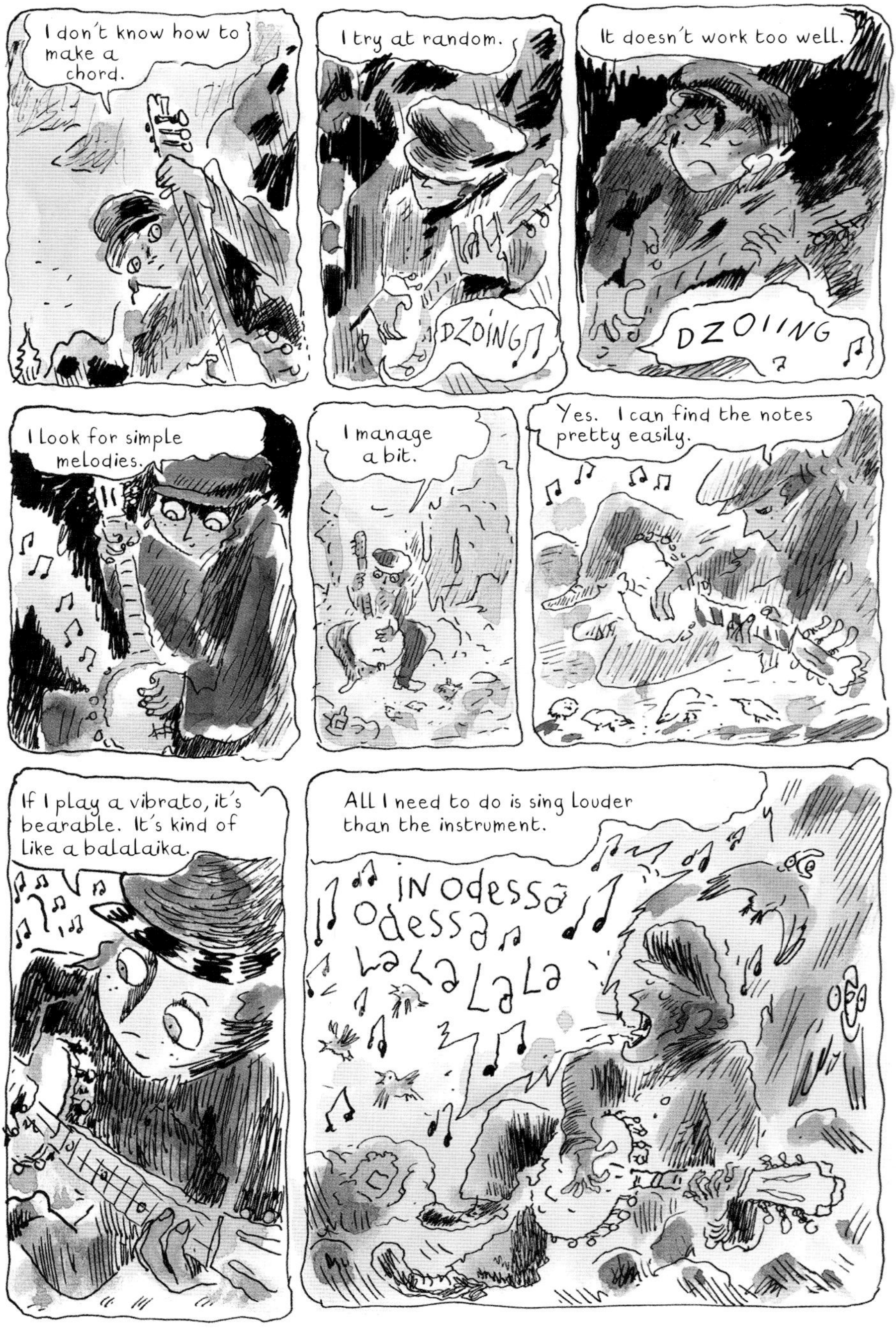

I don't know how to make a chord.
I try at random.
DZOING
It doesn't work too well.
DZOIING
I look for simple melodies.
I manage a bit.
Yes. I can find the notes pretty easily.
If I play a vibrato, it's bearable. It's kind of like a balalaika.
All I need to do is sing louder than the instrument.
IN odessa
odessa
La La La La

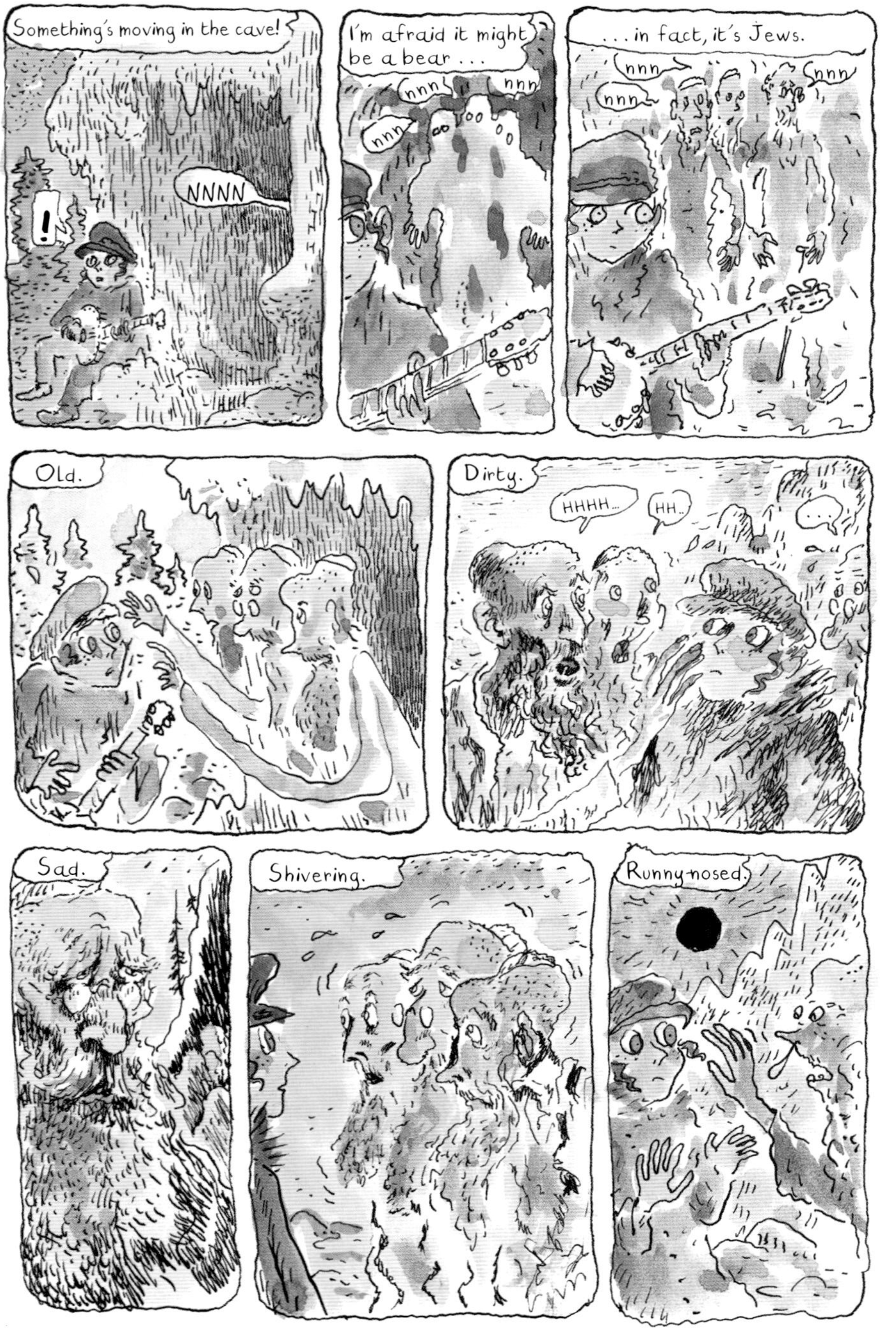
Something's moving in the cave!
!
NNNN
I'm afraid it might be a bear . . .
nnn
nnn
nnn
. . . in fact, it's Jews.
nnn
nnn
nnn
Old.
Dirty.
HHHH...
HH..
Sad.
Shivering.
Runny-nosed.

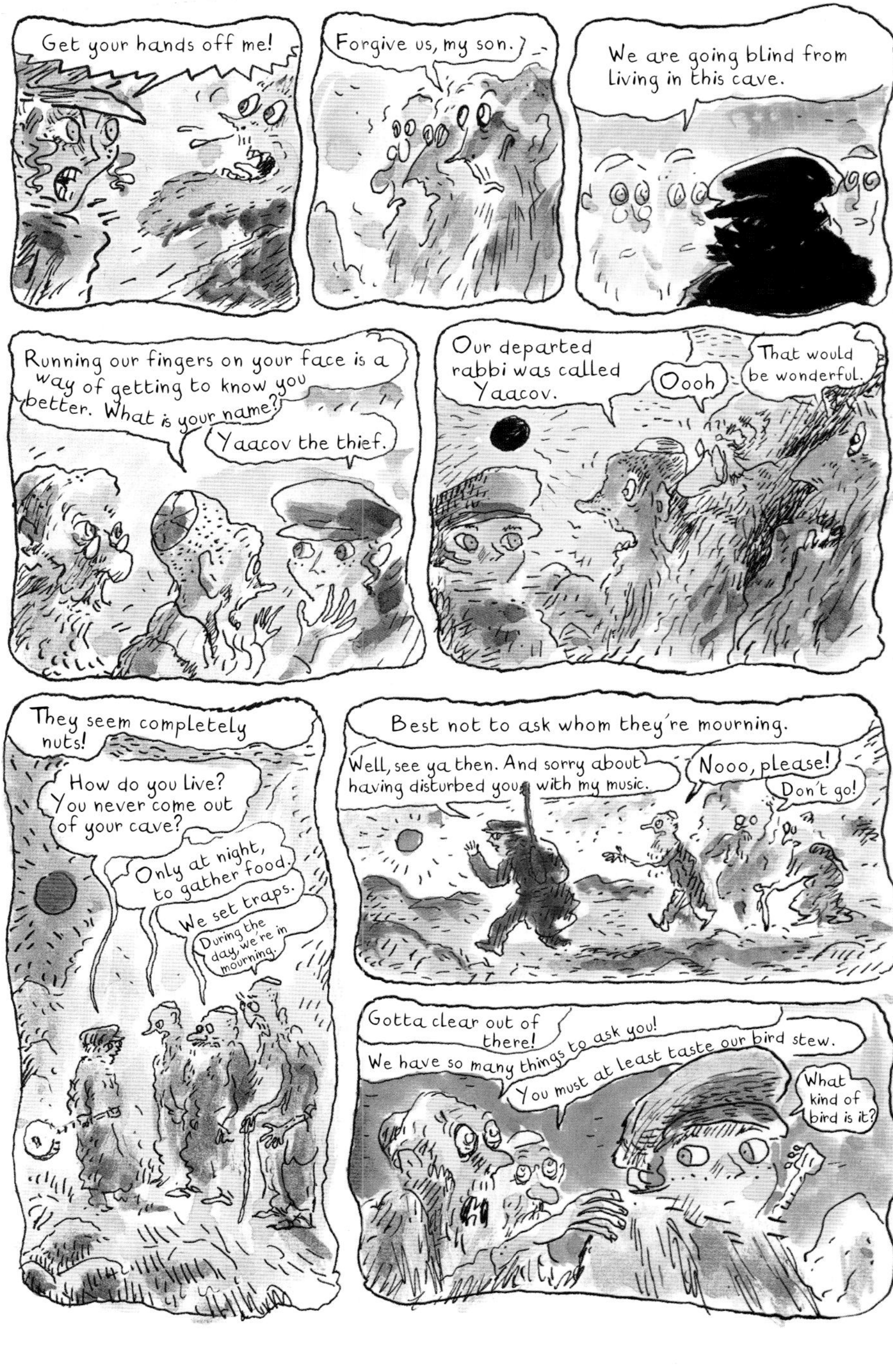

Get your hands off me!
Forgive us, my son.
We are going blind from living in this cave.
Running our fingers on your face is a way of getting to know you better. What is your name?
Yaacov the thief.
Our departed rabbi was called Yaacov.
Oooh
That would be wonderful.
They seem completely nuts!
How do you live? You never come out of your cave?
Only at night, to gather food.
We set traps.
During the day, we're in mourning.
Best not to ask whom they're mourning.
Well, see ya then. And sorry about having disturbed you with my music.
Nooo, please!
Don't go!
Gotta clear out of there!
We have so many things to ask you!
You must at least taste our bird stew.
What kind of bird is it?

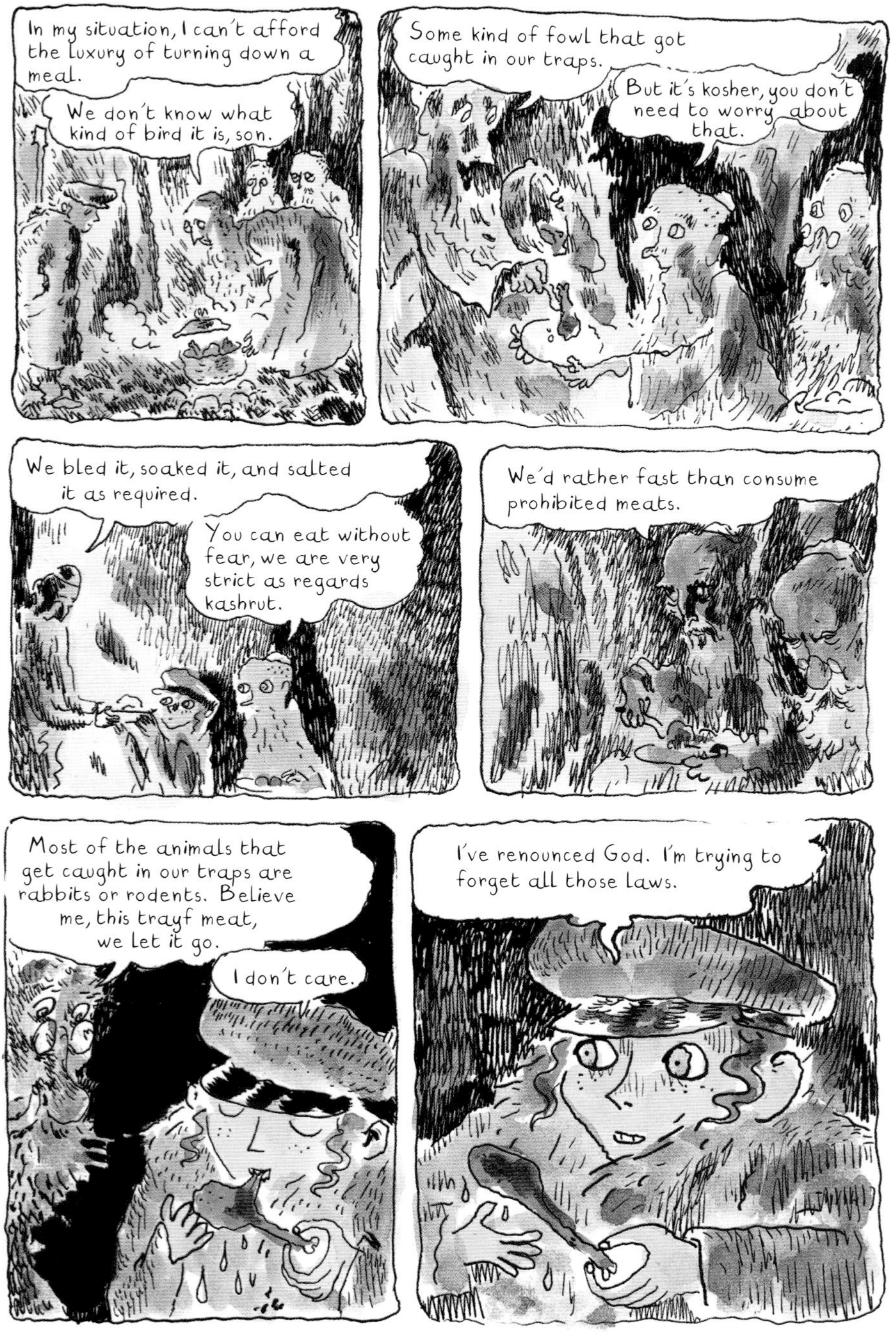
In my situation, I can't afford the luxury of turning down a meal.
We don't know what kind of bird it is, son.
Some kind of fowl that got caught in our traps.
But it's kosher, you don't need to worry about that.
We bled it, soaked it, and salted it as required.
You can eat without fear, we are very strict as regards kashrut.
We'd rather fast than consume prohibited meats.
Most of the animals that get caught in our traps are rabbits or rodents. Believe me, this trayf meat, we let it go.
I don't care.
I've renounced God. I'm trying to forget all those laws.

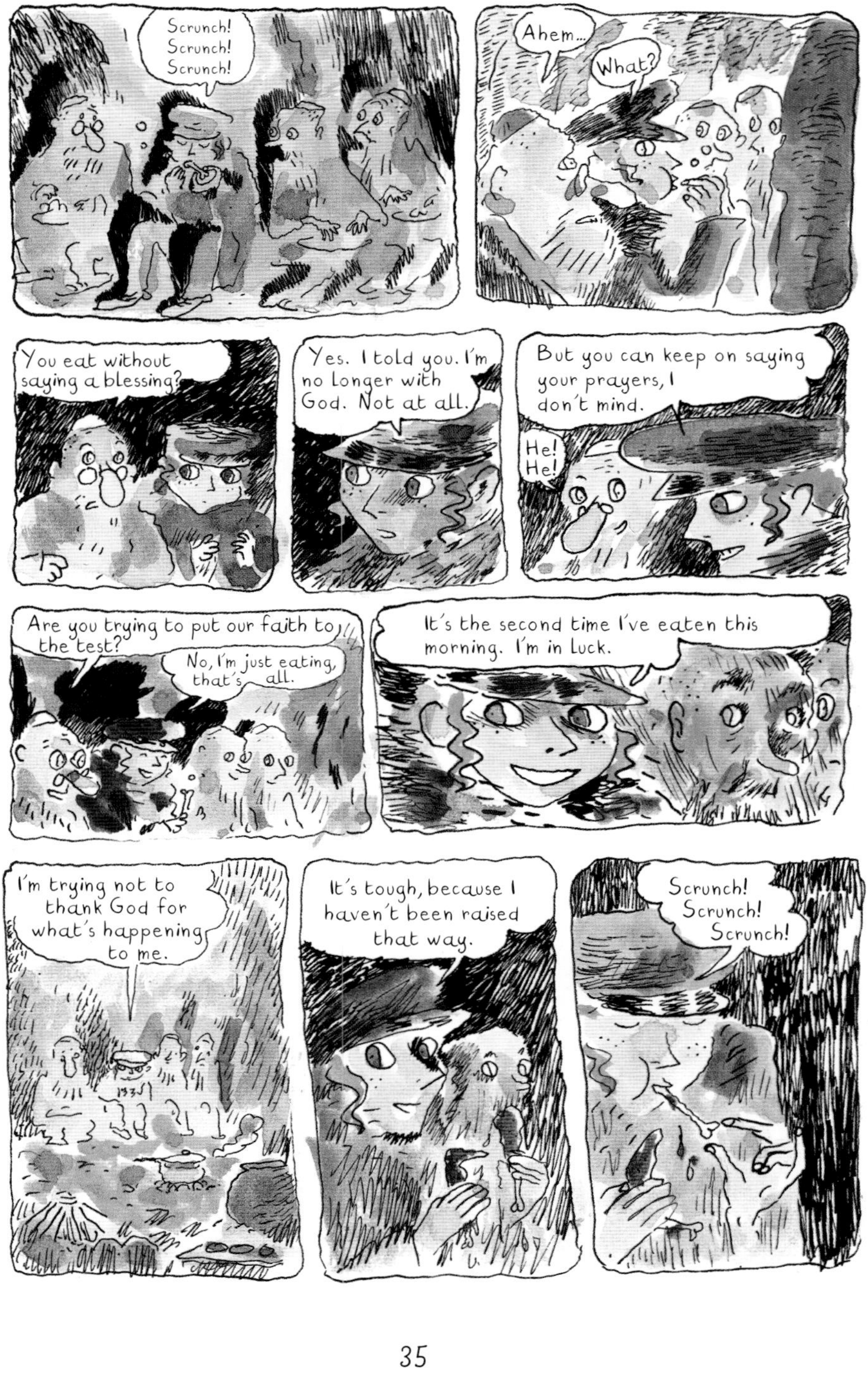
Scrunch!
Scrunch!
Scrunch!
Ahem...
What?
You eat without saying a blessing?
Yes. I told you. I'm no longer with God. Not at all.
But you can keep on saying your prayers, I don't mind.
He! He!
Are you trying to put our faith to the test?
No, I'm just eating, that's all.
It's the second time I've eaten this morning. I'm in luck.
I'm trying not to thank God for what's happening to me.
It's tough, because I haven't been raised that way.
Scrunch!
Scrunch!
Scrunch!

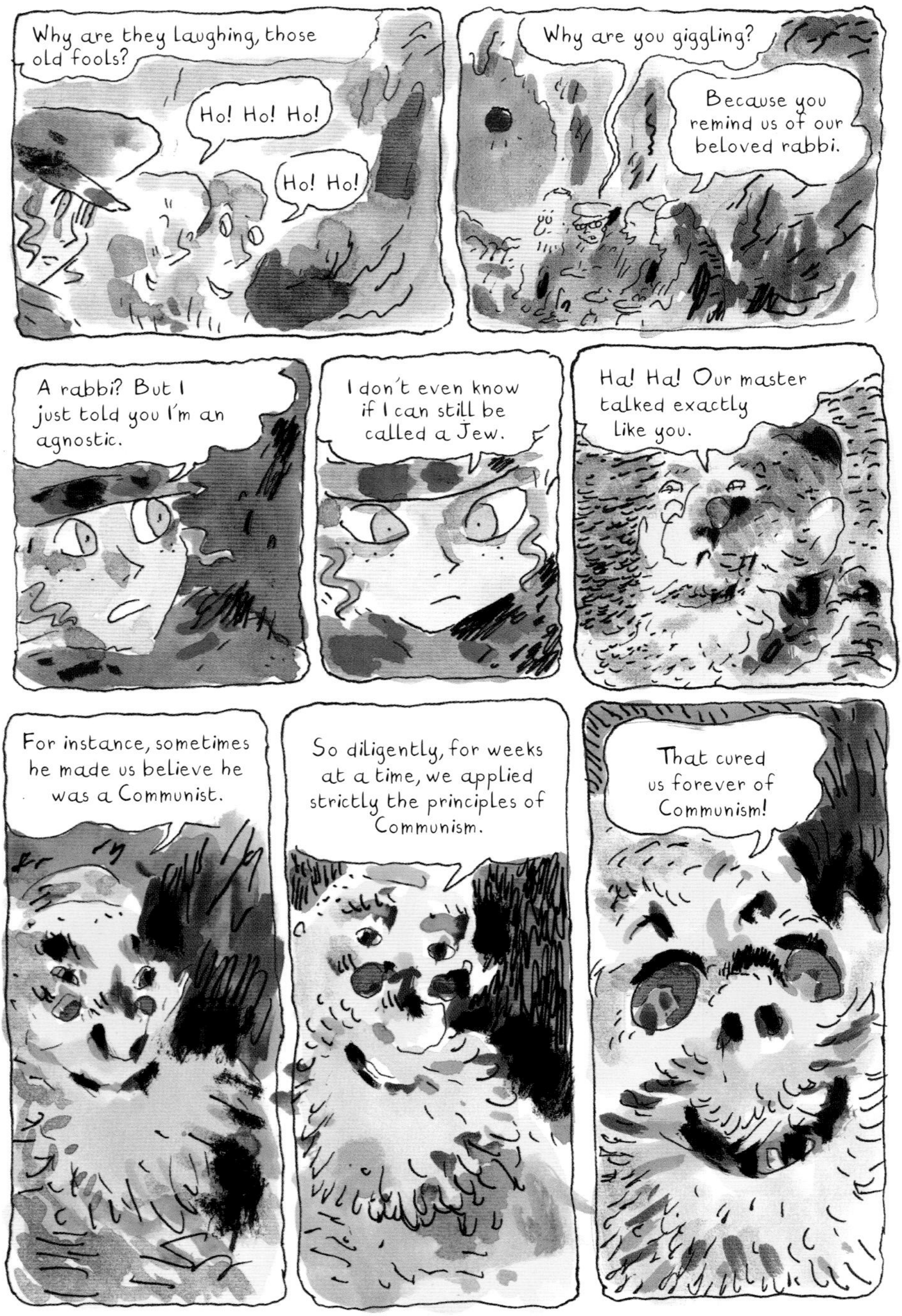
Why are they laughing, those old fools?
Ho! Ho! Ho!
Ho! Ho!
Why are you giggling?
Because you remind us of our beloved rabbi.
A rabbi? But I just told you I'm an agnostic.
I don't even know if I can still be called a Jew.
Ha! Ha! Our master talked exactly like you.
For instance, sometimes he made us believe he was a Communist.
So diligently, for weeks at a time, we applied strictly the principles of Communism.
That cured us forever of Communism!

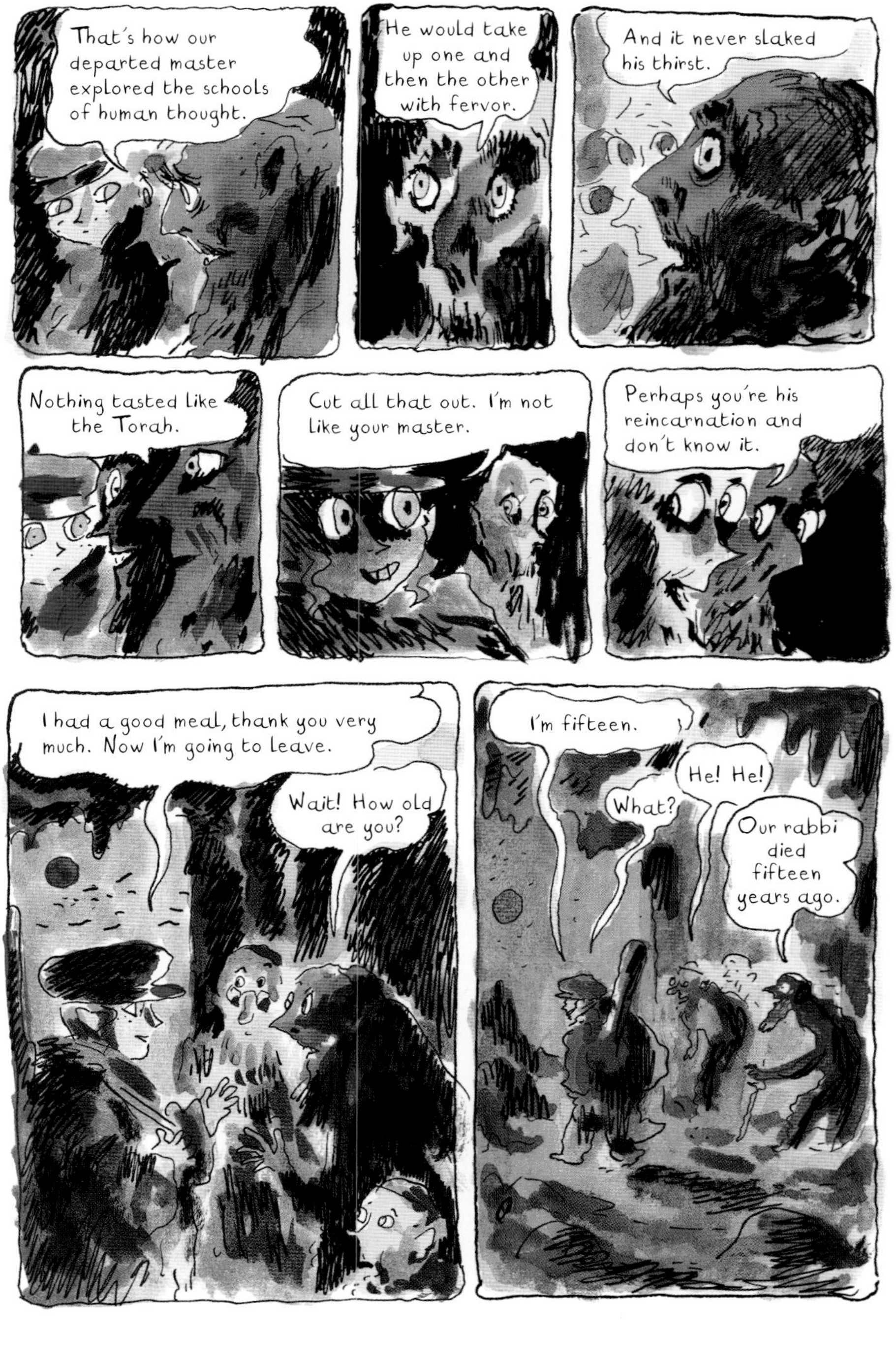
That's how our departed master explored the schools of human thought.
He would take up one and then the other with fervor.
And it never slaked his thirst.
Nothing tasted like the Torah.
Cut all that out. I'm not like your master.
Perhaps you're his reincarnation and don't know it.
I had a good meal, thank you very much. Now I'm going to leave.
Wait! How old are you?
I'm fifteen.
What?
He! He!
Our rabbi died fifteen years ago.

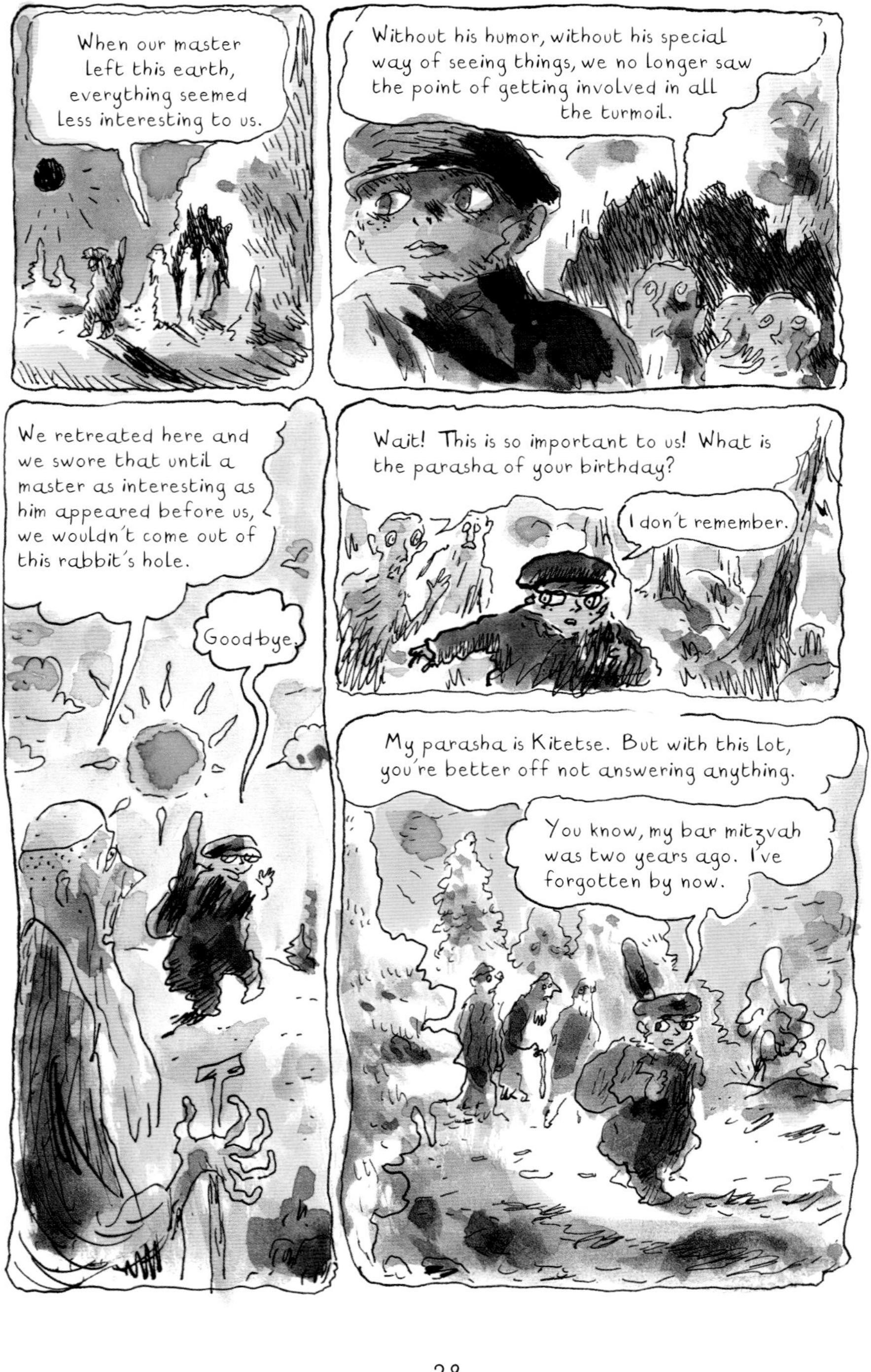

When our master left this earth, everything seemed less interesting to us.
Without his humor, without his special way of seeing things, we no longer saw the point of getting involved in all the turmoil.
We retreated here and we swore that until a master as interesting as him appeared before us, we wouldn't come out of this rabbit's hole.
Goodbye.
Wait! This is so important to us! What is the parasha of your birthday?
I don't remember.
My parasha is Kitetse. But with this lot, you're better off not answering anything.
You know, my bar mitzvah was two years ago. I've forgotten by now.

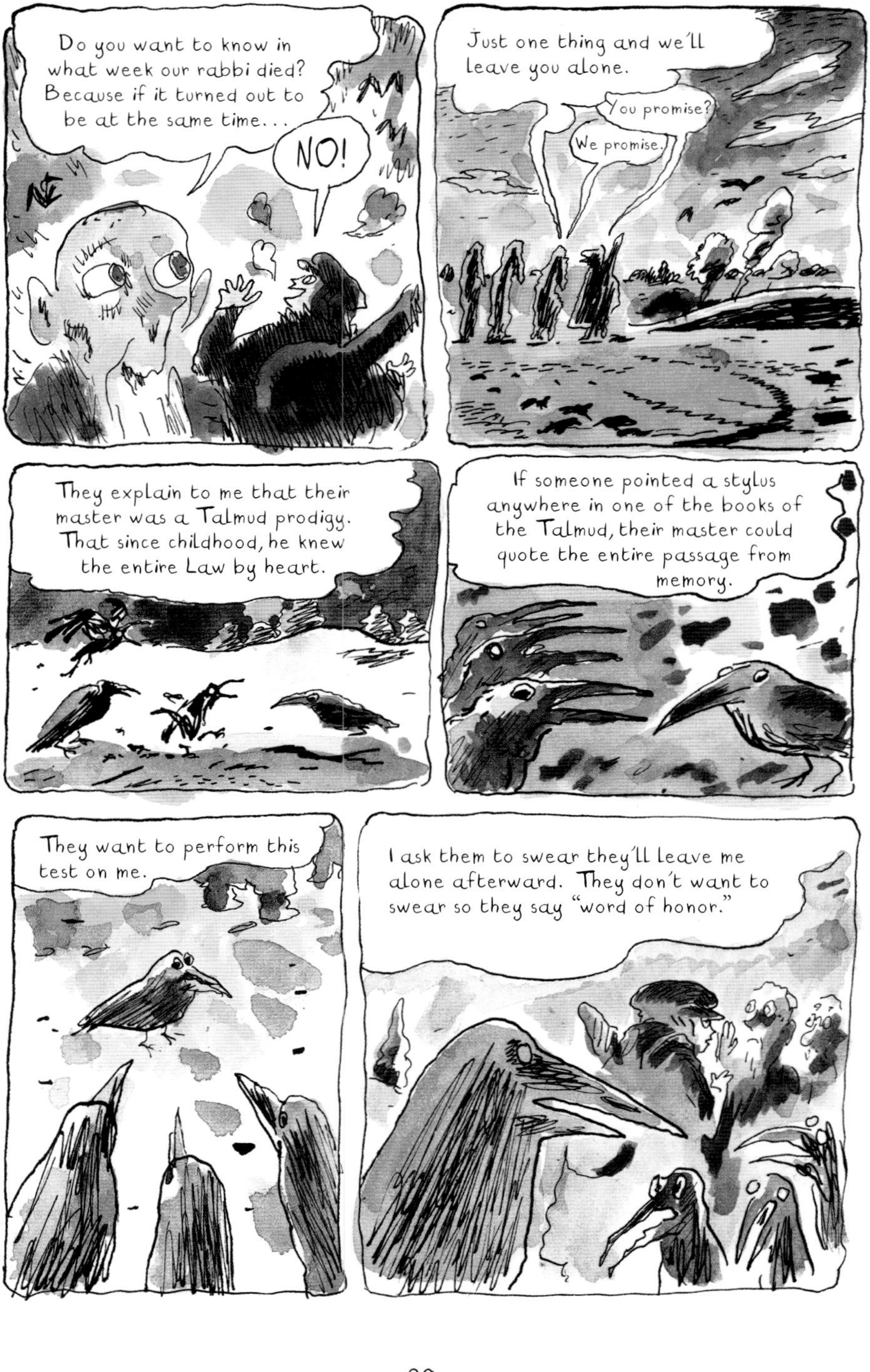
Do you want to know in what week our rabbi died? Because if it turned out to be at the same time...
NO!
Just one thing and we'll leave you alone.
You promise?
We promise.
They explain to me that their master was a Talmud prodigy. That since childhood, he knew the entire Law by heart.
If someone pointed a stylus anywhere in one of the books of the Talmud, their master could quote the entire passage from memory.
They want to perform this test on me.
I ask them to swear they'll leave me alone afterward. They don't want to swear so they say "word of honor."

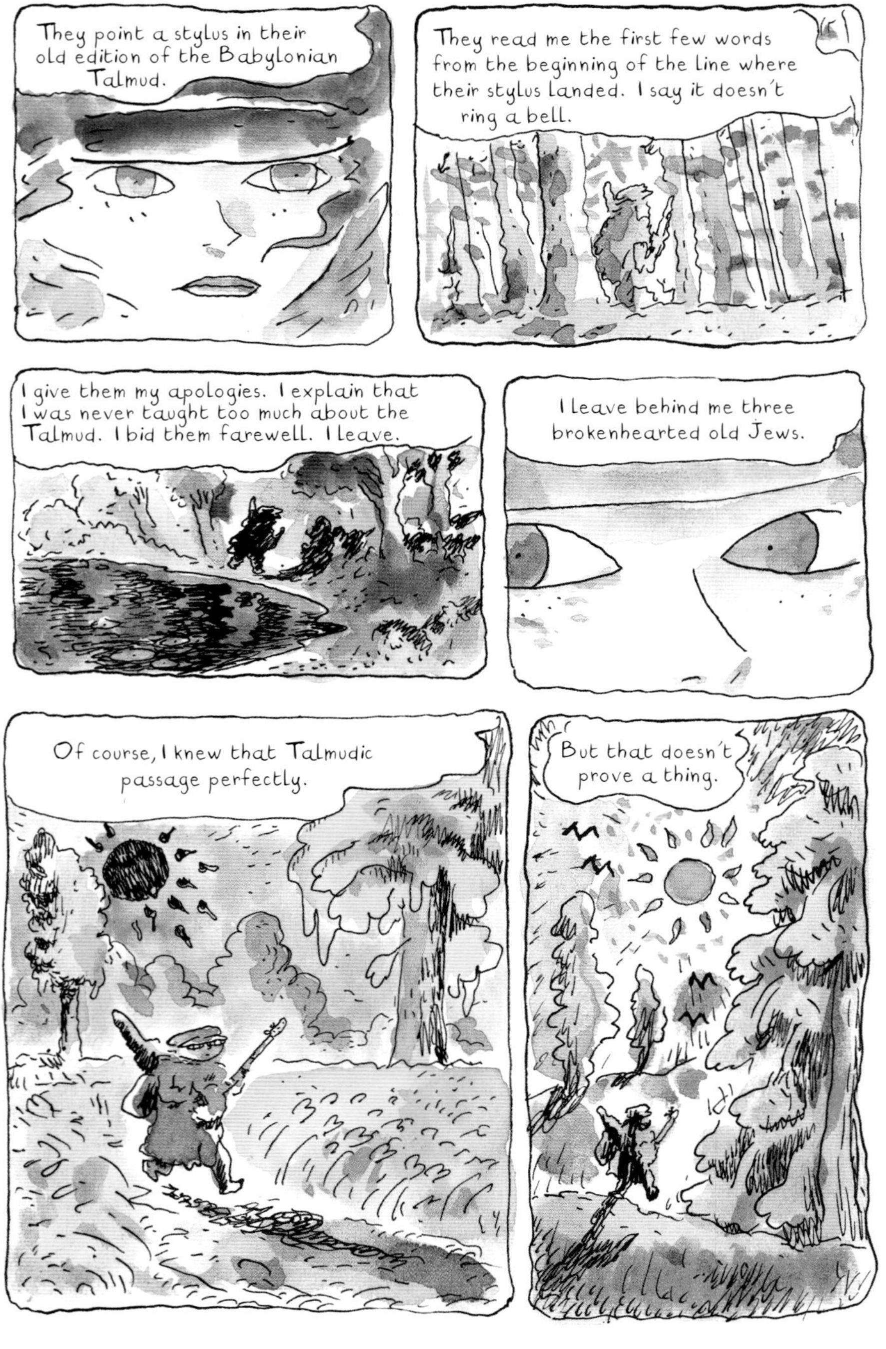
They point a stylus in their old edition of the Babylonian Talmud.
They read me the first few words from the beginning of the line where their stylus landed. I say it doesn't ring a bell.
I give them my apologies. I explain that I was never taught too much about the Talmud. I bid them farewell. I leave.
I leave behind me three brokenhearted old Jews.
Of course, I knew that Talmudic passage perfectly.
But that doesn't prove a thing.

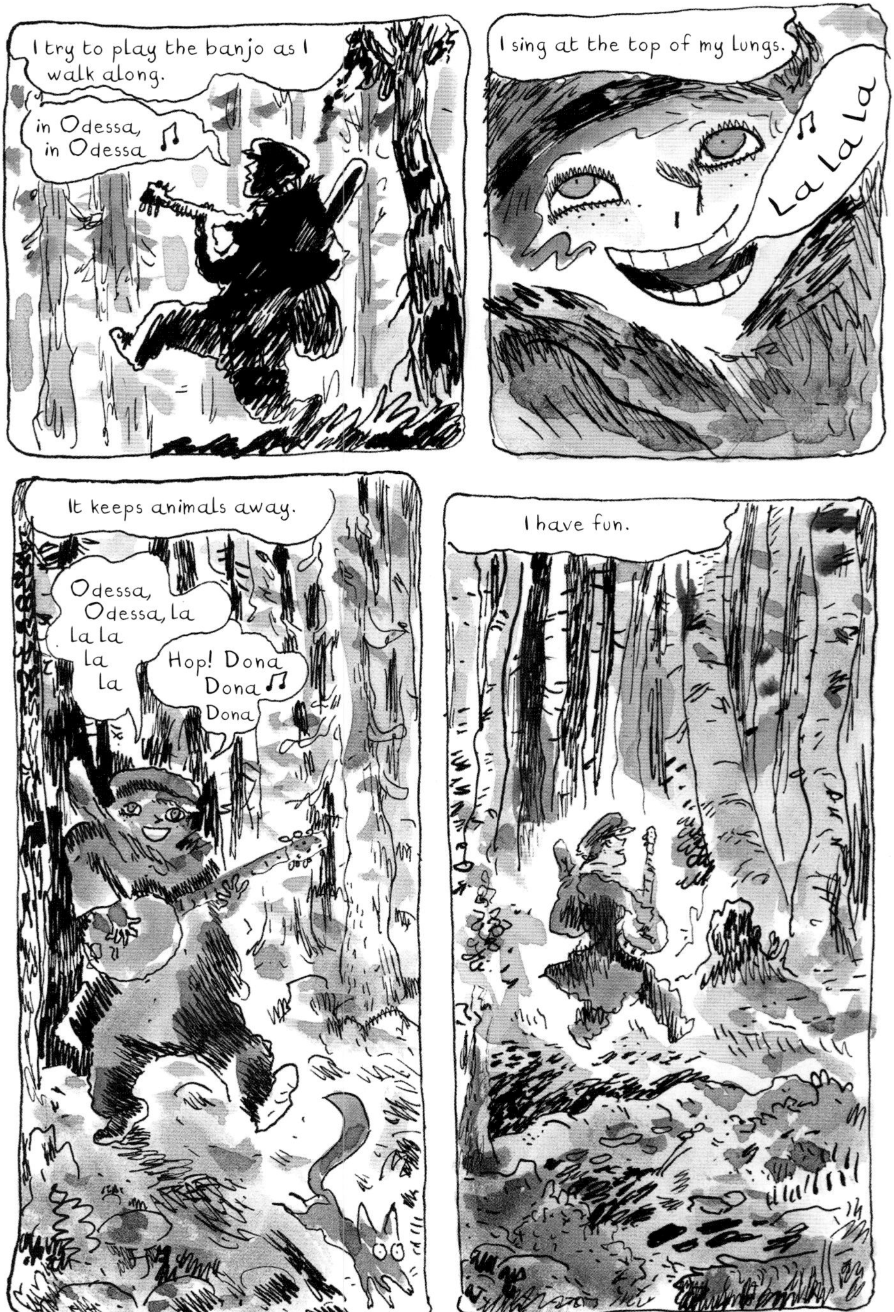
I try to play the banjo as I walk along.
in Odessa, in Odessa ♫
I sing at the top of my lungs.
♫ La La La
It keeps animals away.
Odessa, Odessa, la la la la la
Hop! Dona Dona ♫ Dona
I have fun.

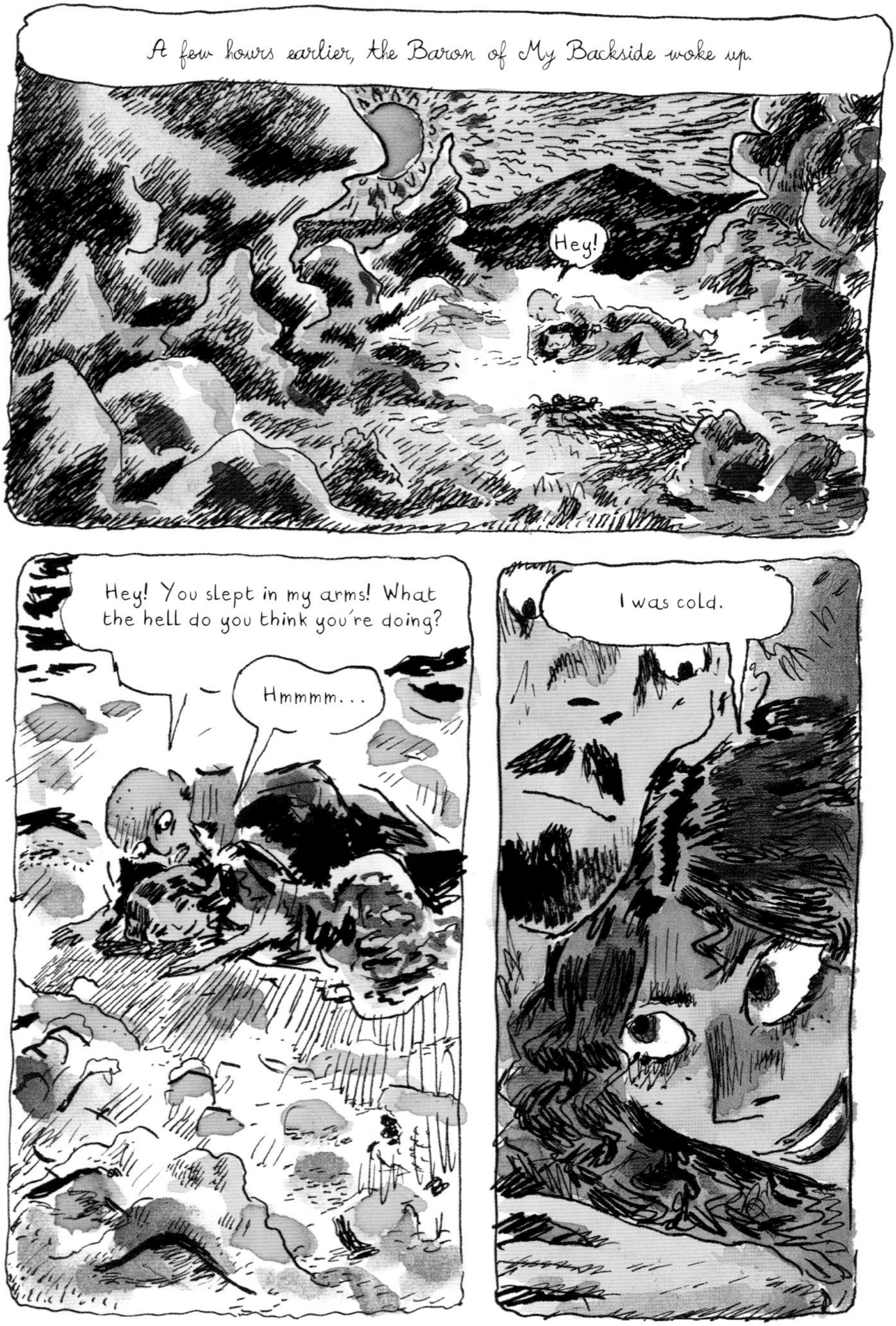
A few hours earlier, the Baron of My Backside woke up.
Hey!
Hey! You slept in my arms! What the hell do you think you're doing?
Hmmmm...
I was cold.

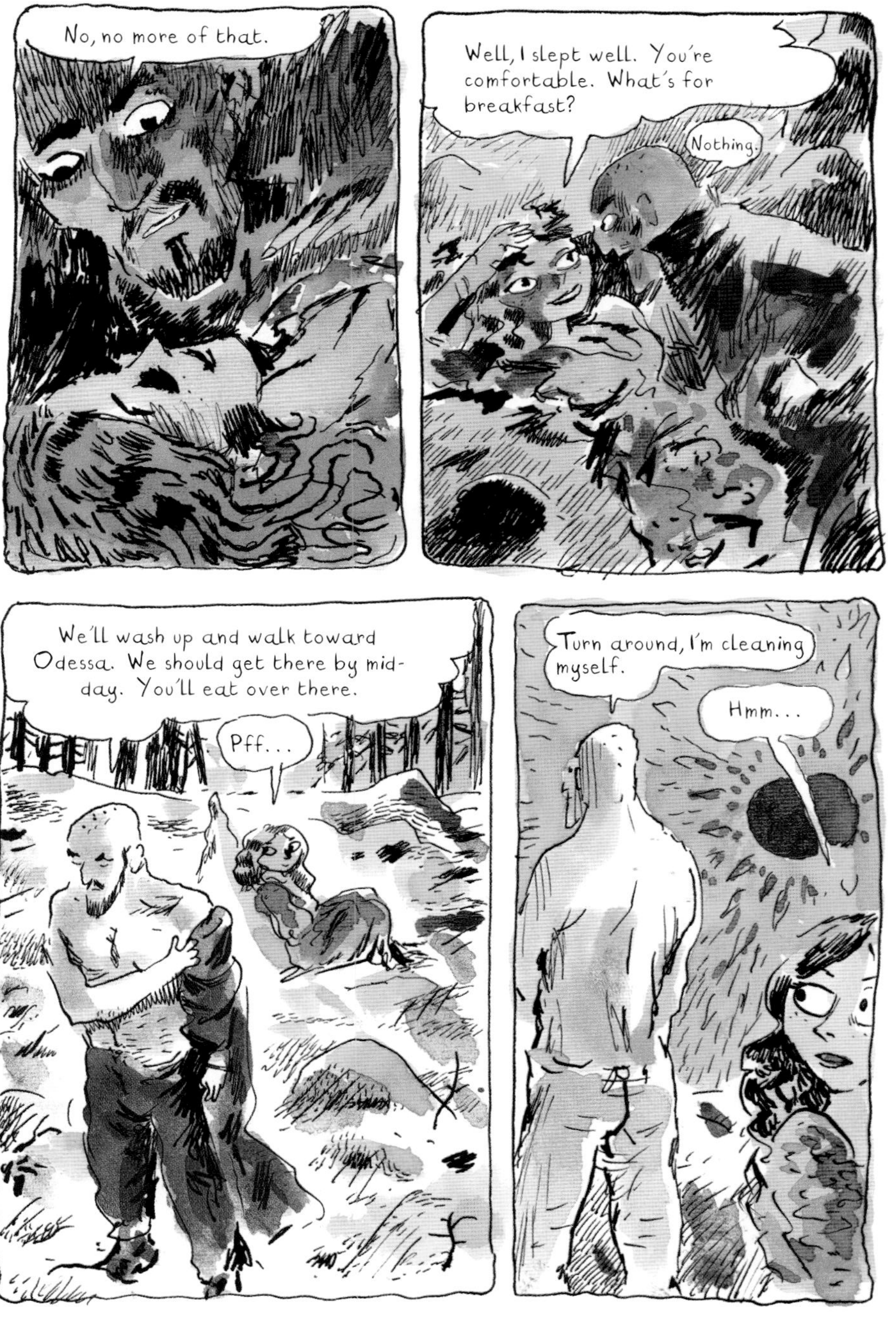
No, no more of that.
Well, I slept well. You're comfortable. What's for breakfast?
Nothing.
We'll wash up and walk toward Odessa. We should get there by mid-day. You'll eat over there.
Pff...
Turn around, I'm cleaning myself.
Hmm...

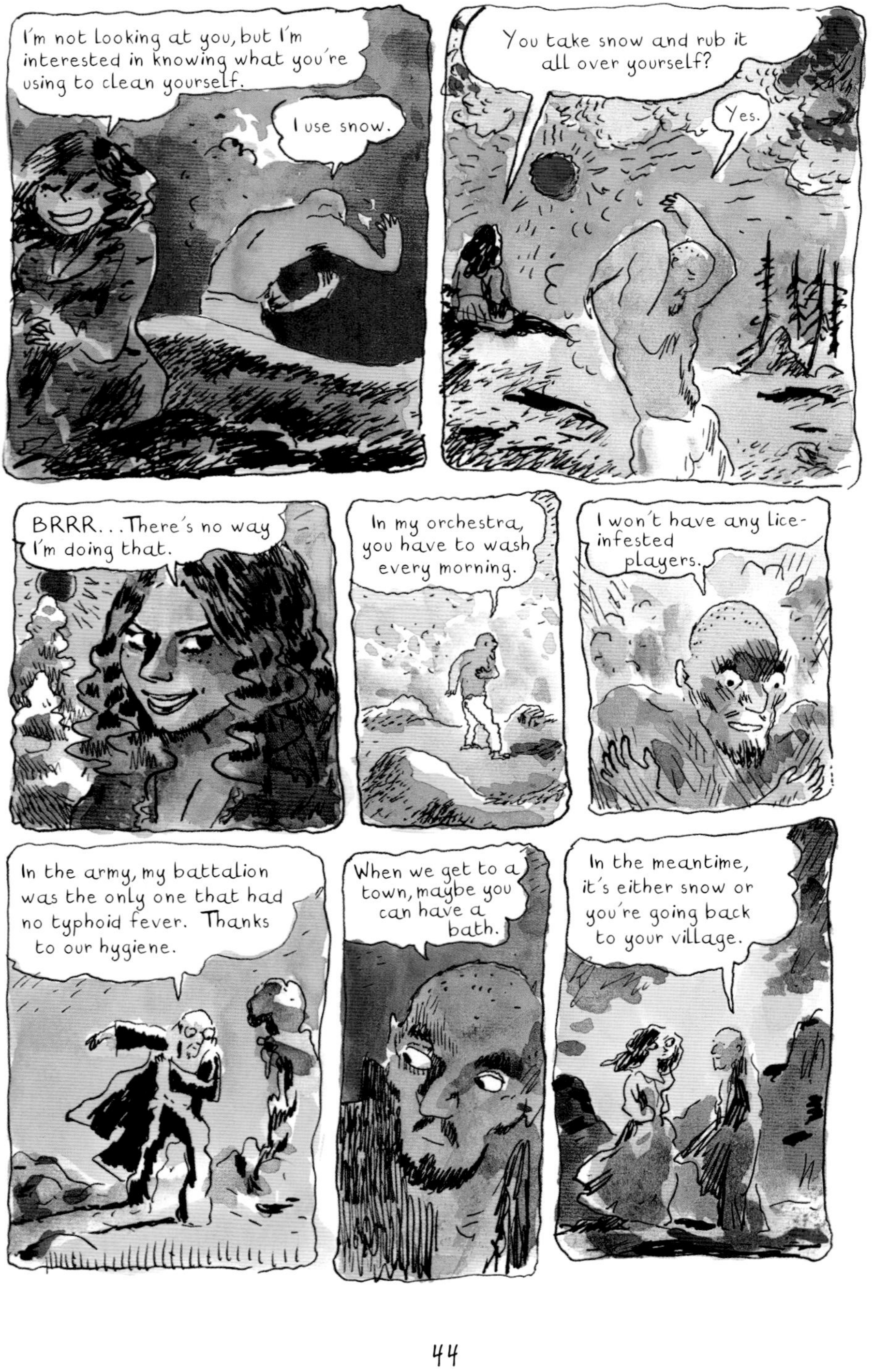
I'm not looking at you, but I'm interested in knowing what you're using to clean yourself.
I use snow.
You take snow and rub it all over yourself?
Yes.
BRRR...There's no way I'm doing that.
In my orchestra, you have to wash every morning.
I won't have any lice-infested players.
In the army, my battalion was the only one that had no typhoid fever. Thanks to our hygiene.
When we get to a town, maybe you can have a bath.
In the meantime, it's either snow or you're going back to your village.

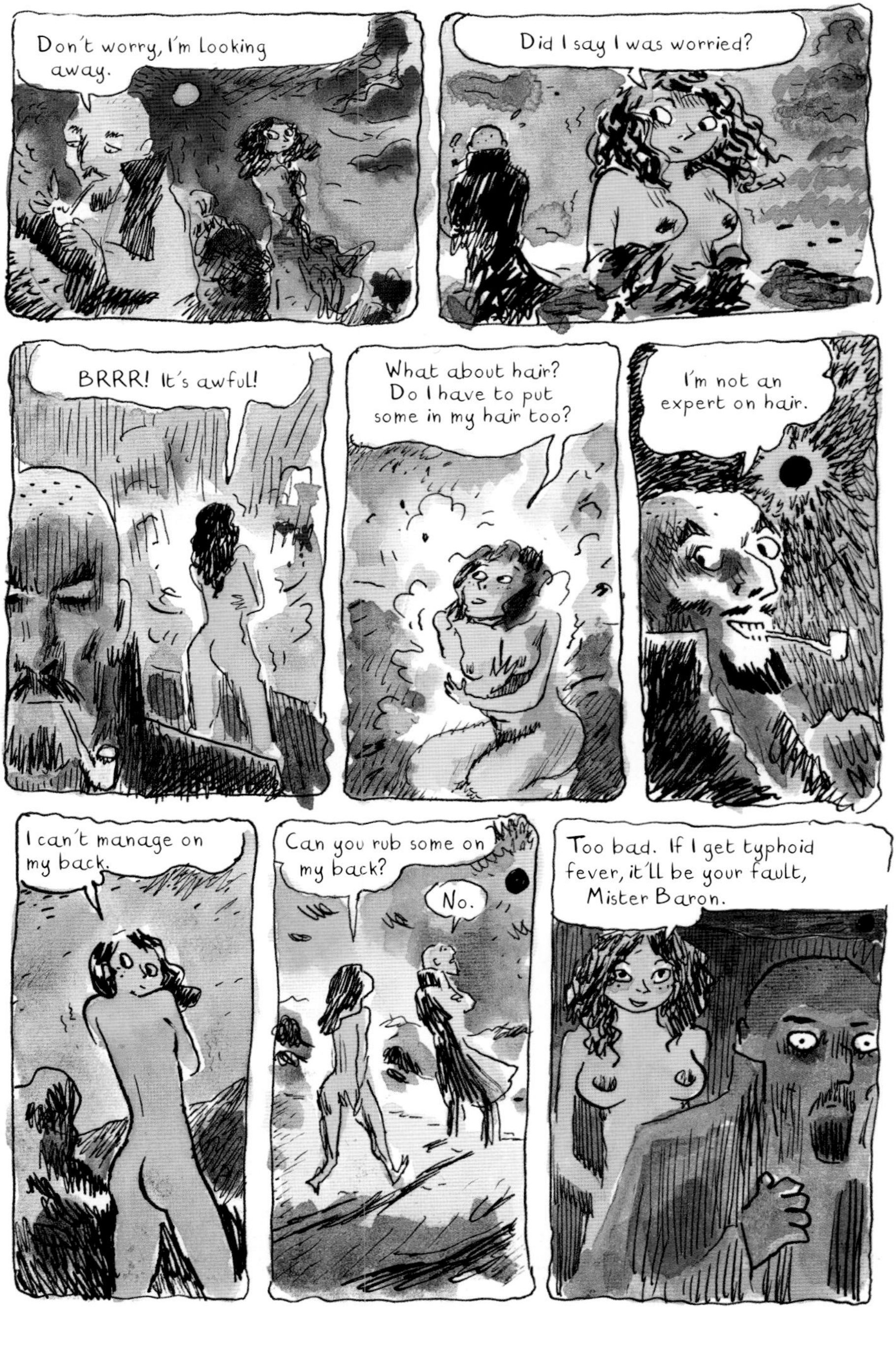
Don't worry, I'm looking away.
Did I say I was worried?
BRRR! It's awful!
What about hair? Do I have to put some in my hair too?
I'm not an expert on hair.
I can't manage on my back.
Can you rub some on my back?
No.
Too bad. If I get typhoid fever, it'll be your fault, Mister Baron.

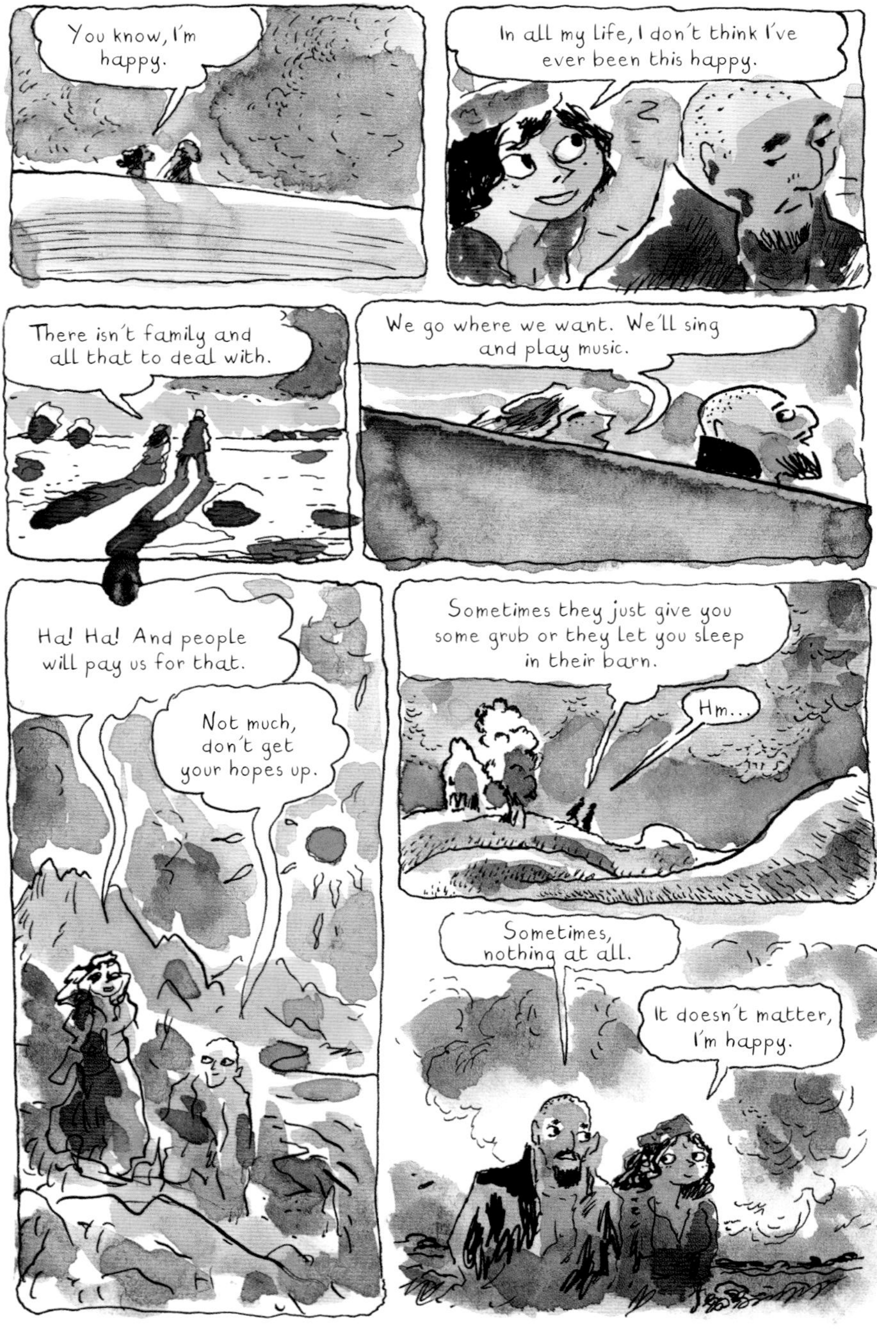
You know, I'm happy.
In all my life, I don't think I've ever been this happy.
There isn't family and all that to deal with.
We go where we want. We'll sing and play music.
Ha! Ha! And people will pay us for that.
Not much, don't get your hopes up.
Sometimes they just give you some grub or they let you sleep in their barn.
Hm...
Sometimes, nothing at all.
It doesn't matter, I'm happy.

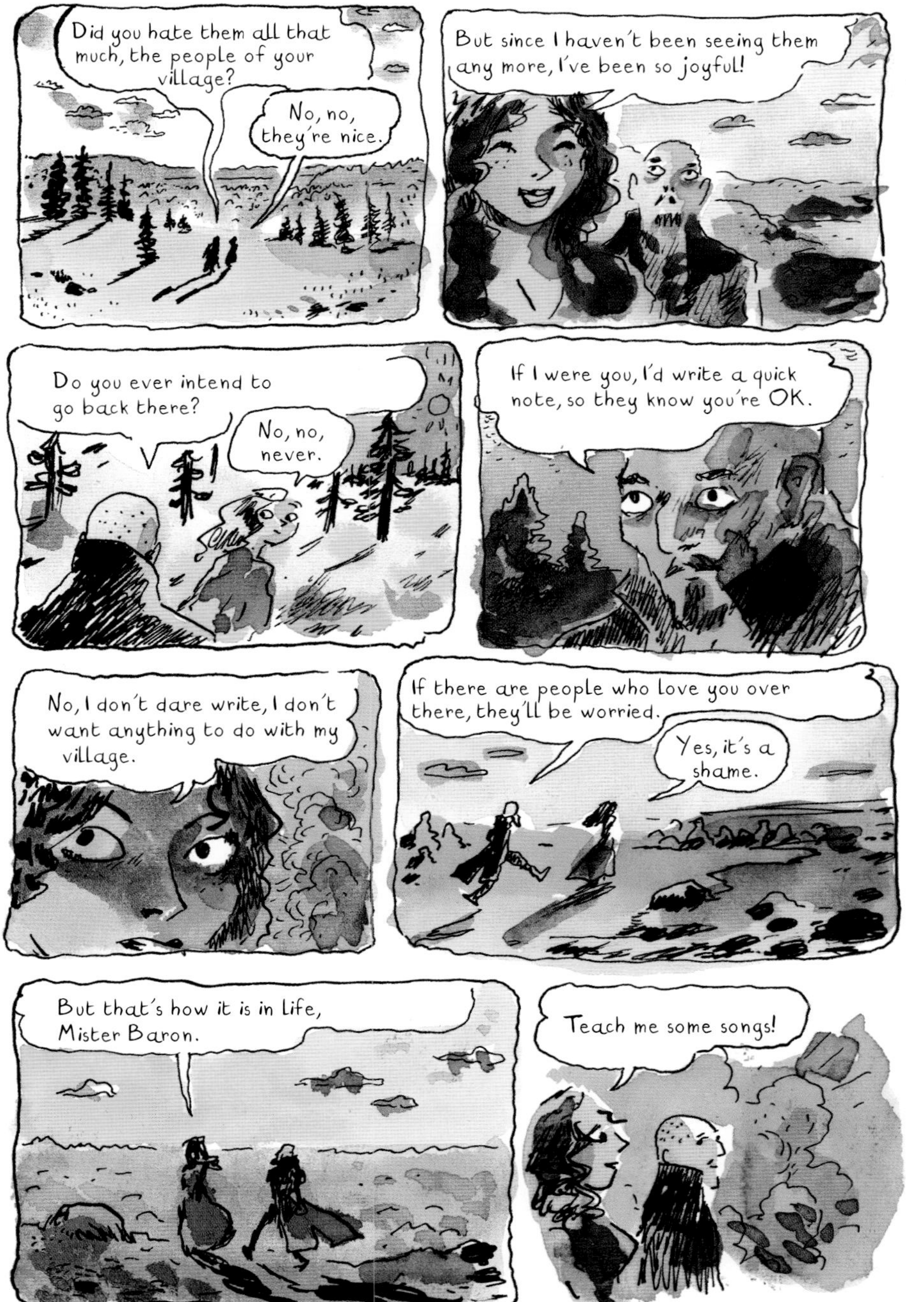
Did you hate them all that much, the people of your village?
No, no, they're nice.
But since I haven't been seeing them any more, I've been so joyful!
Do you ever intend to go back there?
No, no, never.
If I were you, I'd write a quick note, so they know you're OK.
No, I don't dare write, I don't want anything to do with my village.
If there are people who love you over there, they'll be worried.
Yes, it's a shame.
But that's how it is in Life, Mister Baron.
Teach me some songs!

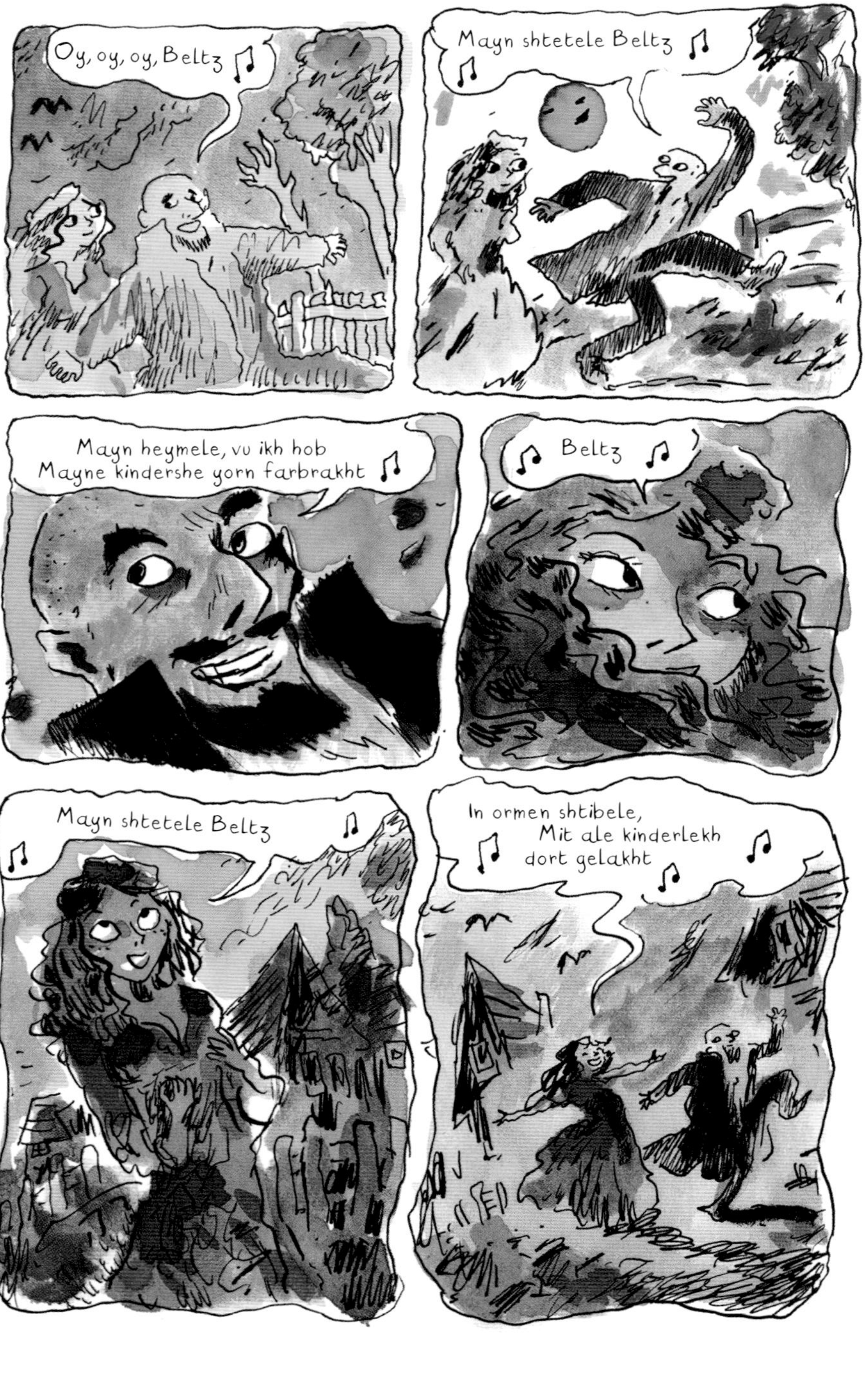
Oy, oy, oy, Beltz
Mayn shtetele Beltz
Mayn heymele, vu ikh hob
Mayne kindershe yorn farbrakht
Beltz
Mayn shtetele Beltz
In ormen shtibele,
Mit ale kinderlekh
dort gelakht

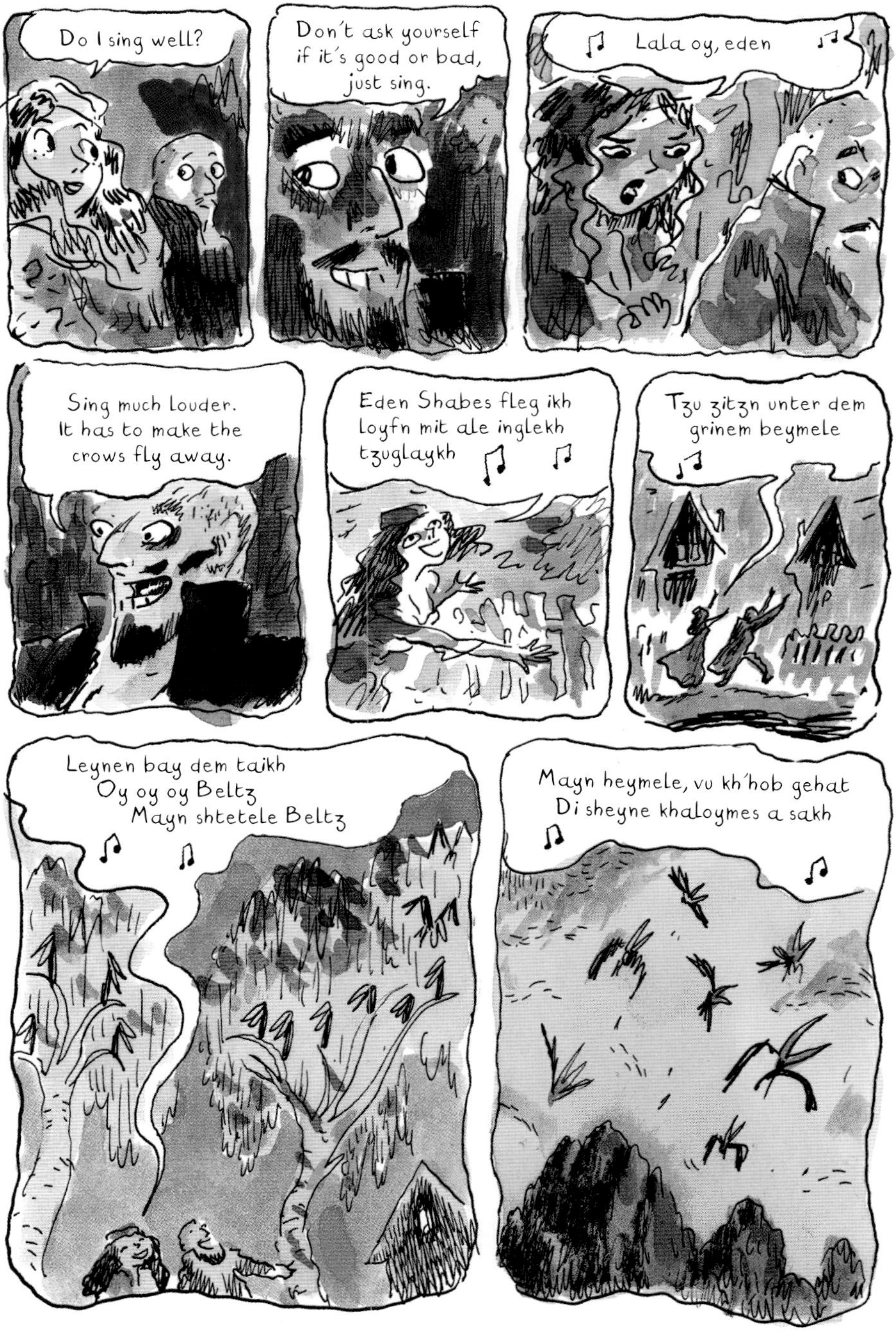
Do I sing well?
Don't ask yourself if it's good or bad, just sing.
Lala oy, eden
Sing much louder. It has to make the crows fly away.
Eden Shabes fleg ikh loyfn mit ale inglekh tzuglaykh
Tzu zitzn unter dem grinem beymele
Leynen bay dem taikh
Oy oy oy Beltz
Mayn shtetele Beltz
Mayn heymele, vu kh'hob gehat
Di sheyne khaloymes a sakh

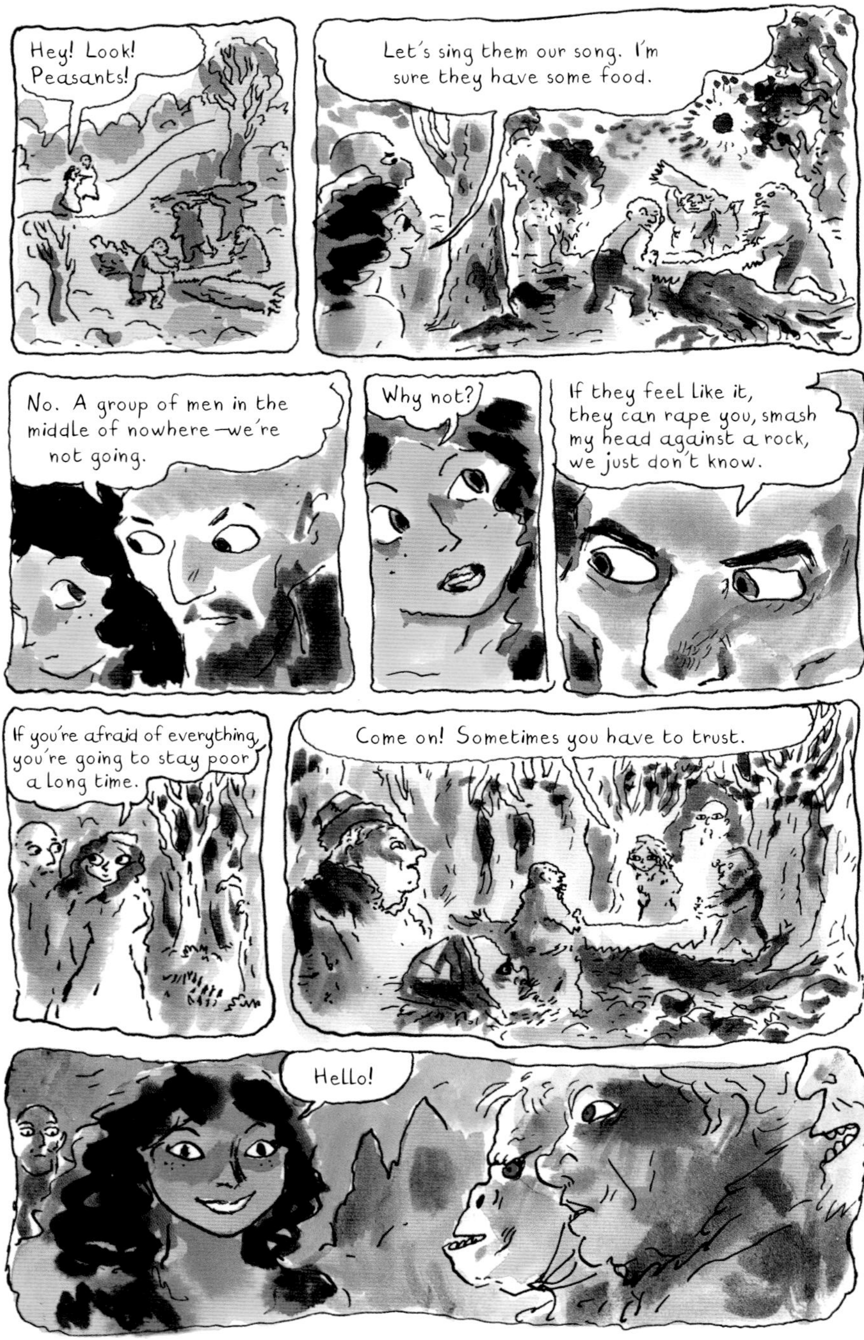
Hey! Look! Peasants!
Let's sing them our song. I'm sure they have some food.
No. A group of men in the middle of nowhere—we're not going.
Why not?
If they feel like it, they can rape you, smash my head against a rock, we just don't know.
If you're afraid of everything, you're going to stay poor a long time.
Come on! Sometimes you have to trust.
Hello!

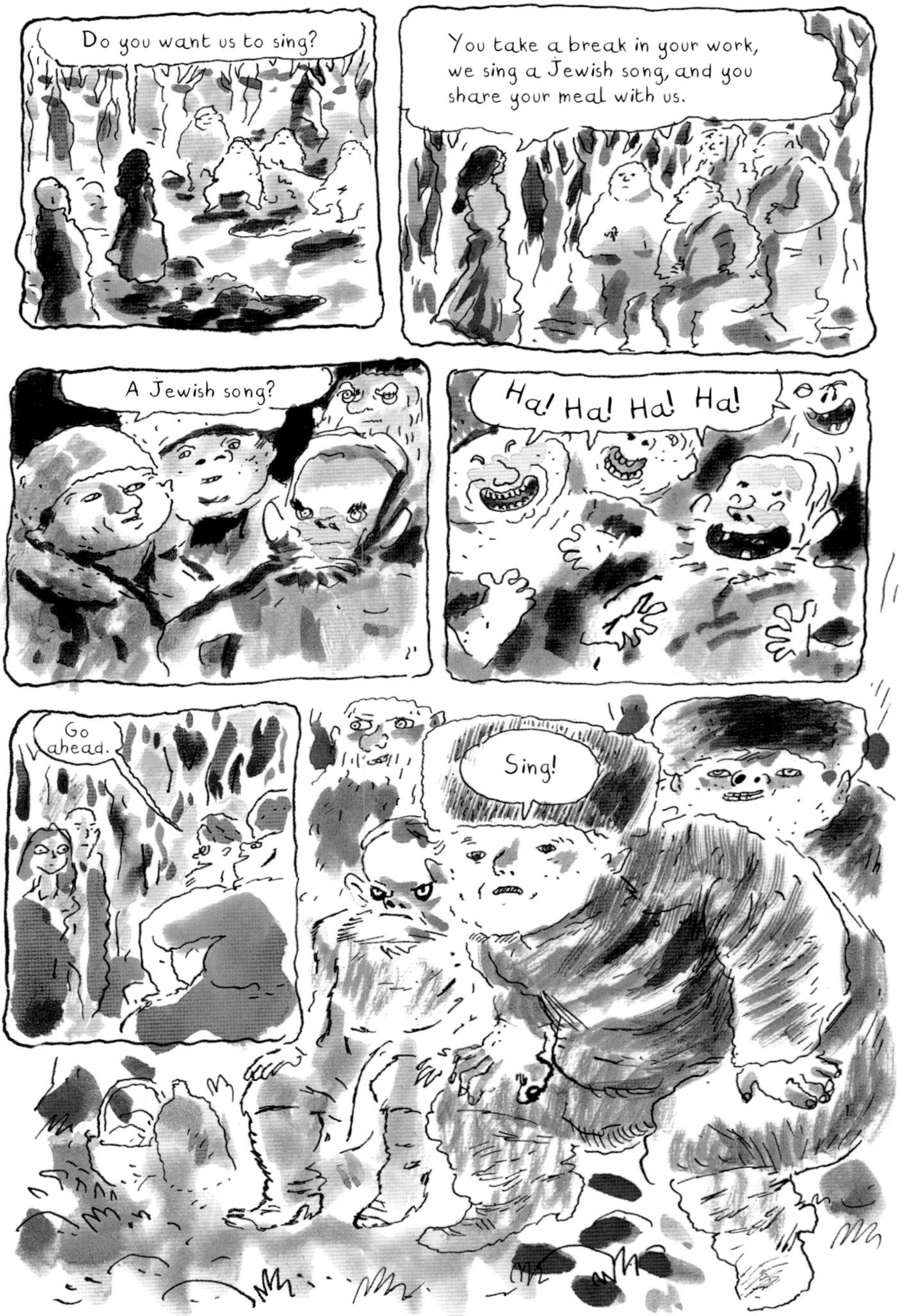
Do you want us to sing?
You take a break in your work, we sing a Jewish song, and you share your meal with us.
A Jewish song?
Ha! Ha! Ha! Ha!
Go ahead.
Sing!

She sings. The Baron accompanies her on the harmonica.

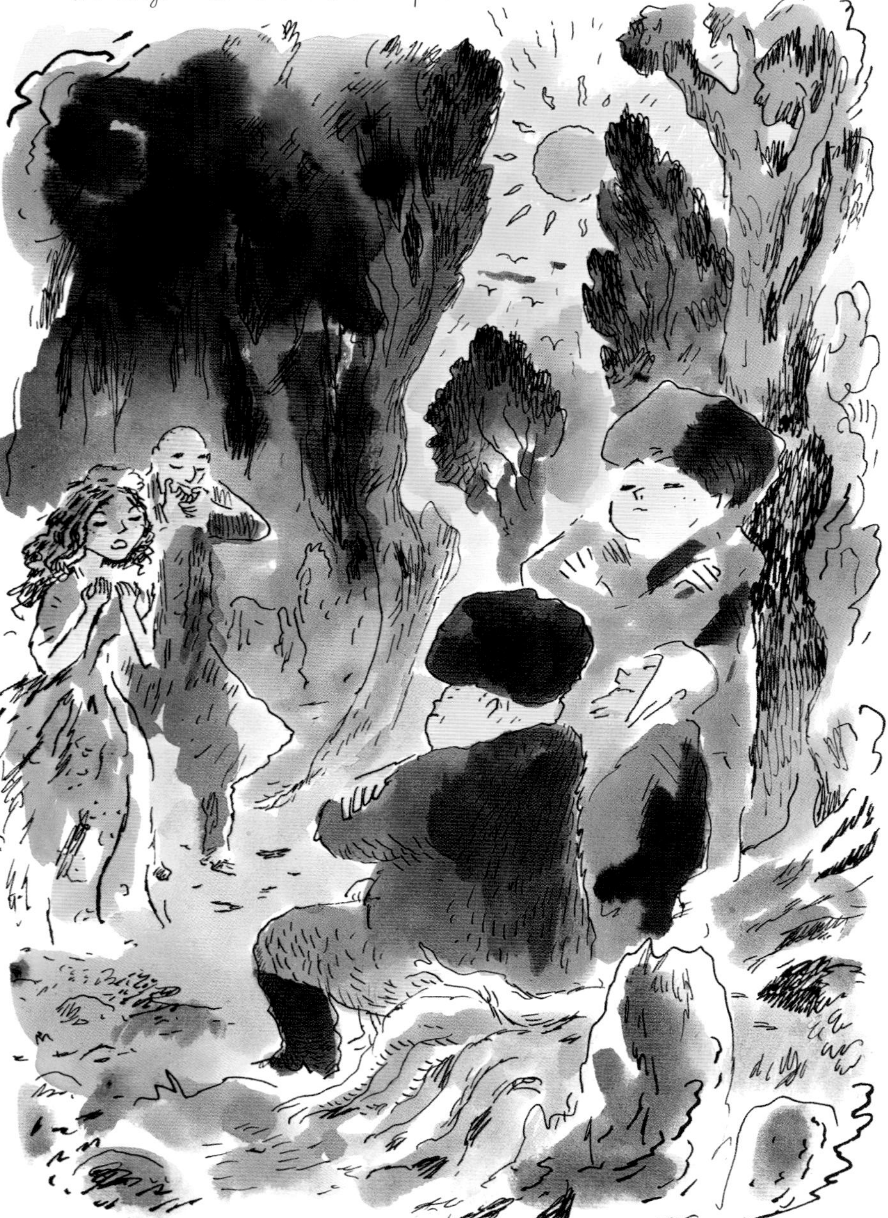

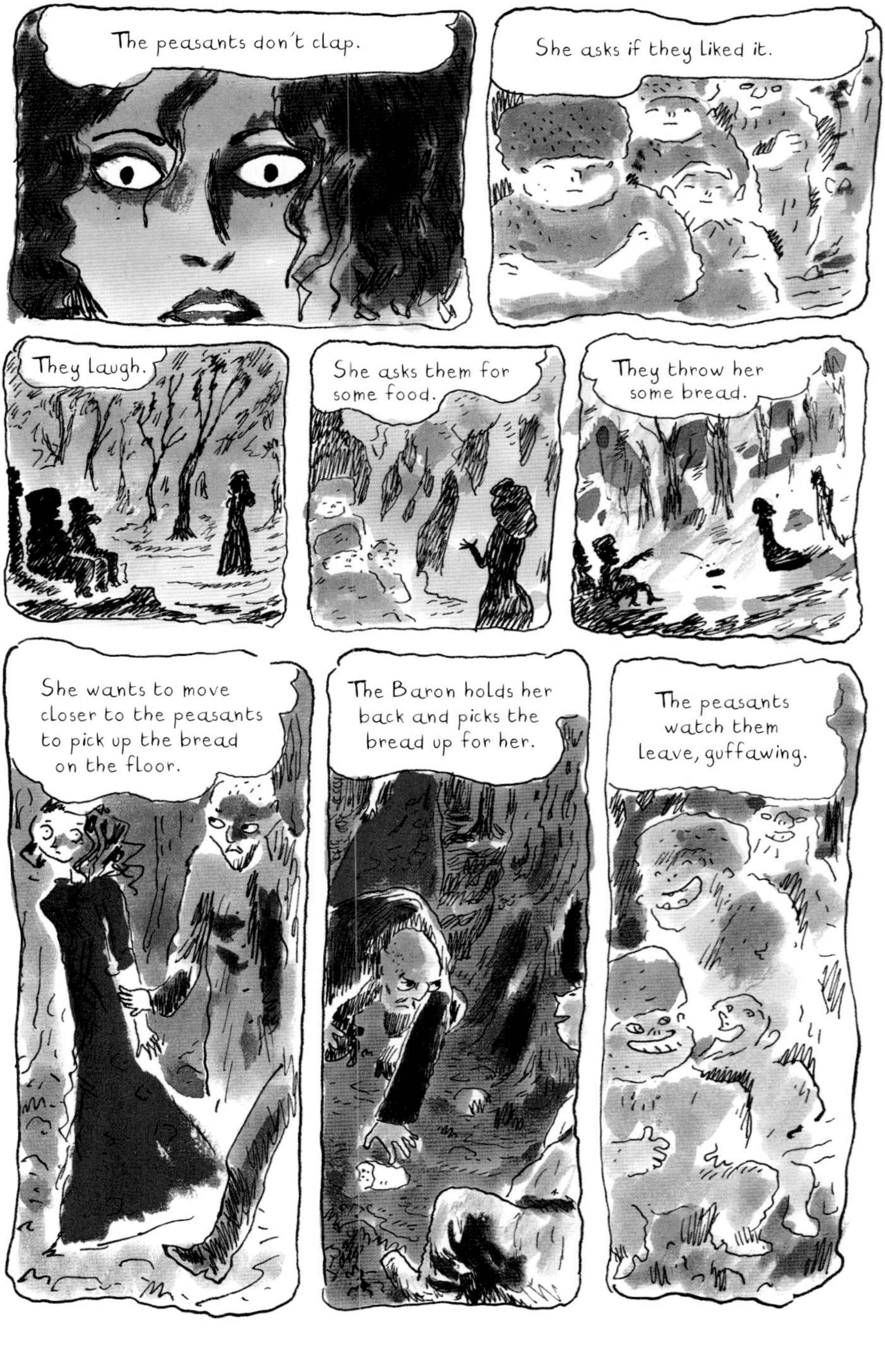
The peasants don't clap.
She asks if they liked it.
They laugh.
She asks them for some food.
They throw her some bread.
She wants to move closer to the peasants to pick up the bread on the floor.
The Baron holds her back and picks the bread up for her.
The peasants watch them leave, guffawing.

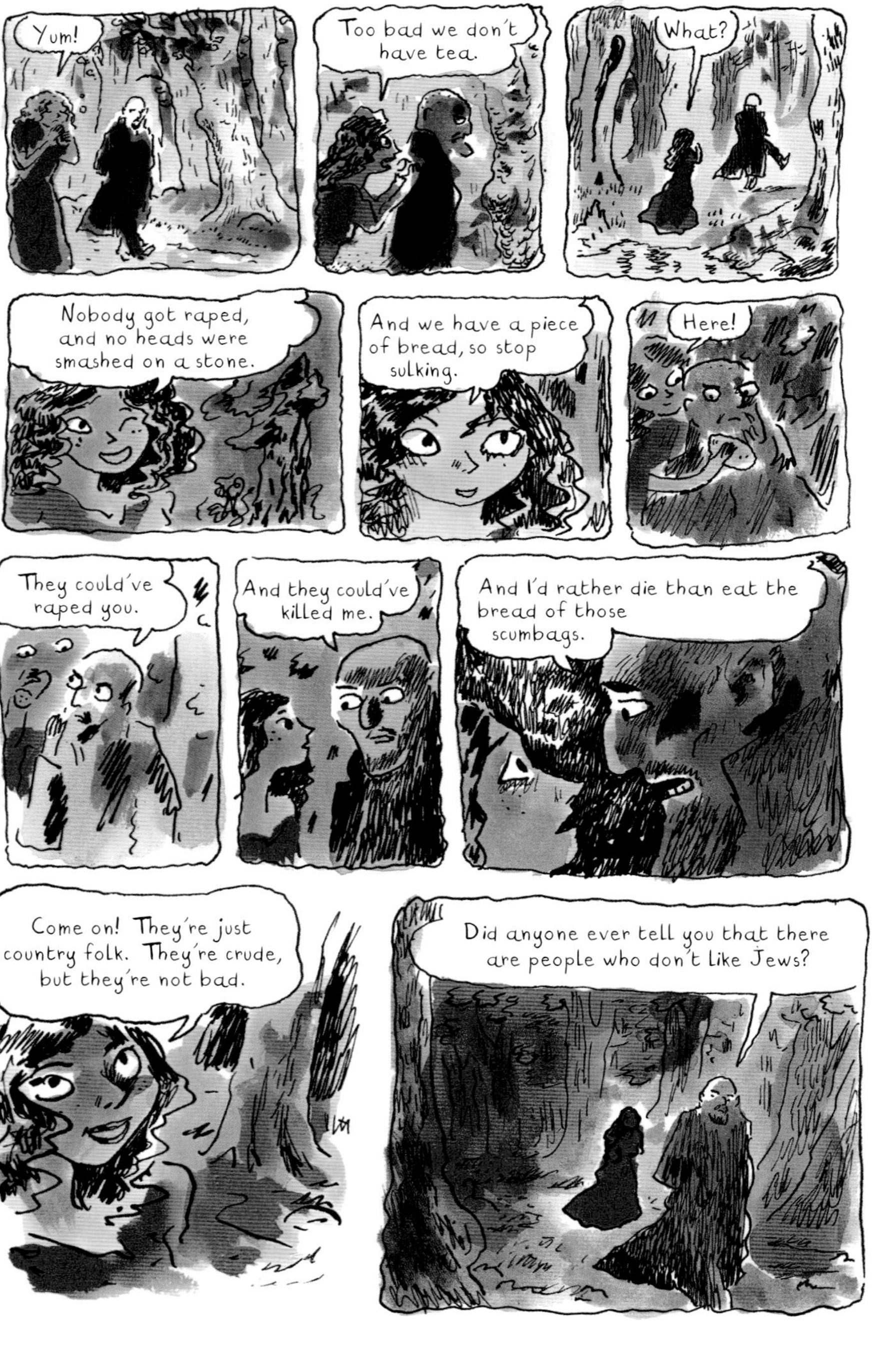
Yum!
Too bad we don't have tea.
What?
Nobody got raped, and no heads were smashed on a stone.
And we have a piece of bread, so stop sulking.
Here!
They could've raped you.
And they could've killed me.
And I'd rather die than eat the bread of those scumbags.
Come on! They're just country folk. They're crude, but they're not bad.
Did anyone ever tell you that there are people who don't like Jews?

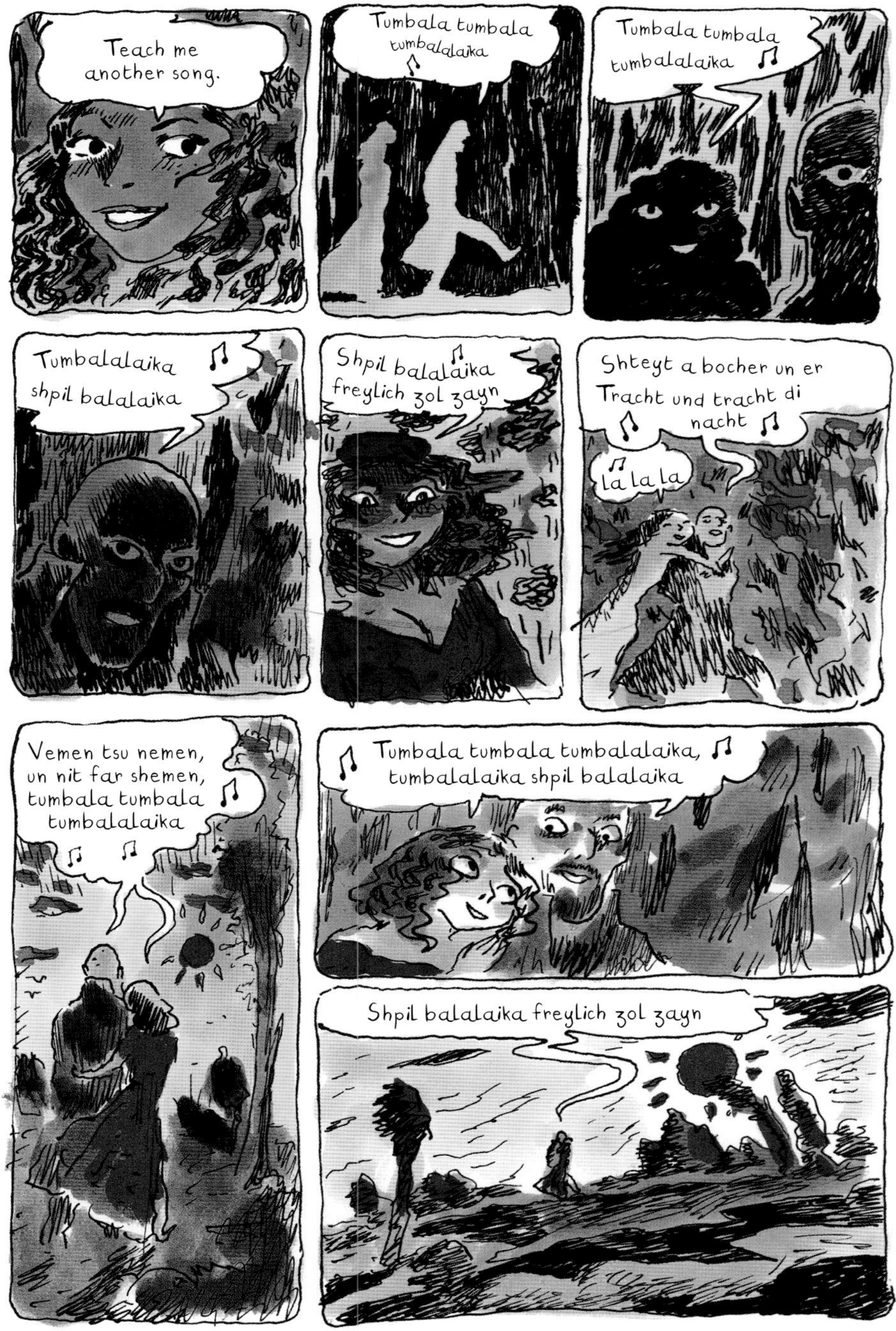
Teach me another song.
Tumbala tumbala tumbalalaika
Tumbala tumbala tumbalalaika
Tumbalalaika shpil balalaika
Shpil balalaika freylich zol zayn
Shteyt a bocher un er Tracht und tracht di nacht
la la la
Vemen tsu nemen, un nit far shemen, tumbala tumbala tumbalalaika
Tumbala tumbala tumbalalaika, tumbalalaika shpil balalaika
Shpil balalaika freylich zol zayn

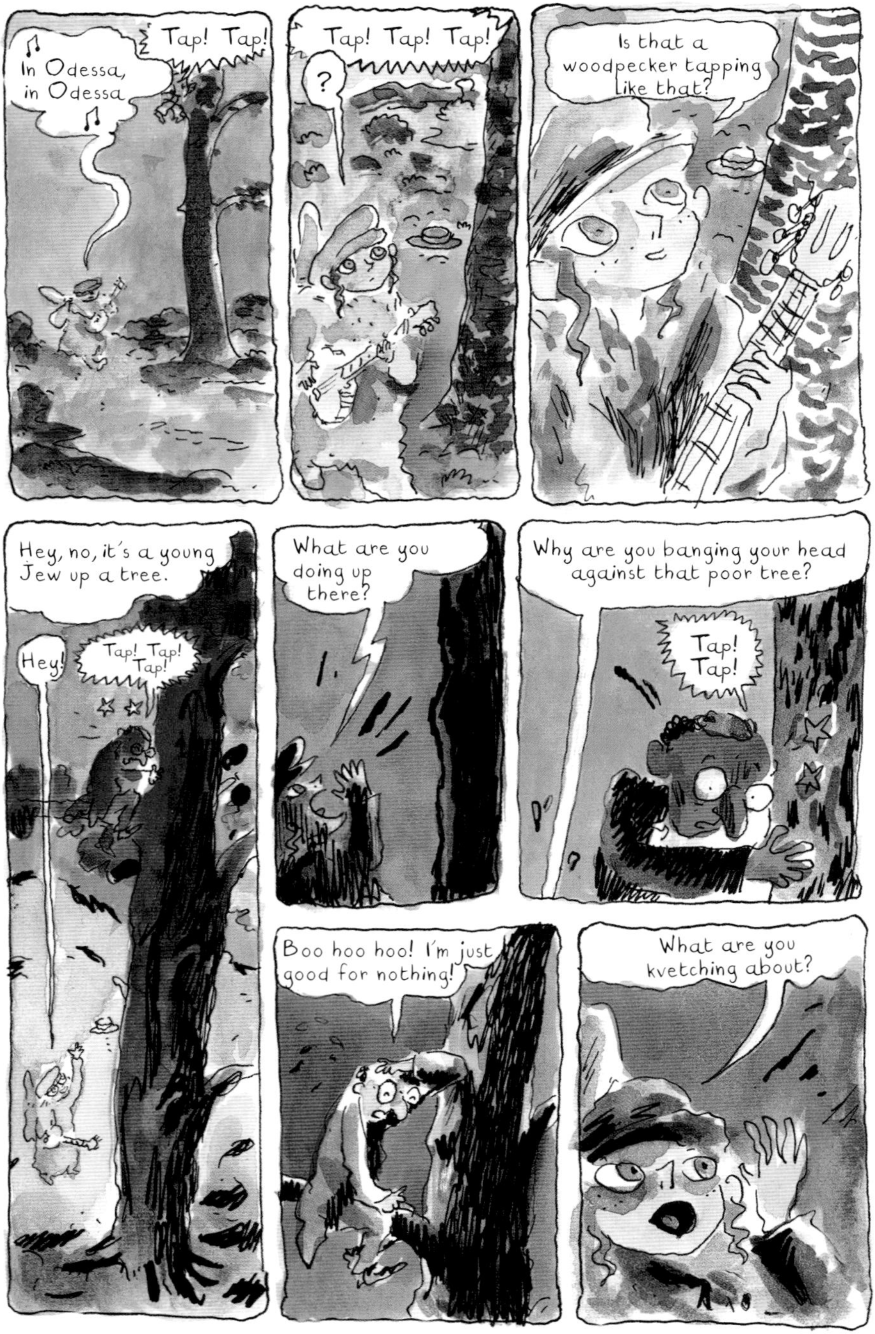

In Odessa, in Odessa
Tap! Tap!
Tap! Tap! Tap!
?
Is that a woodpecker tapping like that?
Hey, no, it's a young Jew up a tree.
Hey!
Tap! Tap! Tap!
What are you doing up there?
Why are you banging your head against that poor tree?
Tap! Tap!
Boo hoo hoo! I'm just good for nothing!
What are you kvetching about?

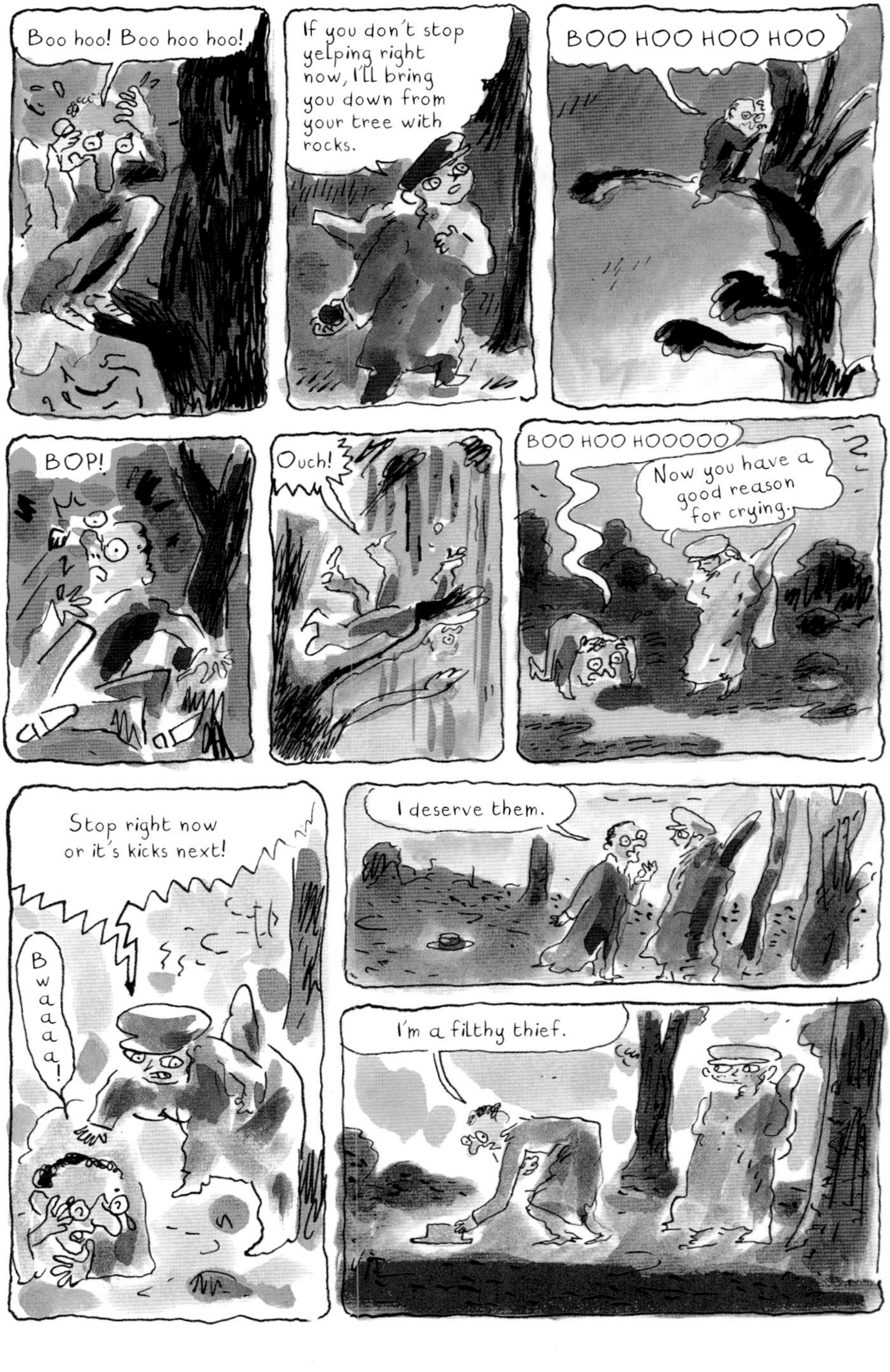
Boo hoo! Boo hoo hoo!
If you don't stop yelping right now, I'll bring you down from your tree with rocks.
BOO HOO HOO HOO
BOP!
Ouch!
BOO HOO HOOOOO
Now you have a good reason for crying.
Stop right now or it's kicks next!
Bwaaaa!
I deserve them.
I'm a filthy thief.

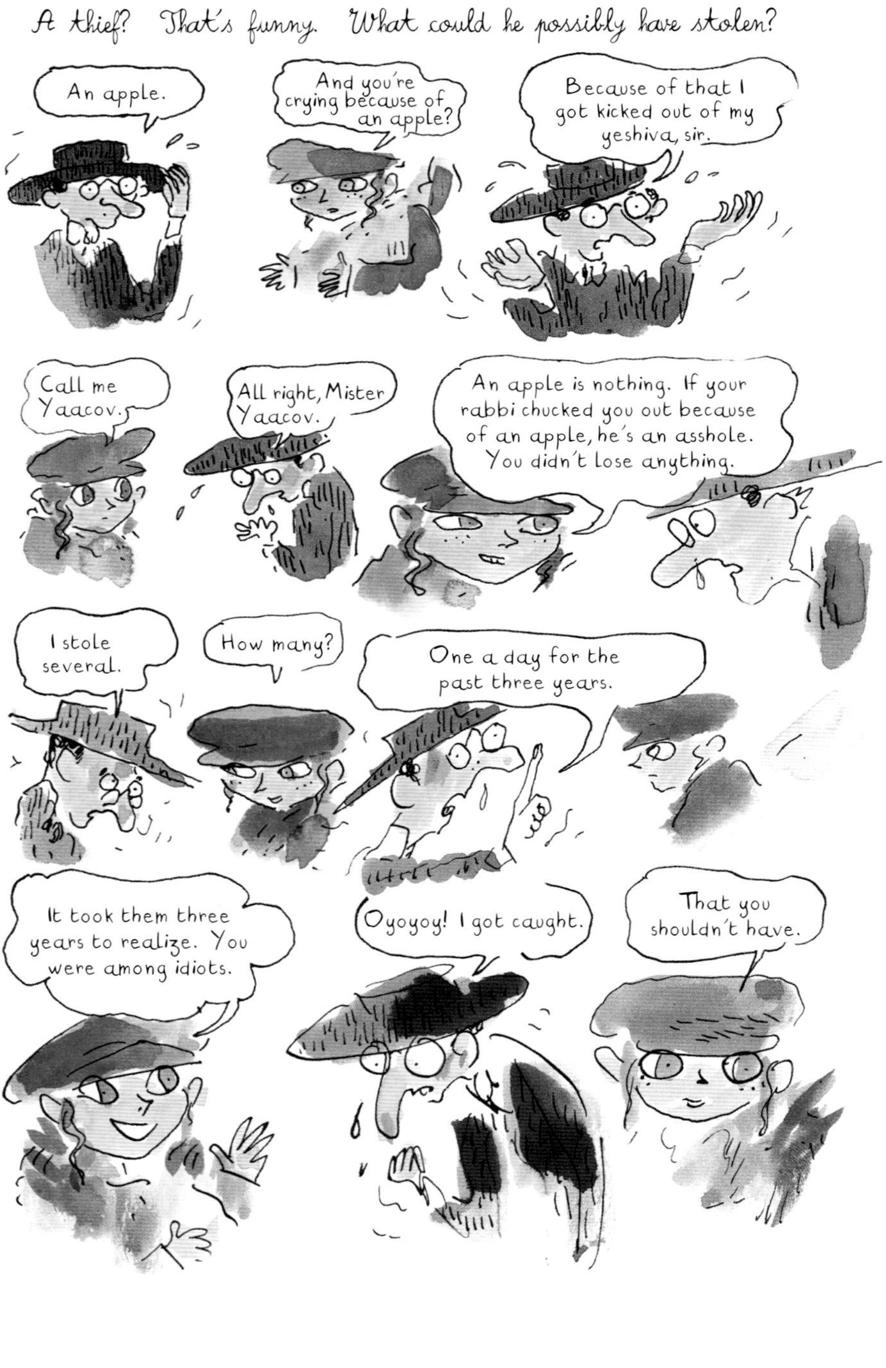
A thief? That's funny. What could he possibly have stolen?
An apple.
And you're crying because of an apple?
Because of that I got kicked out of my yeshiva, sir.
Call me Yaacov.
All right, Mister Yaacov.
An apple is nothing. If your rabbi chucked you out because of an apple, he's an asshole. You didn't lose anything.
I stole several.
How many?
One a day for the past three years.
It took them three years to realize. You were among idiots.
Oyoyoy! I got caught.
That you shouldn't have.

When you're a thief, the only important thing is not getting caught. If you're crying because you're a clumsy oaf, that's a valid reason.

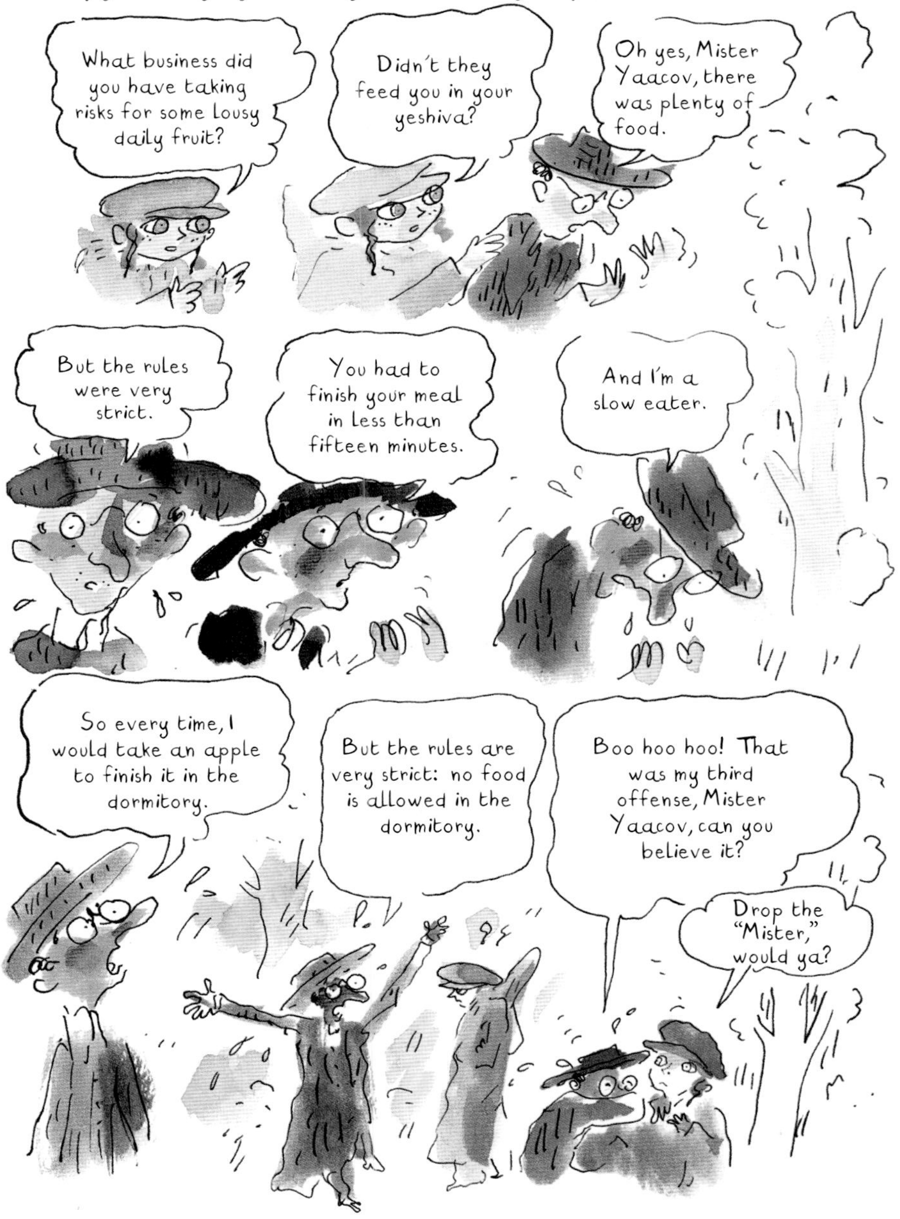

What business did you have taking risks for some lousy daily fruit?
Didn't they feed you in your yeshiva?
Oh yes, Mister Yaacov, there was plenty of food.
But the rules were very strict.
You had to finish your meal in less than fifteen minutes.
And I'm a slow eater.
So every time, I would take an apple to finish it in the dormitory.
But the rules are very strict: no food is allowed in the dormitory.
Boo hoo hoo! That was my third offense, Mister Yaacov, can you believe it?
Drop the "Mister," would ya?

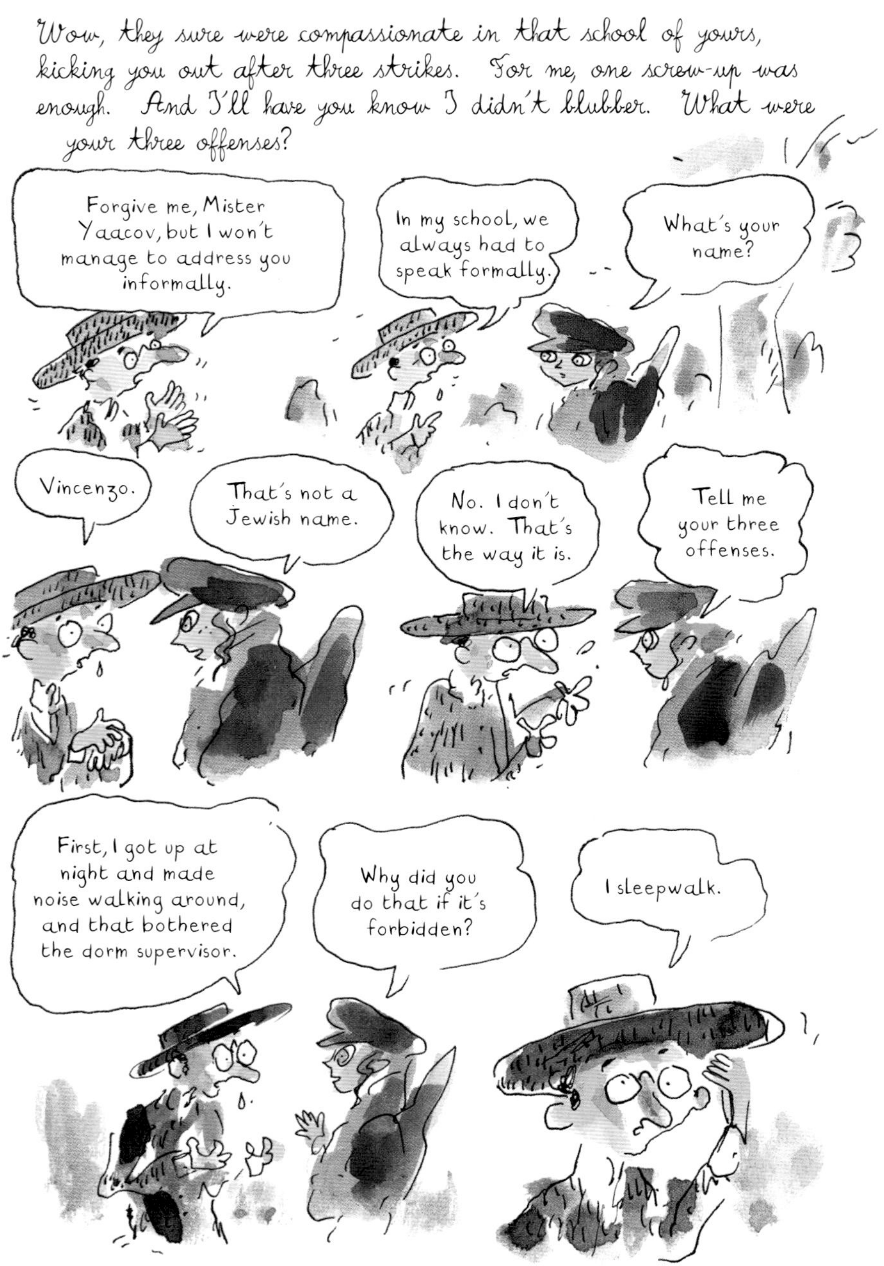
Wow, they sure were compassionate in that school of yours, kicking you out after three strikes. For me, one screw-up was enough. And I'll have you know I didn't blubber. What were your three offenses?
Forgive me, Mister Yaacov, but I won't manage to address you informally.
In my school, we always had to speak formally.
What's your name?
Vincenzo.
That's not a Jewish name.
No. I don't know. That's the way it is.
Tell me your three offenses.
First, I got up at night and made noise walking around, and that bothered the dorm supervisor.
Why did you do that if it's forbidden?
I sleepwalk.

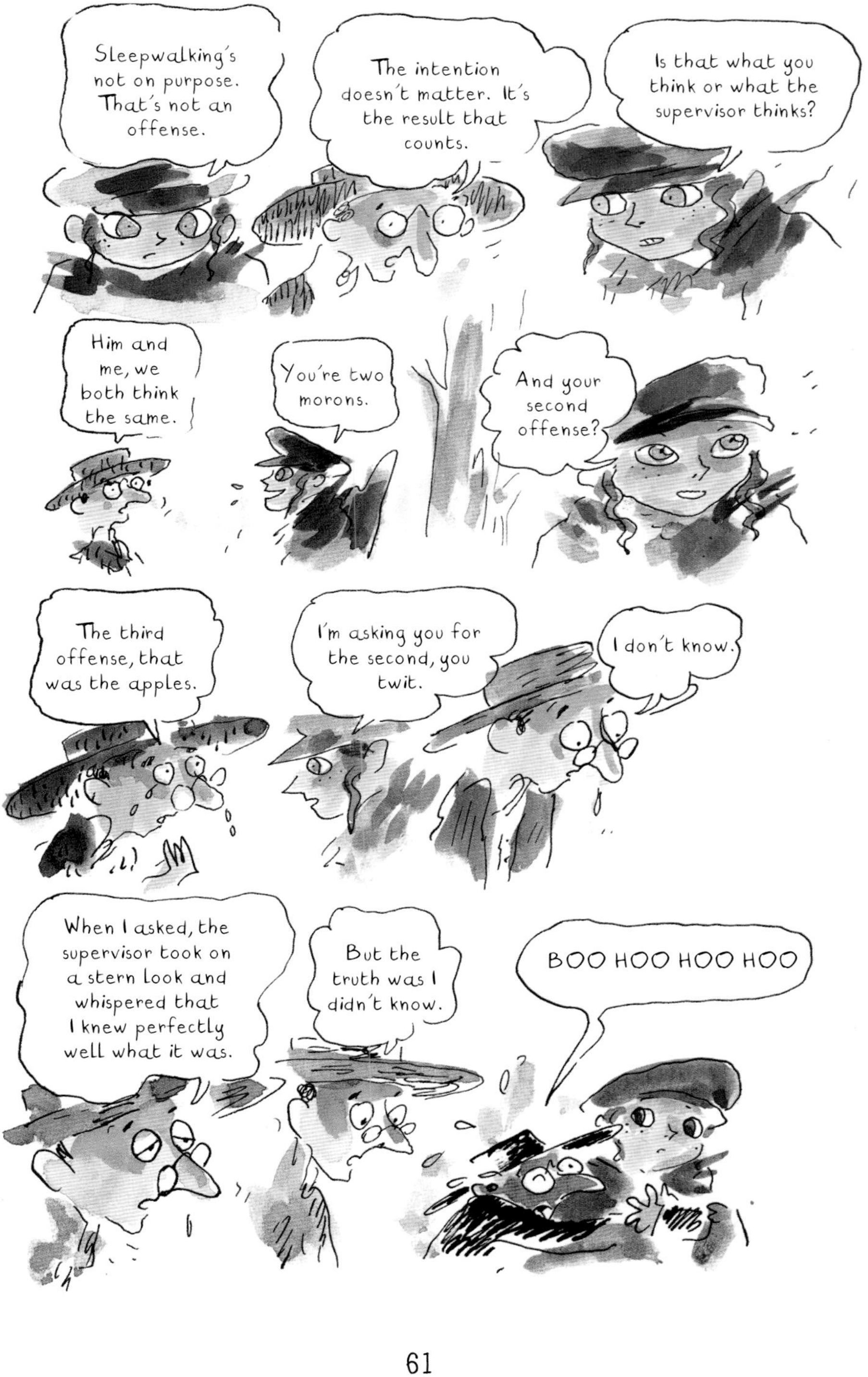
Sleepwalking's not on purpose. That's not an offense.
The intention doesn't matter. It's the result that counts.
Is that what you think or what the supervisor thinks?
Him and me, we both think the same.
You're two morons.
And your second offense?
The third offense, that was the apples.
I'm asking you for the second, you twit.
I don't know.
When I asked, the supervisor took on a stern look and whispered that I knew perfectly well what it was.
But the truth was I didn't know.
BOO HOO HOO HOO

Stop whimpering. Seems to me that they were just fed up with having a sleepwalker among them, so they found the first excuse to chuck you out.

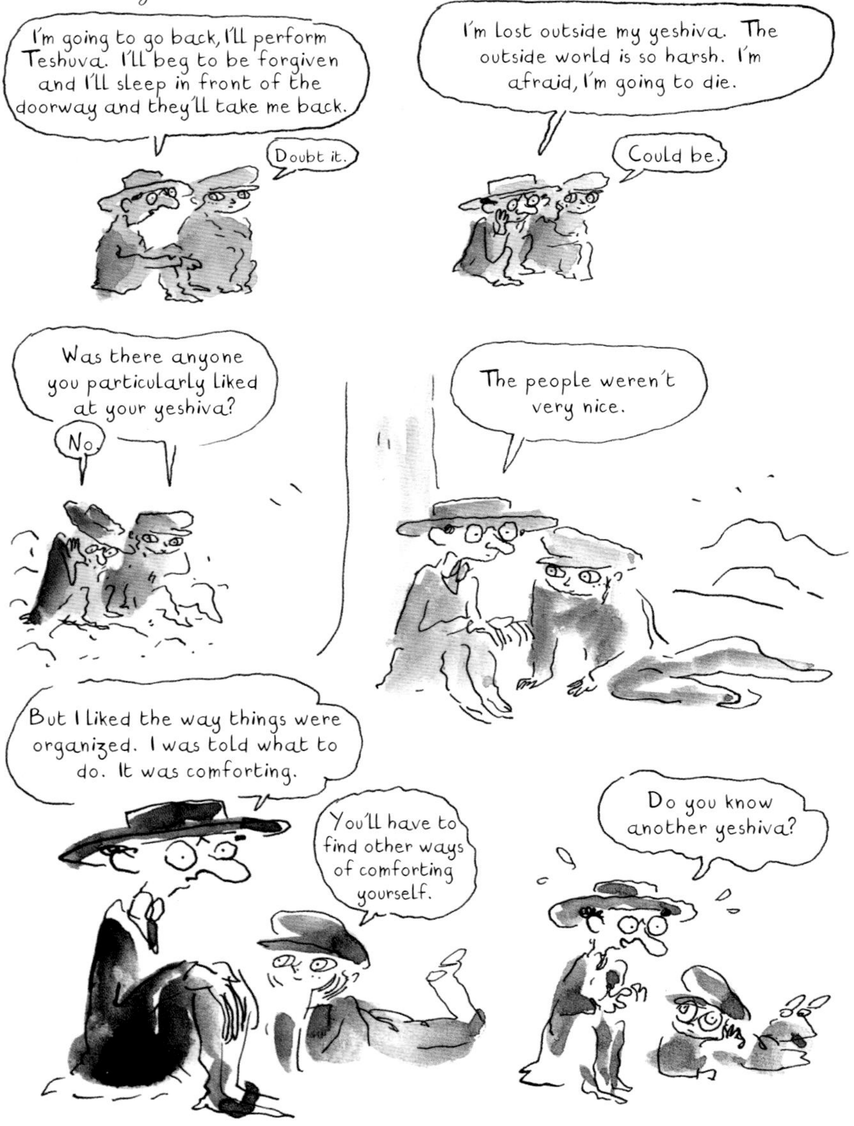
I'm going to go back, I'll perform Teshuva. I'll beg to be forgiven and I'll sleep in front of the doorway and they'll take me back.
Doubt it.
I'm lost outside my yeshiva. The outside world is so harsh. I'm afraid, I'm going to die.
Could be.
Was there anyone you particularly liked at your yeshiva?
No.
The people weren't very nice.
But I liked the way things were organized. I was told what to do. It was comforting.
You'll have to find other ways of comforting yourself.
Do you know another yeshiva?

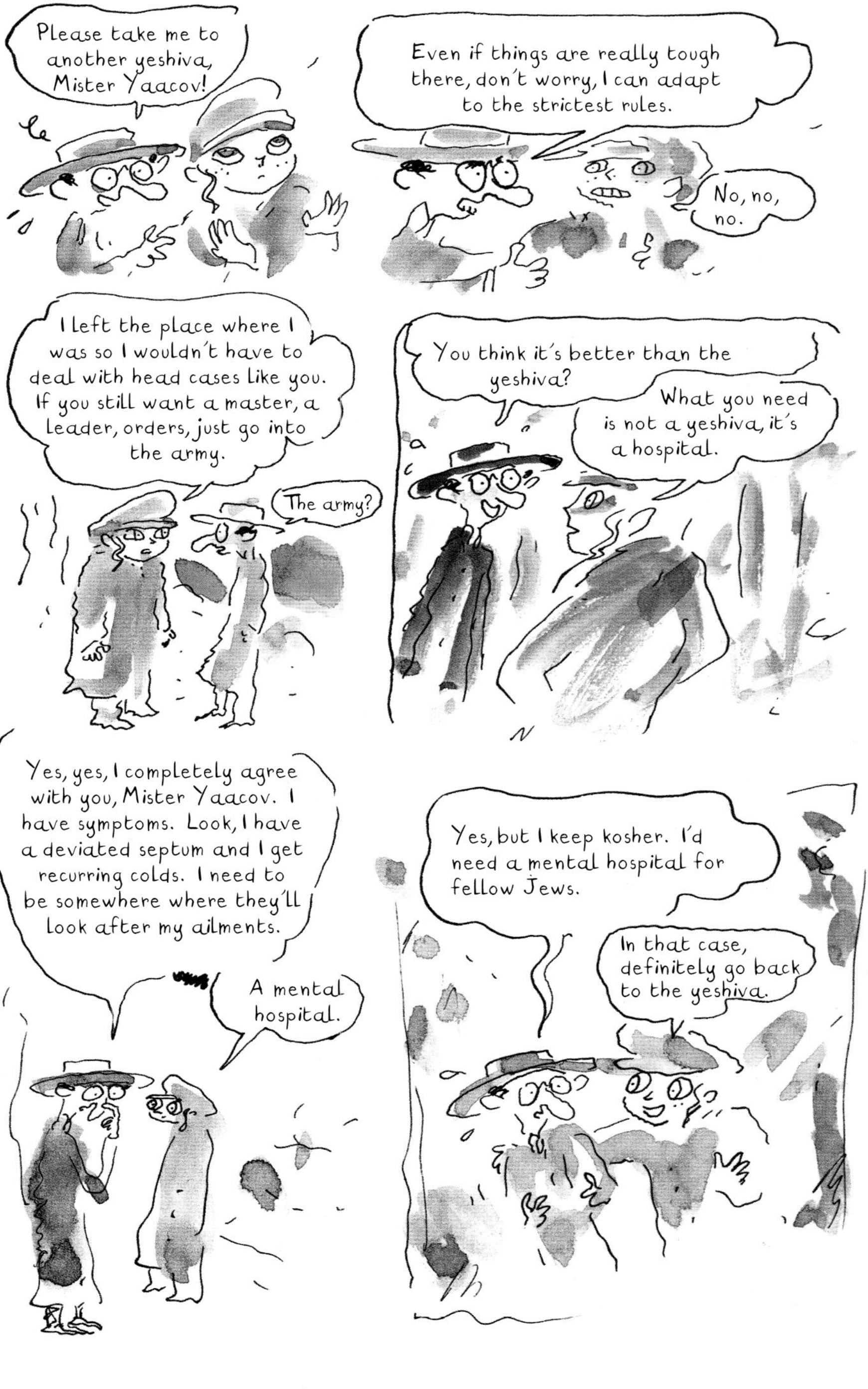
Please take me to another yeshiva, Mister Yaacov!
Even if things are really tough there, don't worry, I can adapt to the strictest rules.
No, no, no.
I left the place where I was so I wouldn't have to deal with head cases like you. If you still want a master, a leader, orders, just go into the army.
The army?
You think it's better than the yeshiva?
What you need is not a yeshiva, it's a hospital.
Yes, yes, I completely agree with you, Mister Yaacov. I have symptoms. Look, I have a deviated septum and I get recurring colds. I need to be somewhere where they'll look after my ailments.
A mental hospital.
Yes, but I keep kosher. I'd need a mental hospital for fellow Jews.
In that case, definitely go back to the yeshiva.

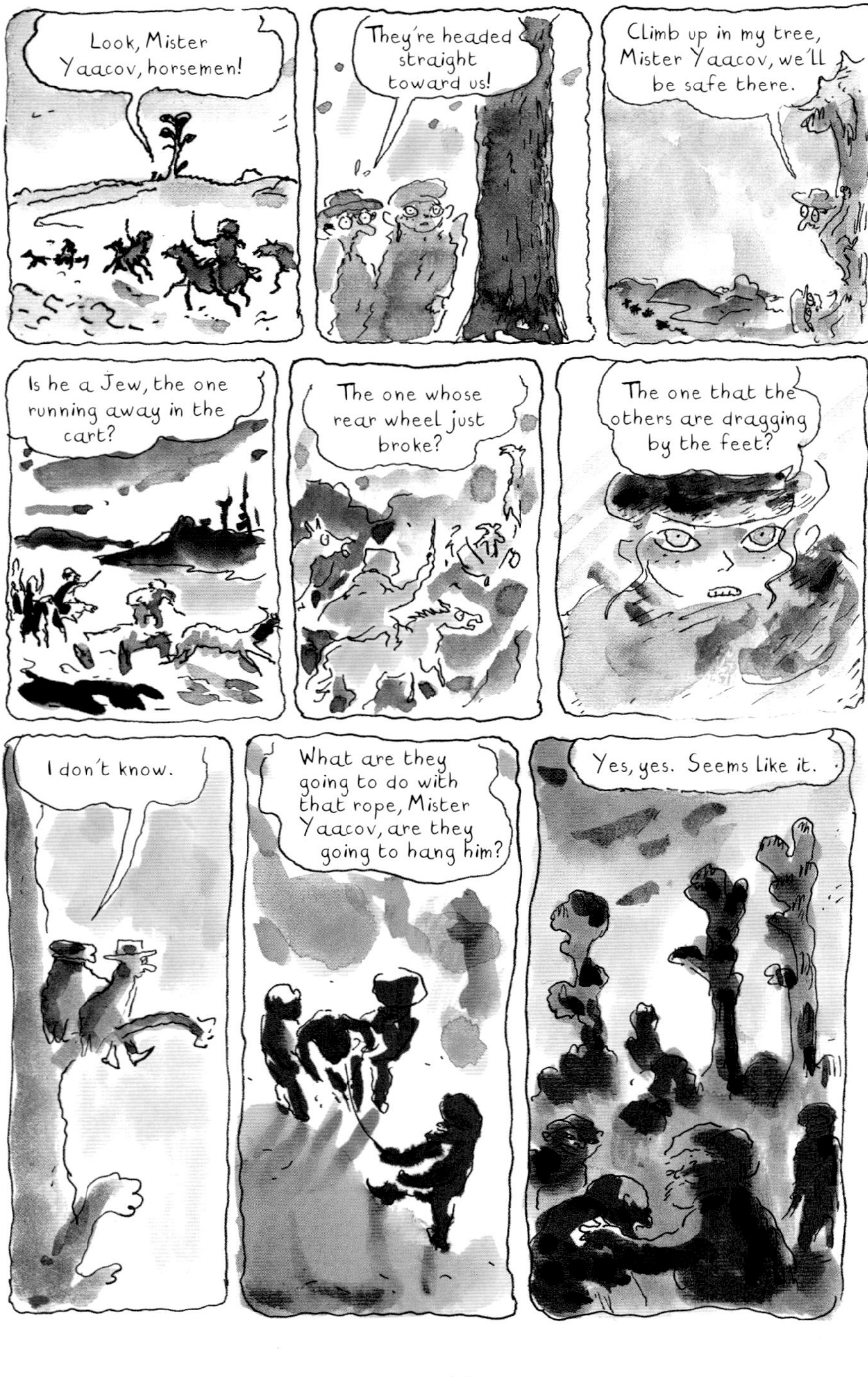
Look, Mister Yaacov, horsemen!
They're headed straight toward us!
Climb up in my tree, Mister Yaacov, we'll be safe there.
Is he a Jew, the one running away in the cart?
The one whose rear wheel just broke?
The one that the others are dragging by the feet?
I don't know.
What are they going to do with that rope, Mister Yaacov, are they going to hang him?
Yes, yes. Seems like it.

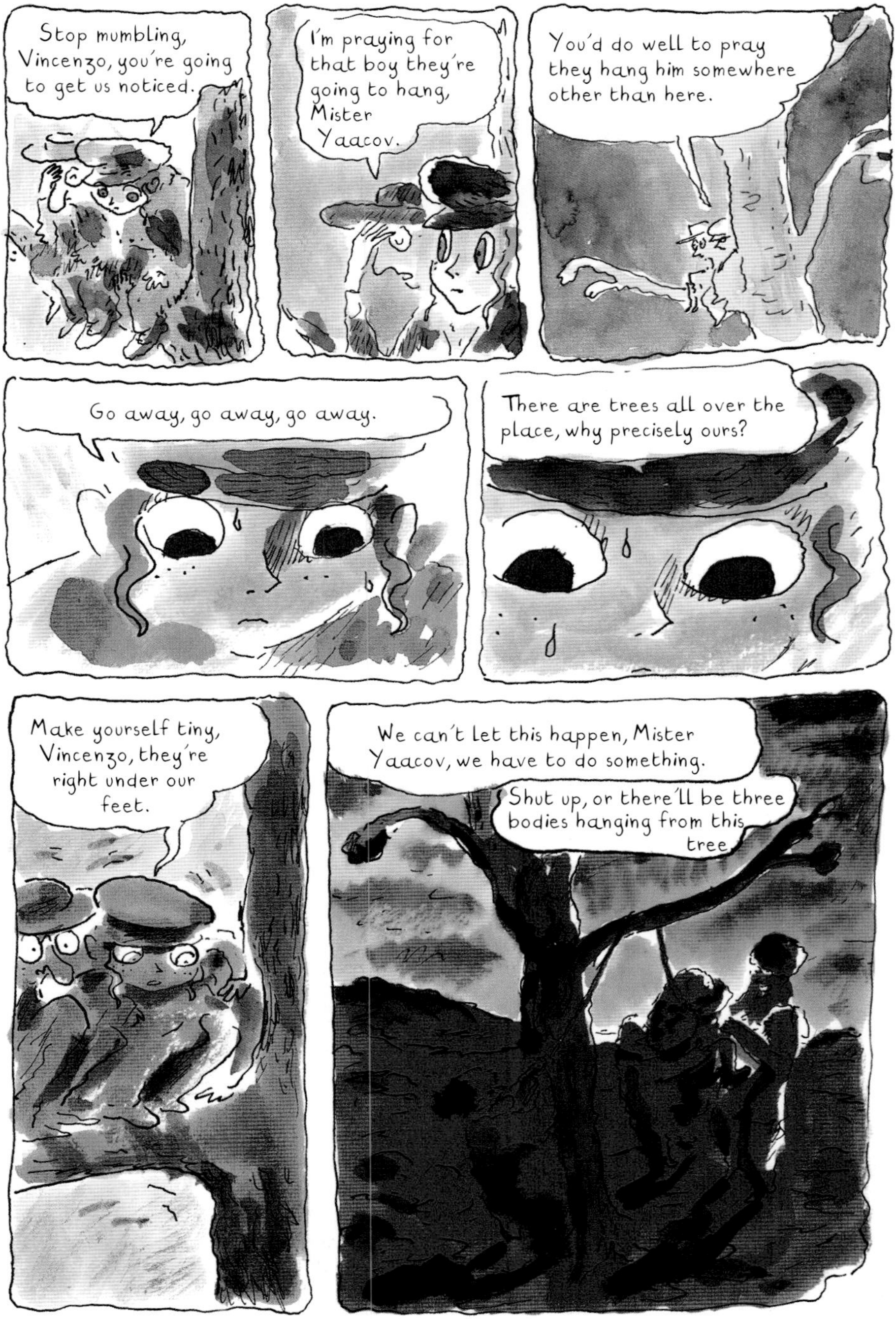
Stop mumbling, Vincenzo, you're going to get us noticed.
I'm praying for that boy they're going to hang, Mister Yaacov.
You'd do well to pray they hang him somewhere other than here.
Go away, go away, go away.
There are trees all over the place, why precisely ours?
Make yourself tiny, Vincenzo, they're right under our feet.
We can't let this happen, Mister Yaacov, we have to do something.
Shut up, or there'll be three bodies hanging from this tree

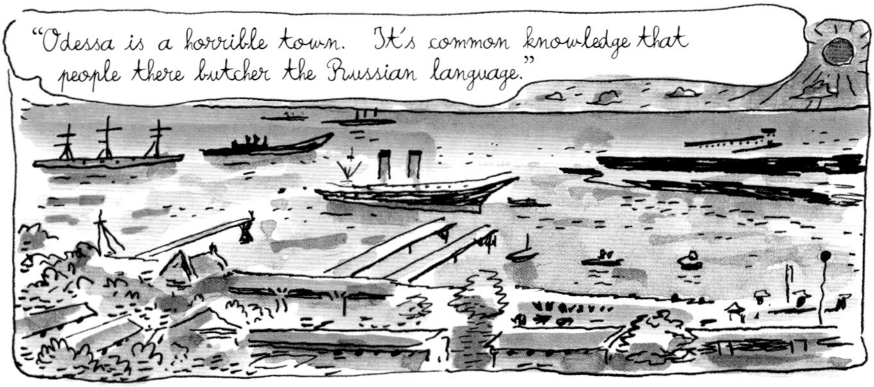
"Odessa is a horrible town. It's common knowledge that people there butcher the Russian language."

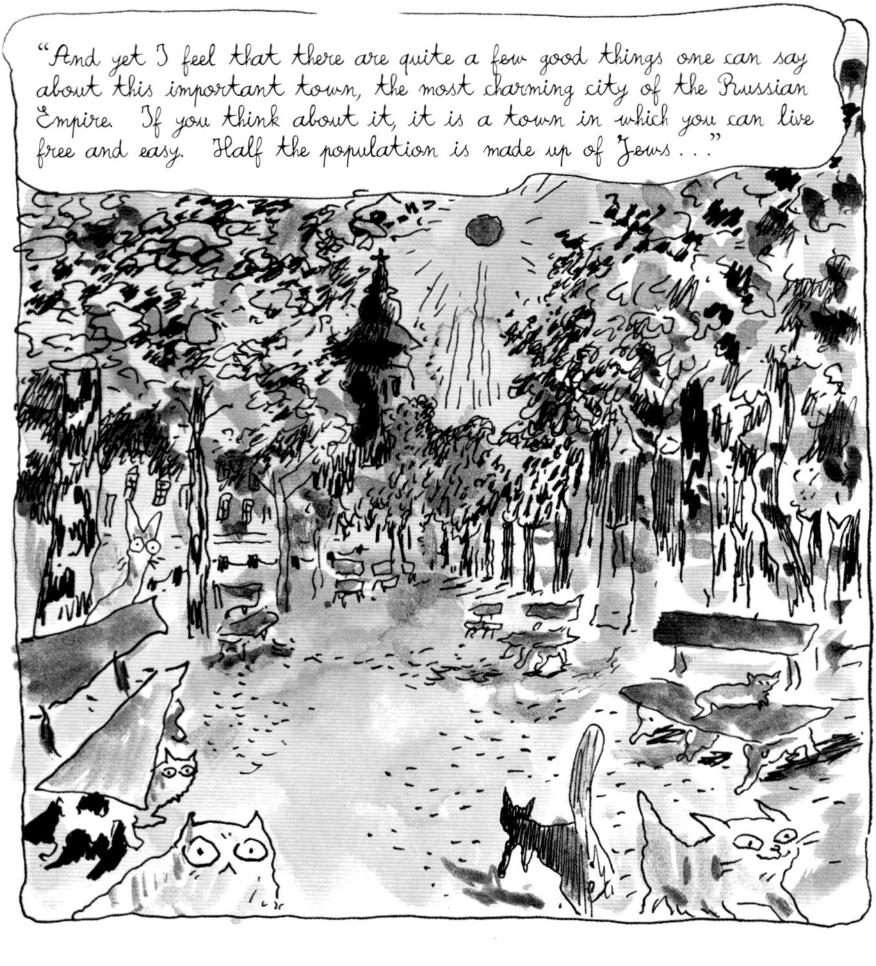
"And yet I feel that there are quite a few good things one can say about this important town, the most charming city of the Russian Empire. If you think about it, it is a town in which you can live free and easy. Half the population is made up of Jews..."

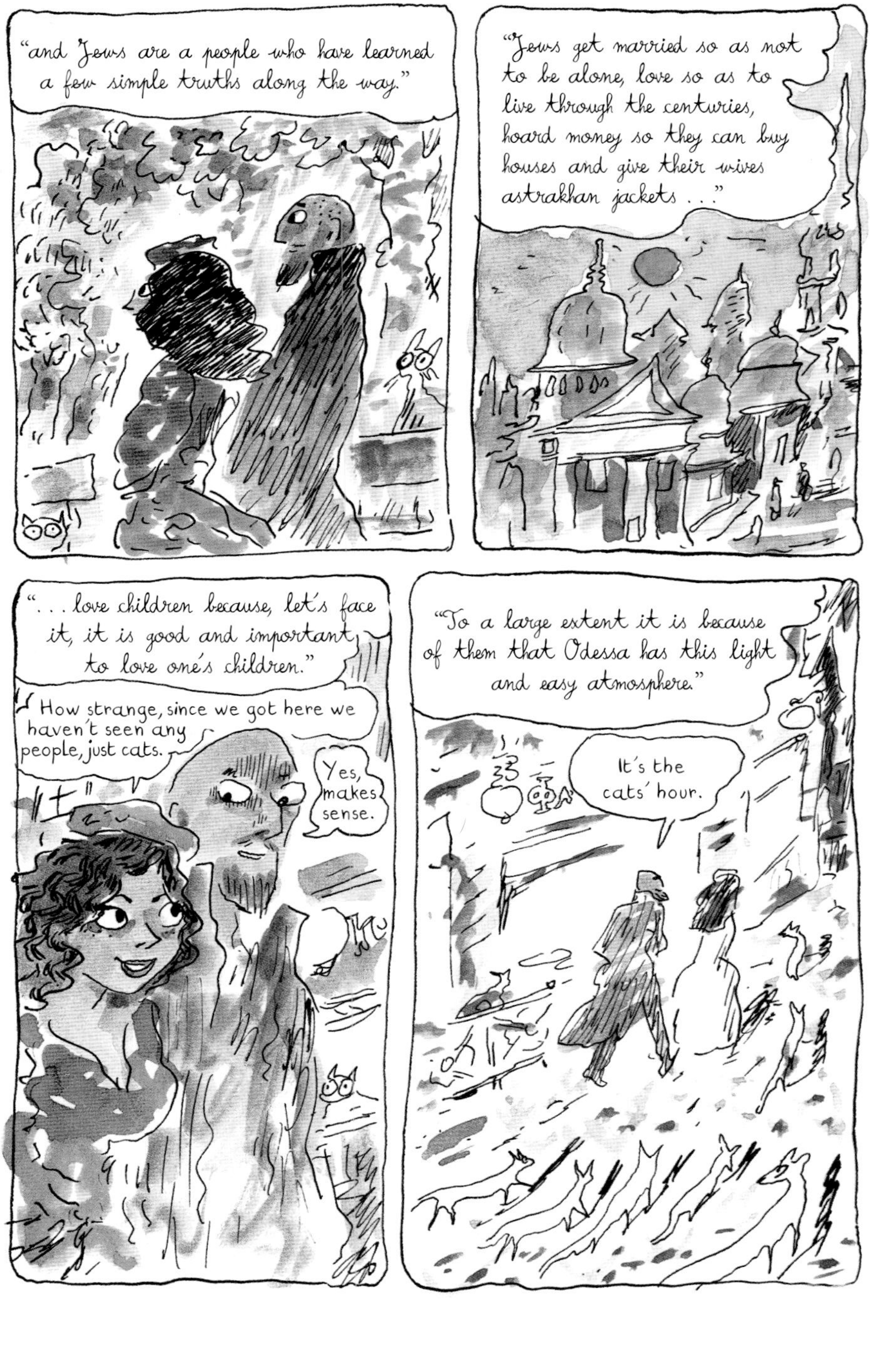
"and Jews are a people who have learned a few simple truths along the way."
"Jews get married so as not to be alone, love so as to live through the centuries, hoard money so they can buy houses and give their wives astrakhan jackets . . ."
". . . love children because, let's face it, it is good and important to love one's children."
How strange, since we got here we haven't seen any people, just cats.
Yes, makes sense.
"To a large extent it is because of them that Odessa has this light and easy atmosphere."
It's the cats' hour.

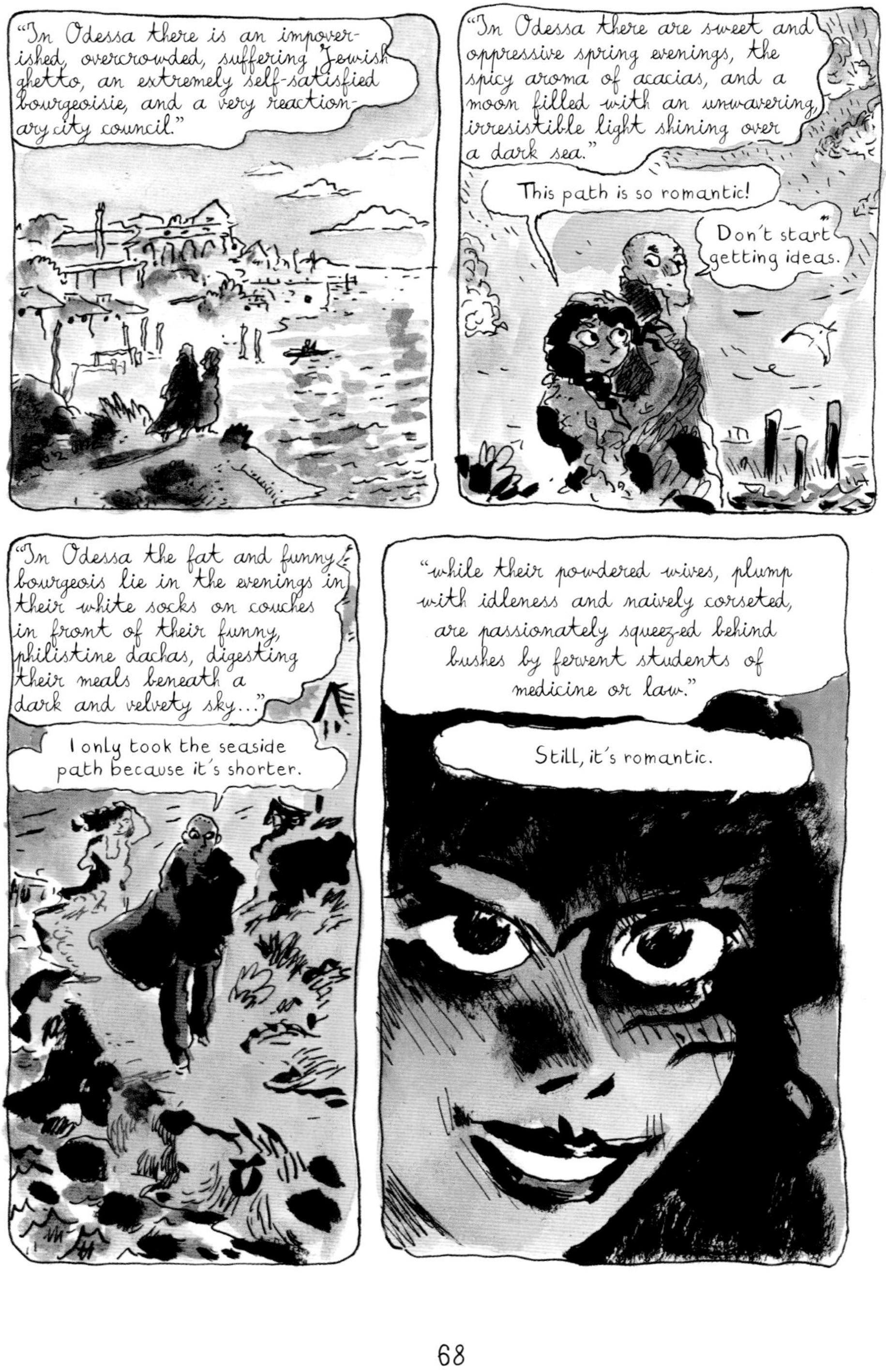
"In Odessa there is an impoverished, overcrowded, suffering Jewish ghetto, an extremely self-satisfied bourgeoisie, and a very reactionary city council."
"In Odessa there are sweet and oppressive spring evenings, the spicy aroma of acacias, and a moon filled with an unwavering, irresistible light shining over a dark sea."
This path is so romantic!
Don't start getting ideas.
"In Odessa the fat and funny bourgeois lie in the evenings in their white socks on couches in front of their funny, philistine dachas, digesting their meals beneath a dark and velvety sky..."
I only took the seaside path because it's shorter.
"while their powdered wives, plump with idleness and naively corseted, are passionately squeez-ed behind bushes by fervent students of medicine or law."
Still, it's romantic.

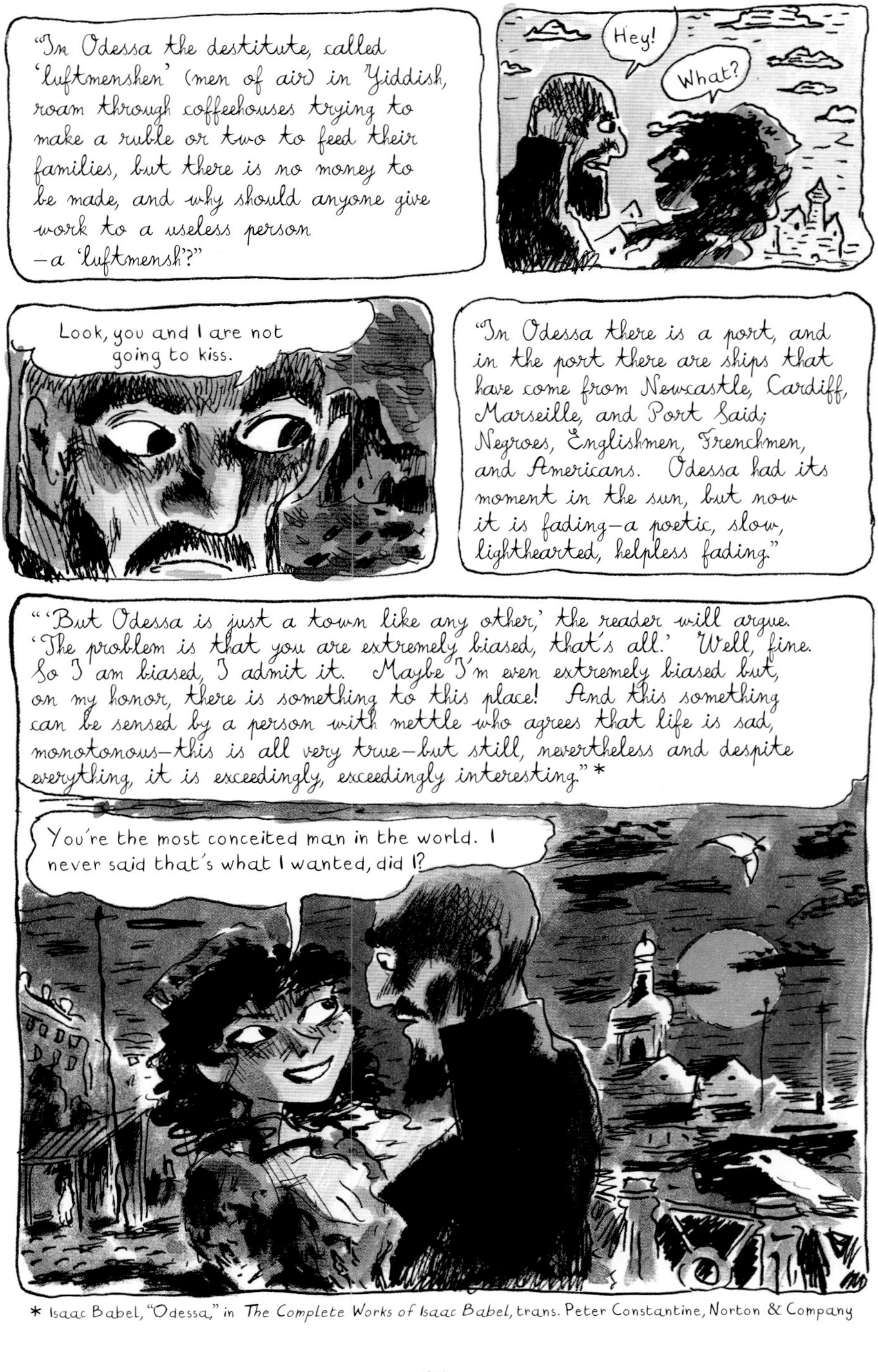
"In Odessa the destitute, called 'luftmenshen' (men of air) in Yiddish, roam through coffeehouses trying to make a ruble or two to feed their families, but there is no money to be made, and why should anyone give work to a useless person —a 'luftmensh'?"
Hey!
What?
Look, you and I are not going to kiss.
"In Odessa there is a port, and in the port there are ships that have come from Newcastle, Cardiff, Marseille, and Port Said; Negroes, Englishmen, Frenchmen, and Americans. Odessa had its moment in the sun, but now it is fading—a poetic, slow, lighthearted, helpless fading."
"'But Odessa is just a town like any other,' the reader will argue. 'The problem is that you are extremely biased, that's all.' Well, fine. So I am biased, I admit it. Maybe I'm even extremely biased but, on my honor, there is something to this place! And this something can be sensed by a person with mettle who agrees that life is sad, monotonous—this is all very true—but still, nevertheless and despite everything, it is exceedingly, exceedingly interesting." *
You're the most conceited man in the world. I never said that's what I wanted, did I?

* Isaac Babel, "Odessa," in *The Complete Works of Isaac Babel*, trans. Peter Constantine, Norton & Company

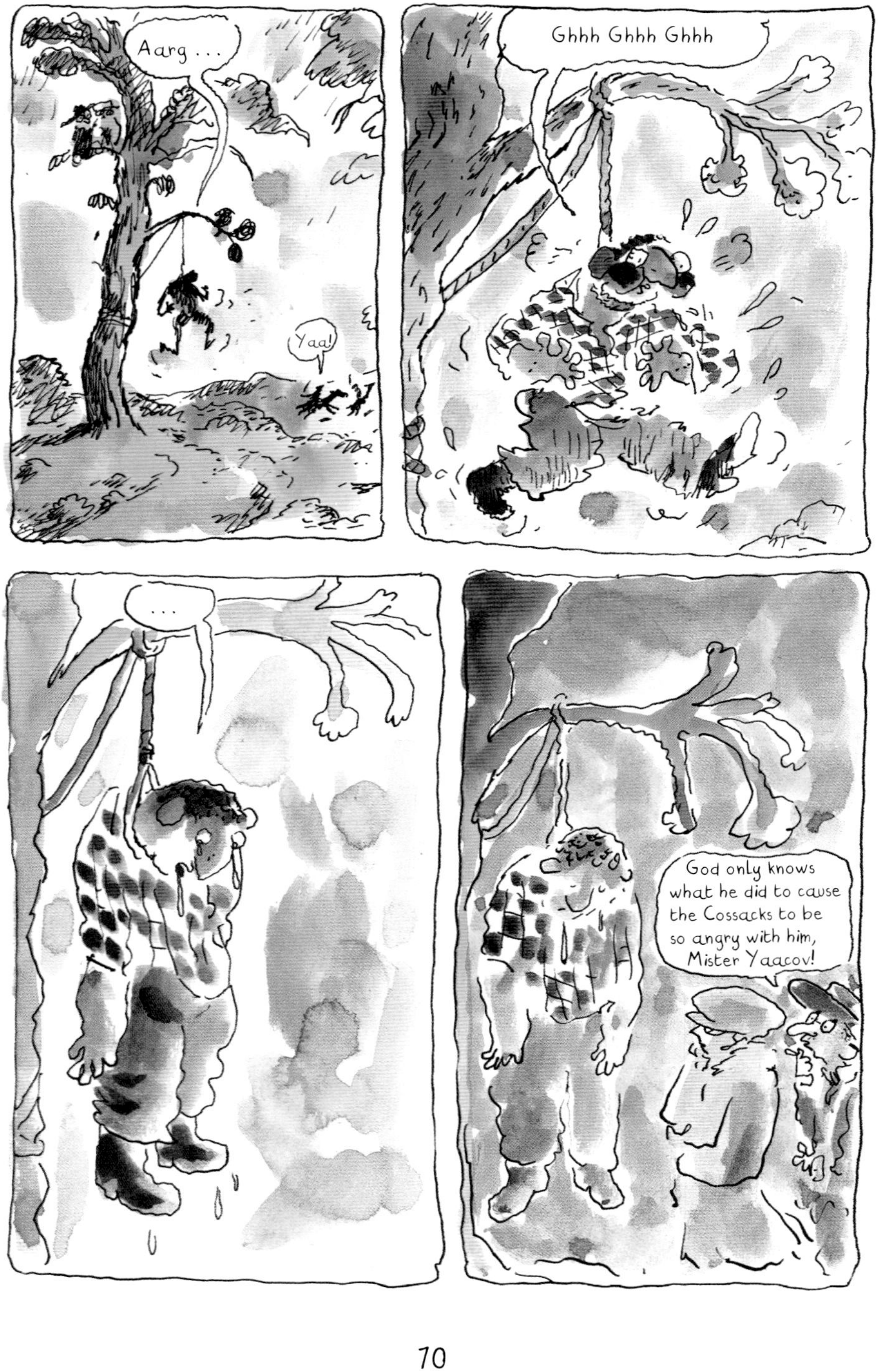
Aarg . . .
Yaa!
Ghhh Ghhh Ghhh
. . .
God only knows what he did to cause the Cossacks to be so angry with him, Mister Yaacov!

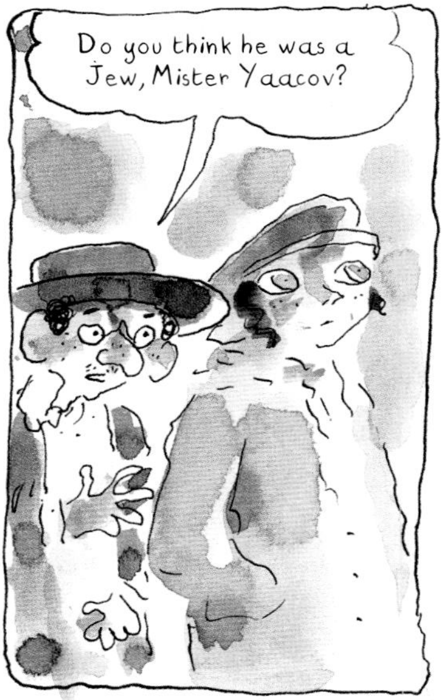
Do you think he was a Jew, Mister Yaacov?

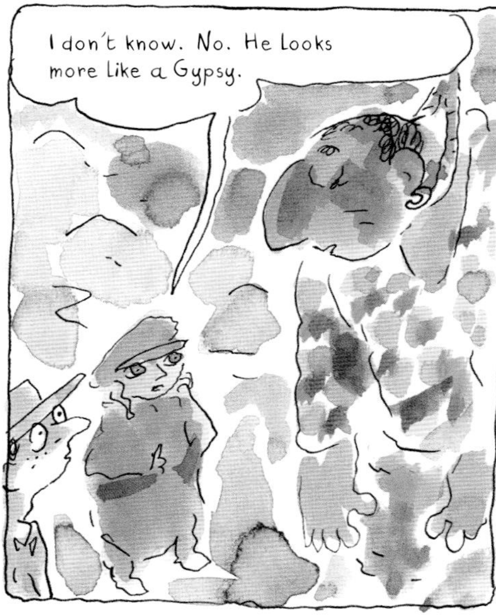
I don't know. No. He looks more like a Gypsy.

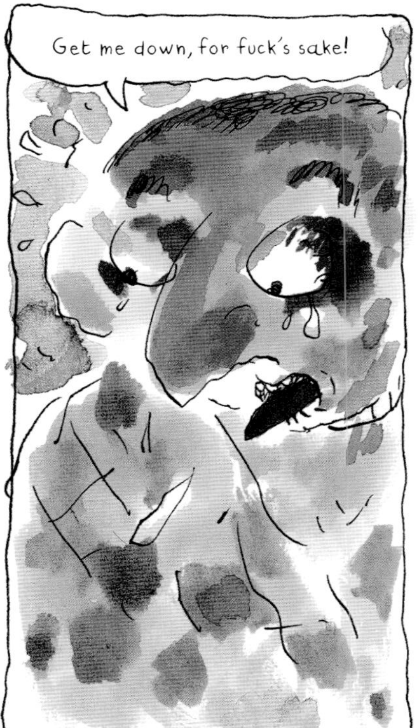
Get me down, for fuck's sake!

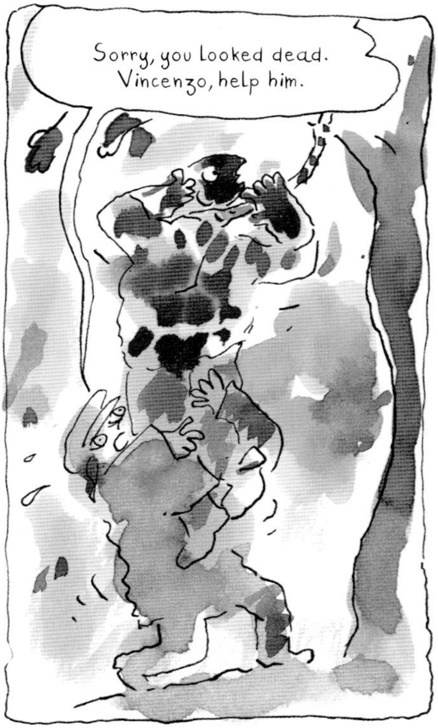
Sorry, you looked dead. Vincenzo, help him.

We took him down. I was right, he's a Gypsy. No older than us, it seems, but tough-looking.

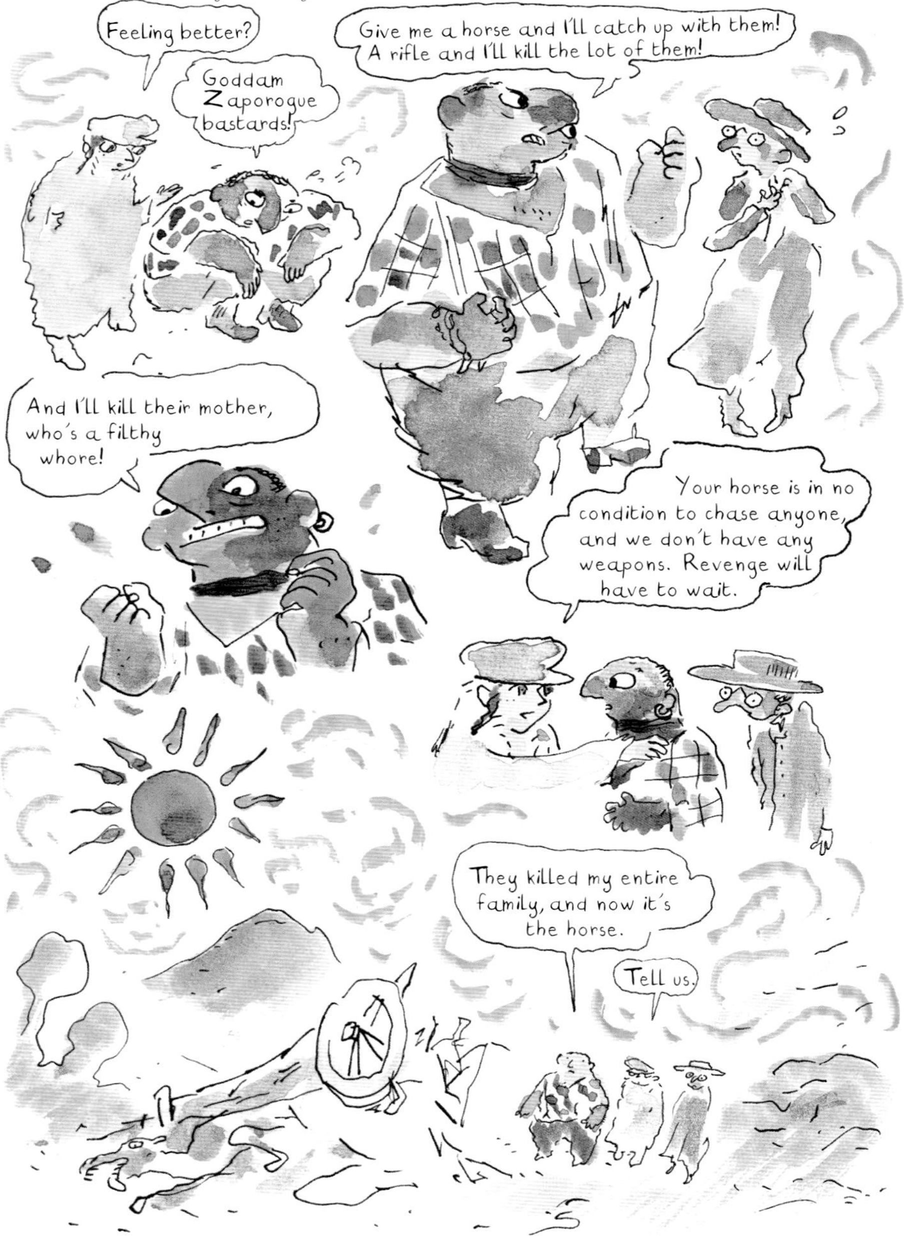
Feeling better?
Goddam Zaporogue bastards!
Give me a horse and I'll catch up with them! A rifle and I'll kill the lot of them!
And I'll kill their mother, who's a filthy whore!
Your horse is in no condition to chase anyone, and we don't have any weapons. Revenge will have to wait.
They killed my entire family, and now it's the horse.
Tell us.

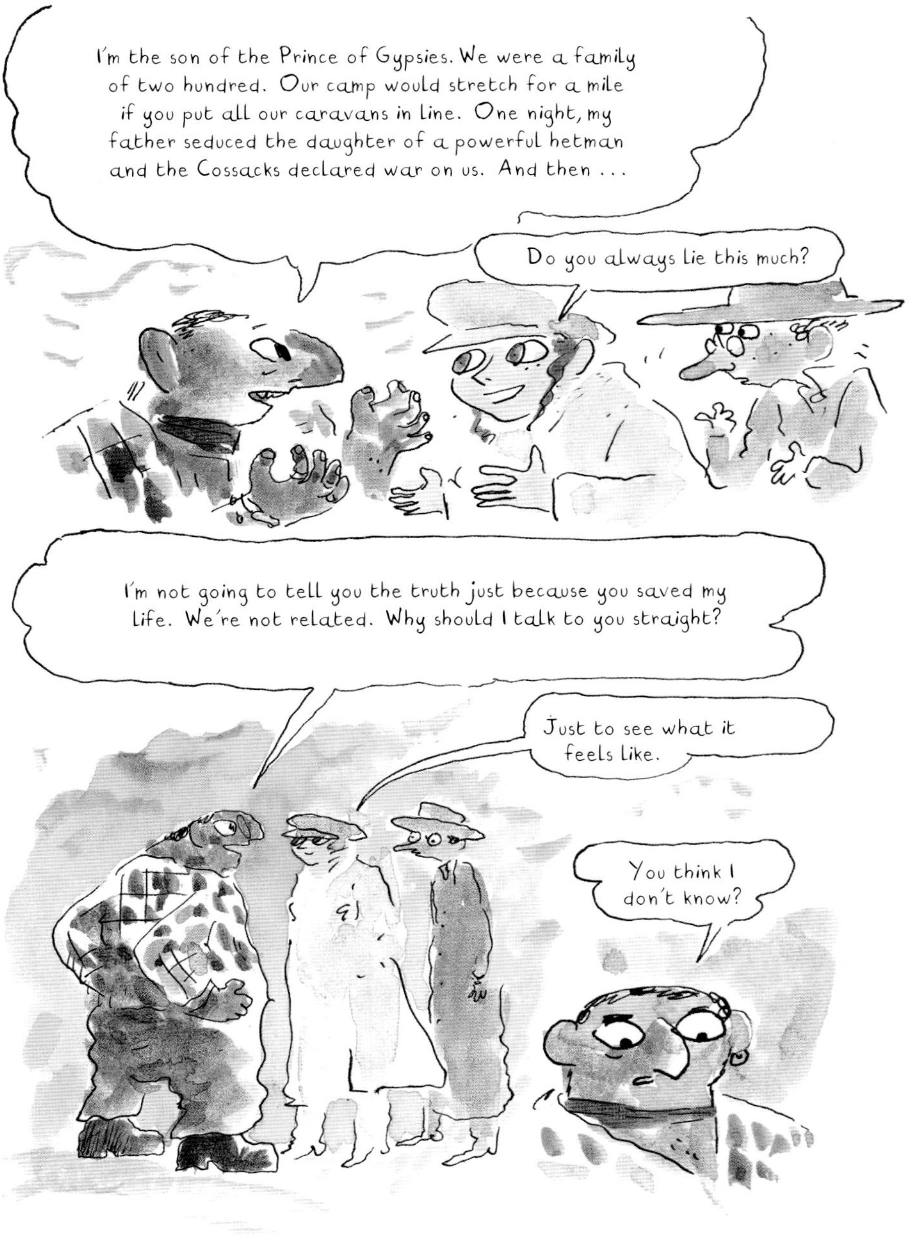
I'm the son of the Prince of Gypsies. We were a family of two hundred. Our camp would stretch for a mile if you put all our caravans in line. One night, my father seduced the daughter of a powerful hetman and the Cossacks declared war on us. And then . . .
Do you always lie this much?
I'm not going to tell you the truth just because you saved my life. We're not related. Why should I talk to you straight?
Just to see what it feels like.
You think I don't know?

Telling things exactly the way they happened is so ugly it ought to be forbidden. I'm inventing you a story, it's the most basic courtesy.

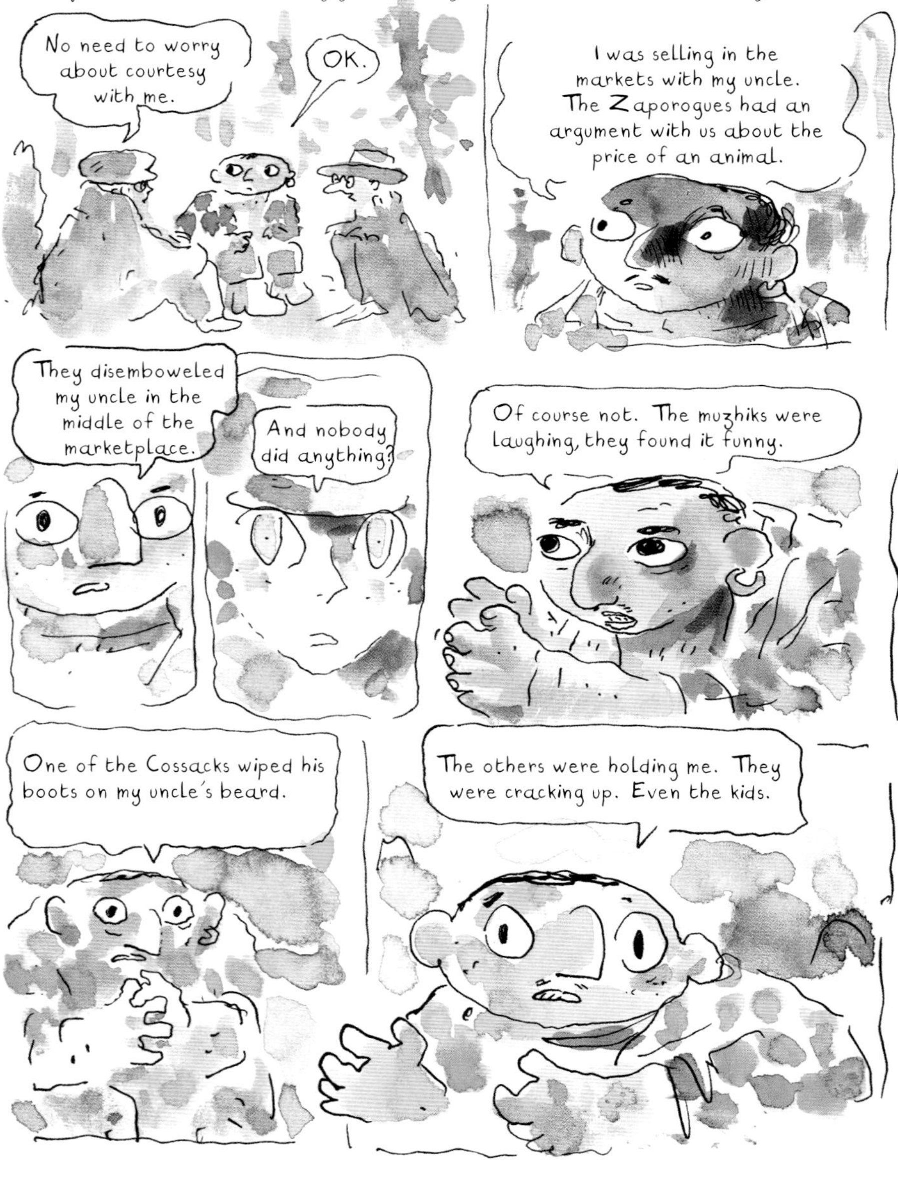
No need to worry about courtesy with me.
OK.
I was selling in the markets with my uncle. The Zaporogues had an argument with us about the price of an animal.
They disemboweled my uncle in the middle of the marketplace.
And nobody did anything?
Of course not. The muzhiks were laughing, they found it funny.
One of the Cossacks wiped his boots on my uncle's beard.
The others were holding me. They were cracking up. Even the kids.

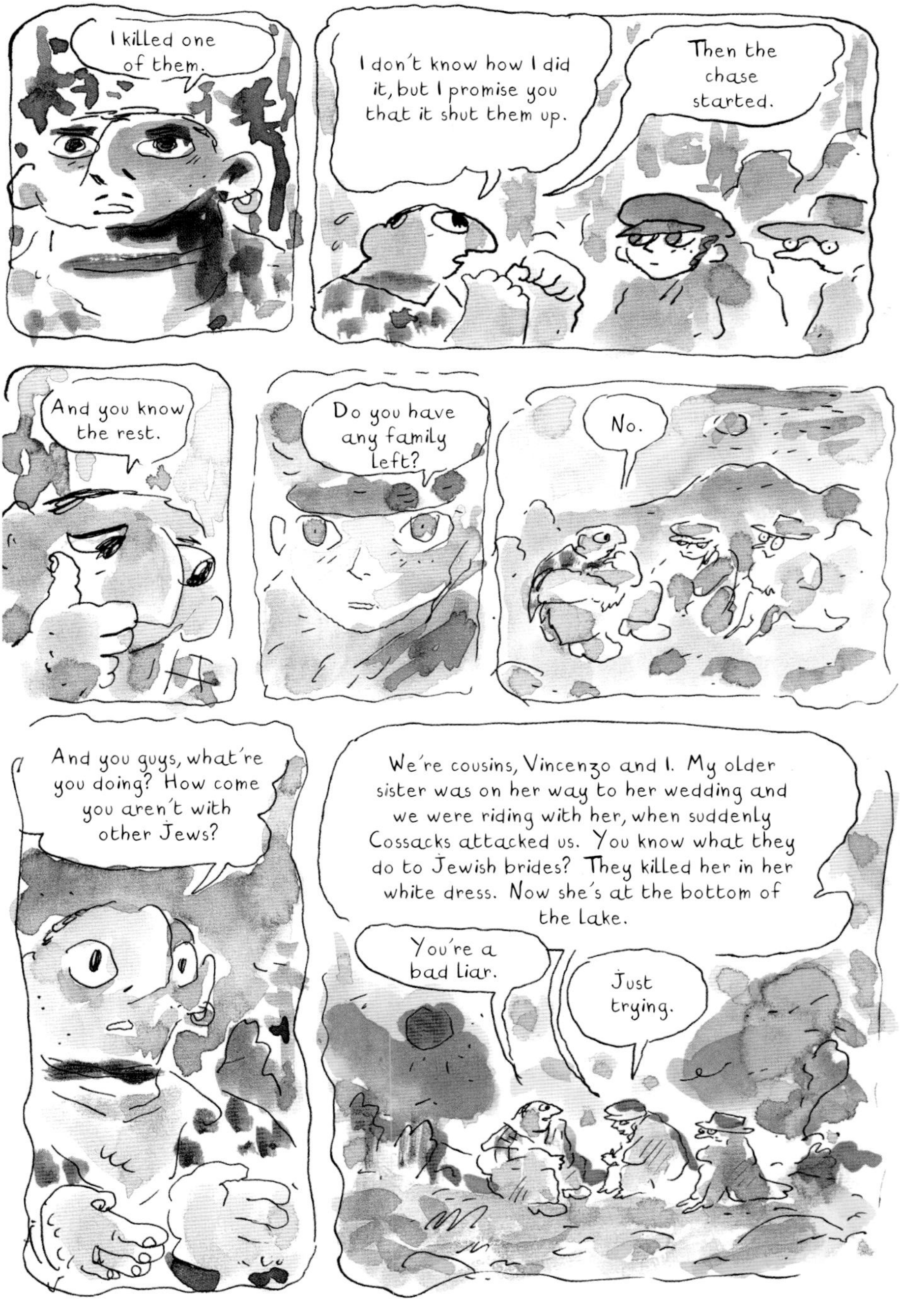
I killed one of them.
I don't know how I did it, but I promise you that it shut them up.
Then the chase started.
And you know the rest.
Do you have any family left?
No.
And you guys, what're you doing? How come you aren't with other Jews?
We're cousins, Vincenzo and I. My older sister was on her way to her wedding and we were riding with her, when suddenly Cossacks attacked us. You know what they do to Jewish brides? They killed her in her white dress. Now she's at the bottom of the lake.
You're a bad liar.
Just trying.

At first, I saw him as a hulk, but actually he's pretty normal. A big guy, but no golem. We live among Jews so much that we get these strange ideas about outsiders.

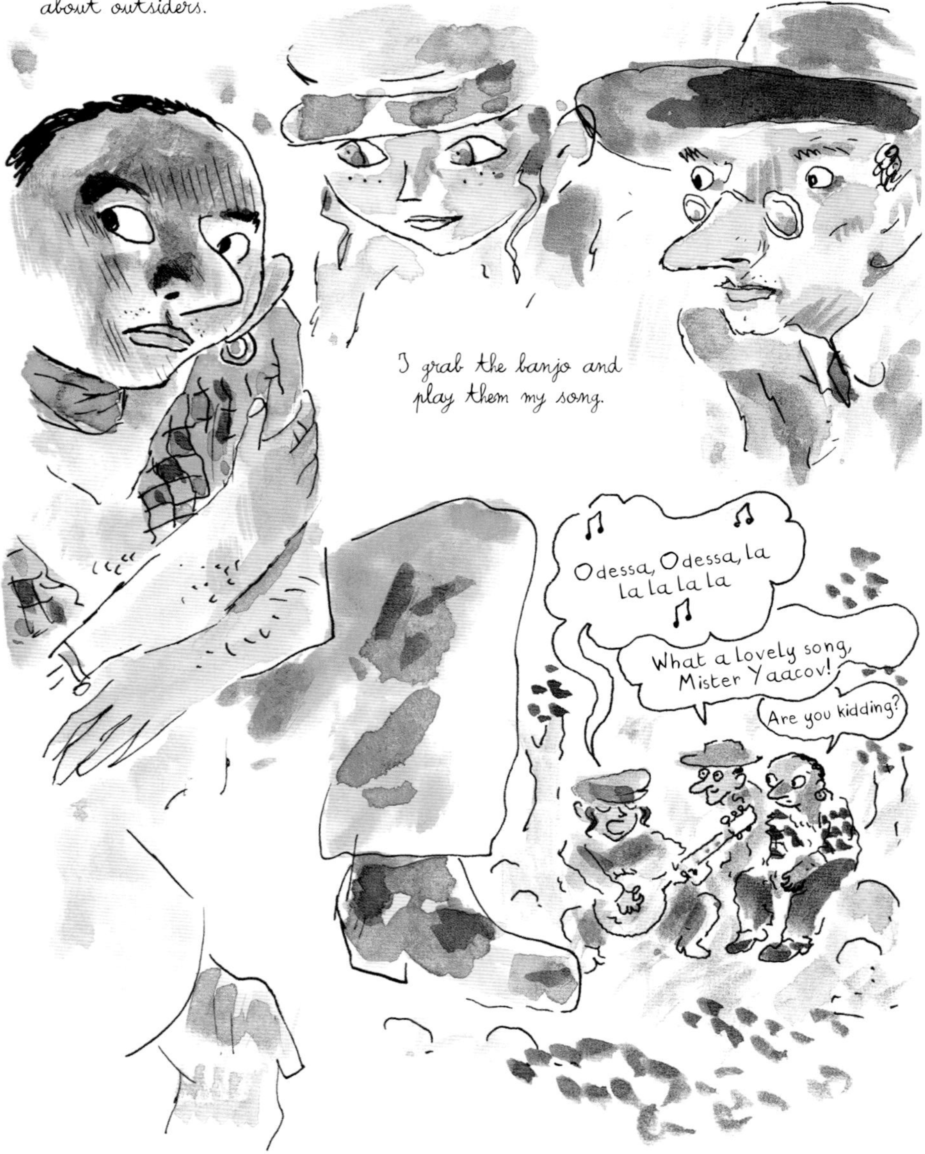
I grab the banjo and play them my song.
Odessa, Odessa, la la la la la
What a lovely song, Mister Yaacov!
Are you kidding?

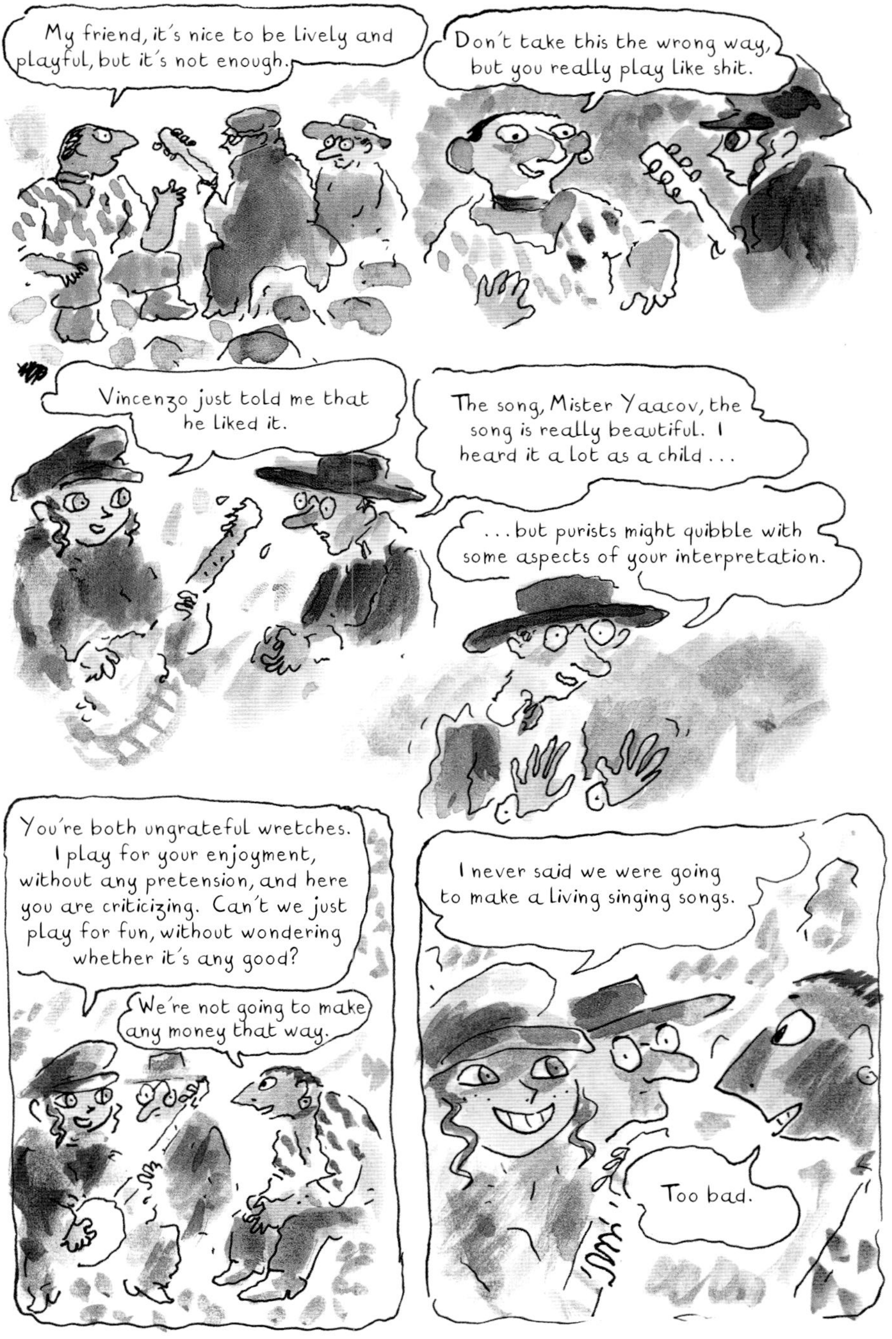

My friend, it's nice to be lively and playful, but it's not enough.
Don't take this the wrong way, but you really play like shit.
Vincenzo just told me that he liked it.
The song, Mister Yaacov, the song is really beautiful. I heard it a lot as a child . . .
. . . but purists might quibble with some aspects of your interpretation.
You're both ungrateful wretches. I play for your enjoyment, without any pretension, and here you are criticizing. Can't we just play for fun, without wondering whether it's any good?
We're not going to make any money that way.
I never said we were going to make a living singing songs.
Too bad.

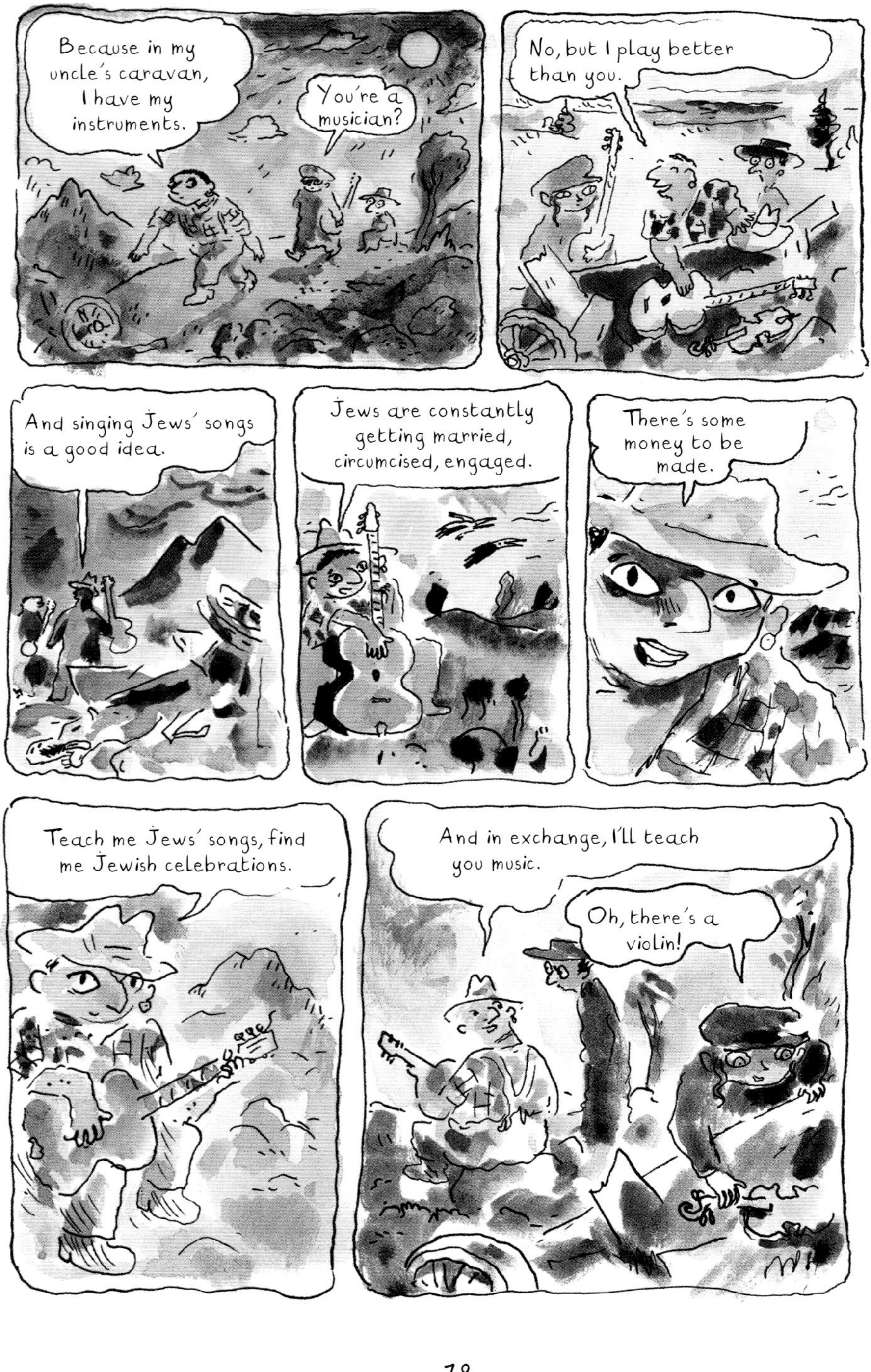
Because in my uncle's caravan, I have my instruments.
You're a musician?
No, but I play better than you.
And singing Jews' songs is a good idea.
Jews are constantly getting married, circumcised, engaged.
There's some money to be made.
Teach me Jews' songs, find me Jewish celebrations.
And in exchange, I'll teach you music.
Oh, there's a violin!

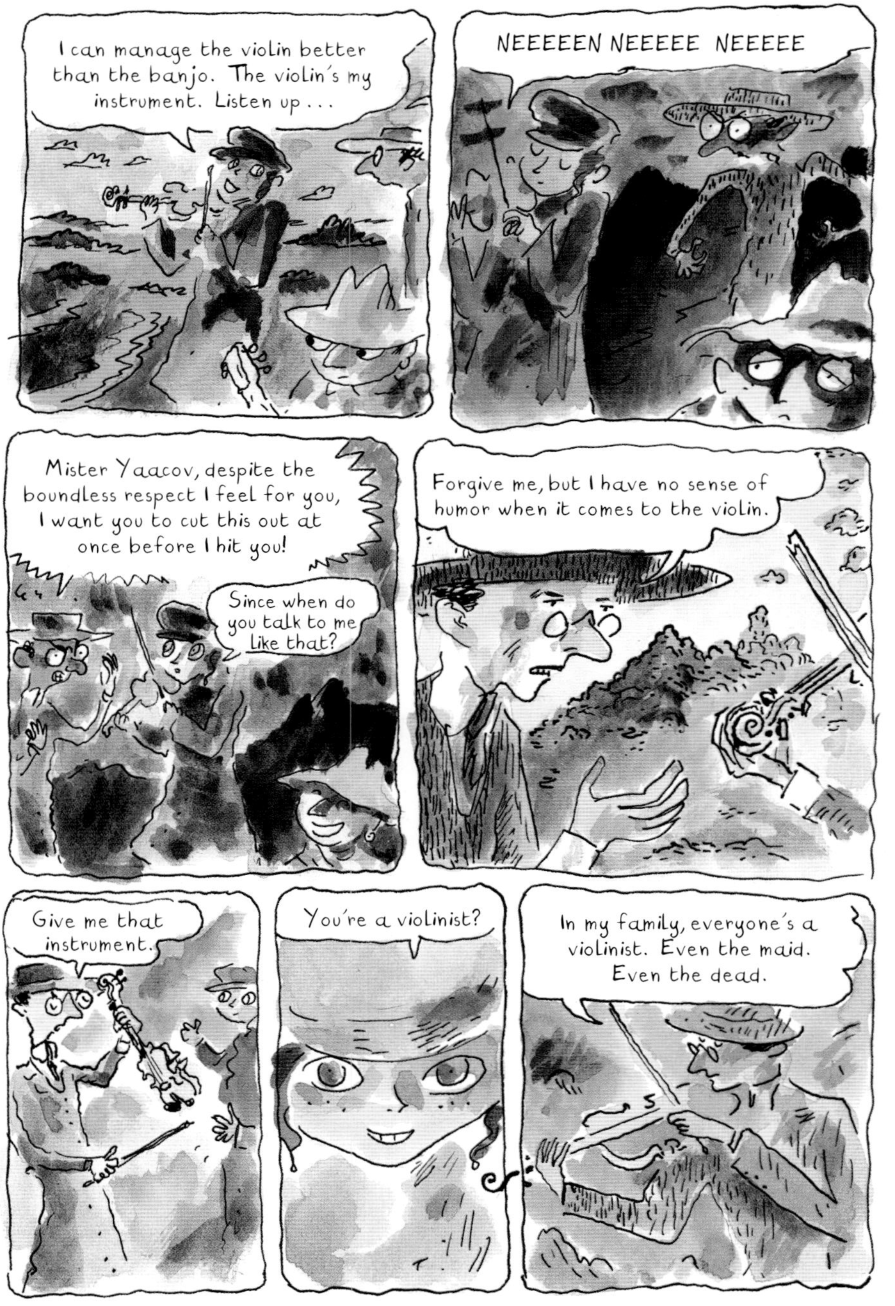
I can manage the violin better than the banjo. The violin's my instrument. Listen up . . .
NEEEEEN NEEEEE NEEEEE
Mister Yaacov, despite the boundless respect I feel for you, I want you to cut this out at once before I hit you!
Since when do you talk to me like that?
Forgive me, but I have no sense of humor when it comes to the violin.
Give me that instrument.
You're a violinist?
In my family, everyone's a violinist. Even the maid. Even the dead.

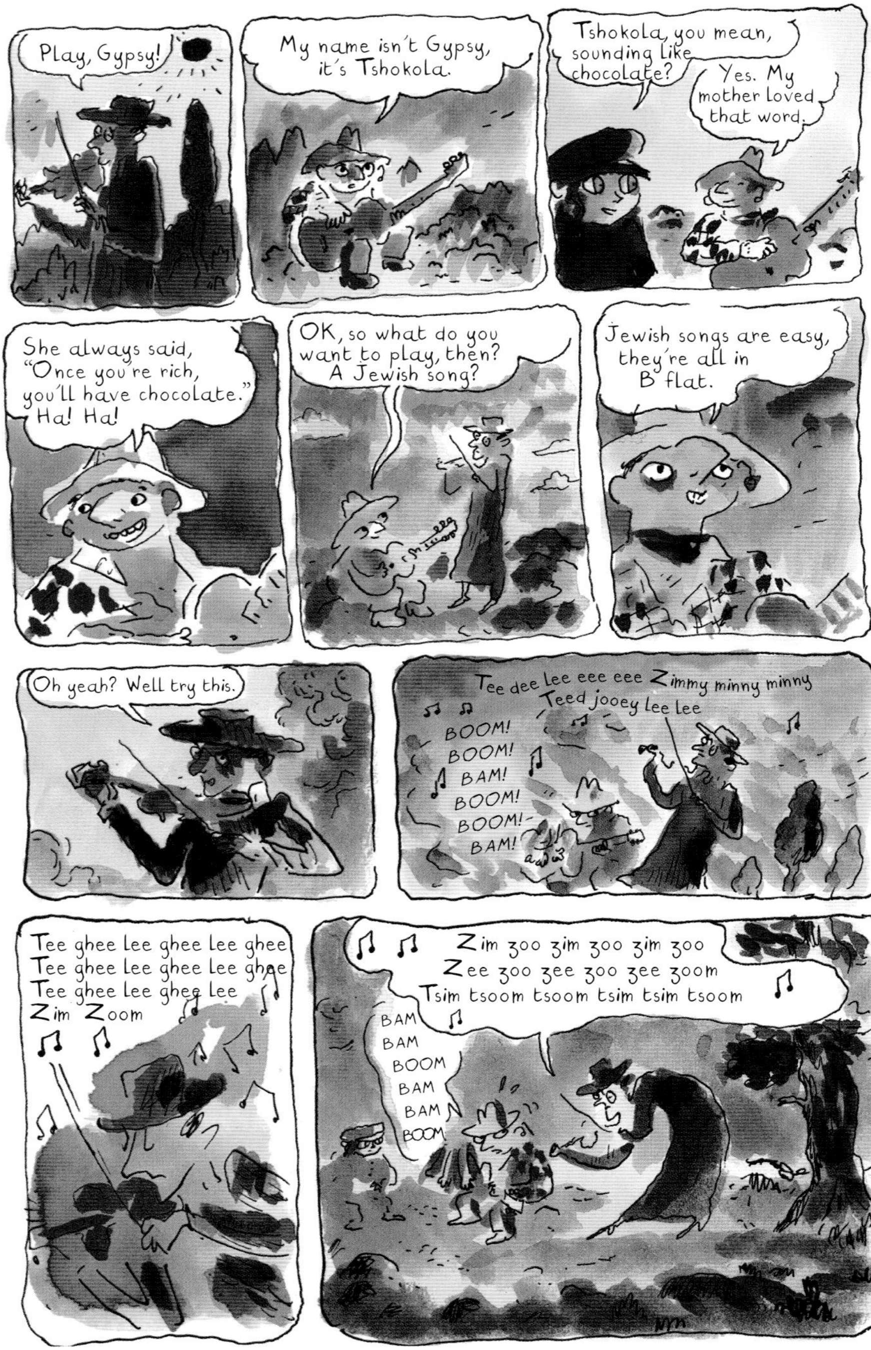
Play, Gypsy!
My name isn't Gypsy, it's Tshokola.
Tshokola, you mean, sounding like chocolate?
Yes. My mother loved that word.
She always said, "Once you're rich, you'll have chocolate." Ha! Ha!
OK, so what do you want to play, then? A Jewish song?
Jewish songs are easy, they're all in B flat.
Oh yeah? Well try this.
Tee dee lee eee eee Zimmy minny minny
Teed jooey lee lee
BOOM! BOOM! BAM! BOOM! BOOM! BAM!
Tee ghee lee ghee lee ghee
Tee ghee lee ghee lee ghee
Tee ghee lee ghee lee
Zim Zoom
Zim zoo zim zoo zim zoo
Zee zoo zee zoo zee zoom
Tsim tsoom tsoom tsim tsim tsoom
BAM BAM BOOM BAM BAM BOOM

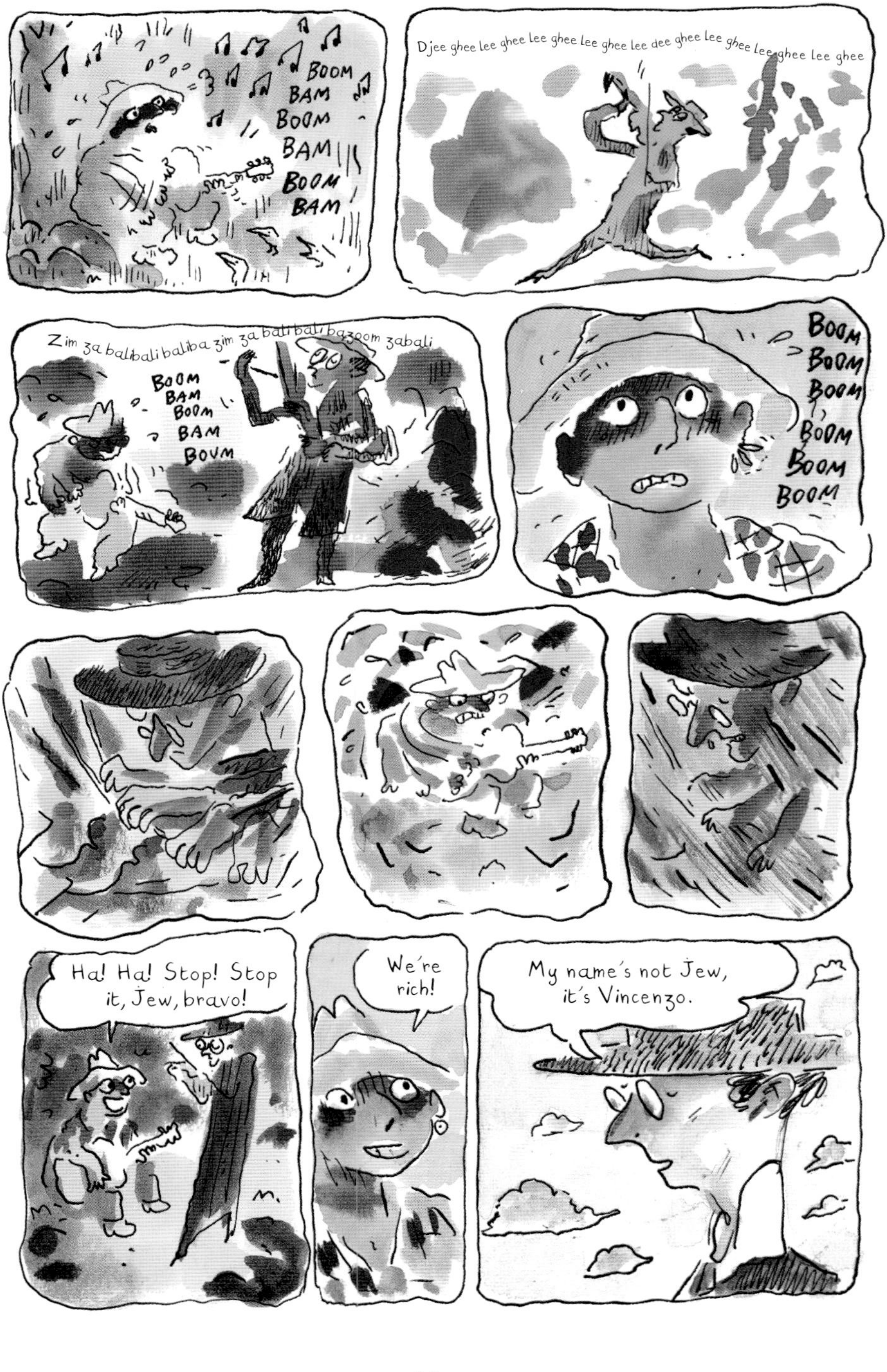
BOOM
BAM
BOOM
BAM
BOOM
BAM
Djee ghee lee ghee lee ghee lee ghee lee dee ghee lee ghee lee ghee lee ghee
Zim za balibali baliba zim za balibali bazoom zabali
BOOM
BAM
BOOM
BAM
BOUM
BOOM
BOOM
BOOM
BOOM
BOOM
BOOM
Ha! Ha! Stop! Stop it, Jew, bravo!
We're rich!
My name's not Jew, it's Vincenzo.

Just then their looks converged on me, and my companions wondered what on earth they were going to be able to do with me.

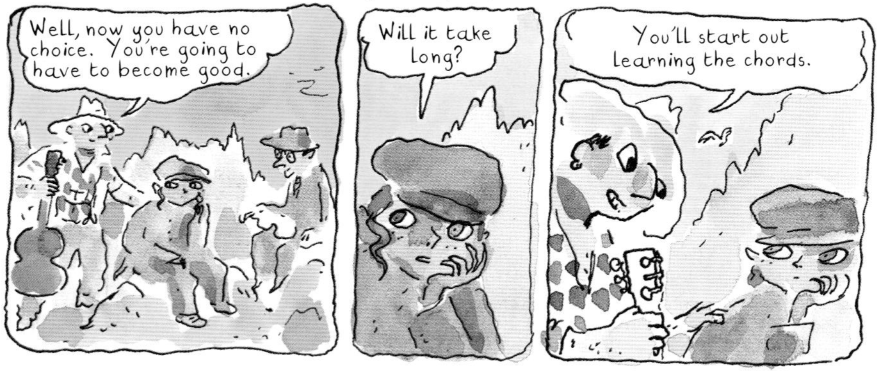
Well, now you have no choice. You're going to have to become good.
Will it take long?
You'll start out learning the chords.

He spent the entire evening teaching me chords. He told me our chord progression was the same and all I needed to do was watch him

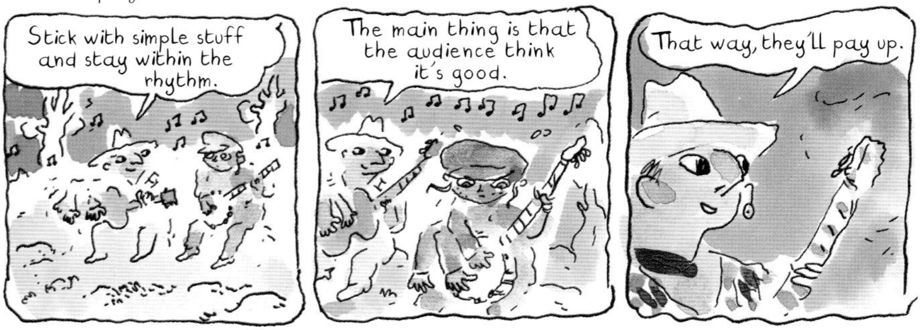
Stick with simple stuff and stay within the rhythm.
The main thing is that the audience think it's good.
That way, they'll pay up.

We had dinner. There were some provisions in the caravan. We played very late, till our fingers hurt. I stuck to the rhythm, and I don't think I disturbed the musicians.

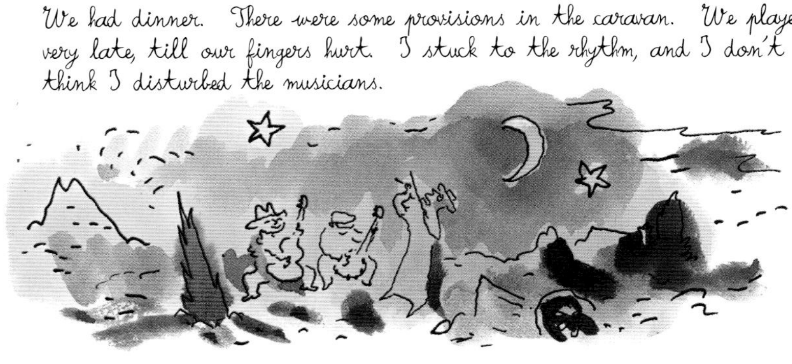

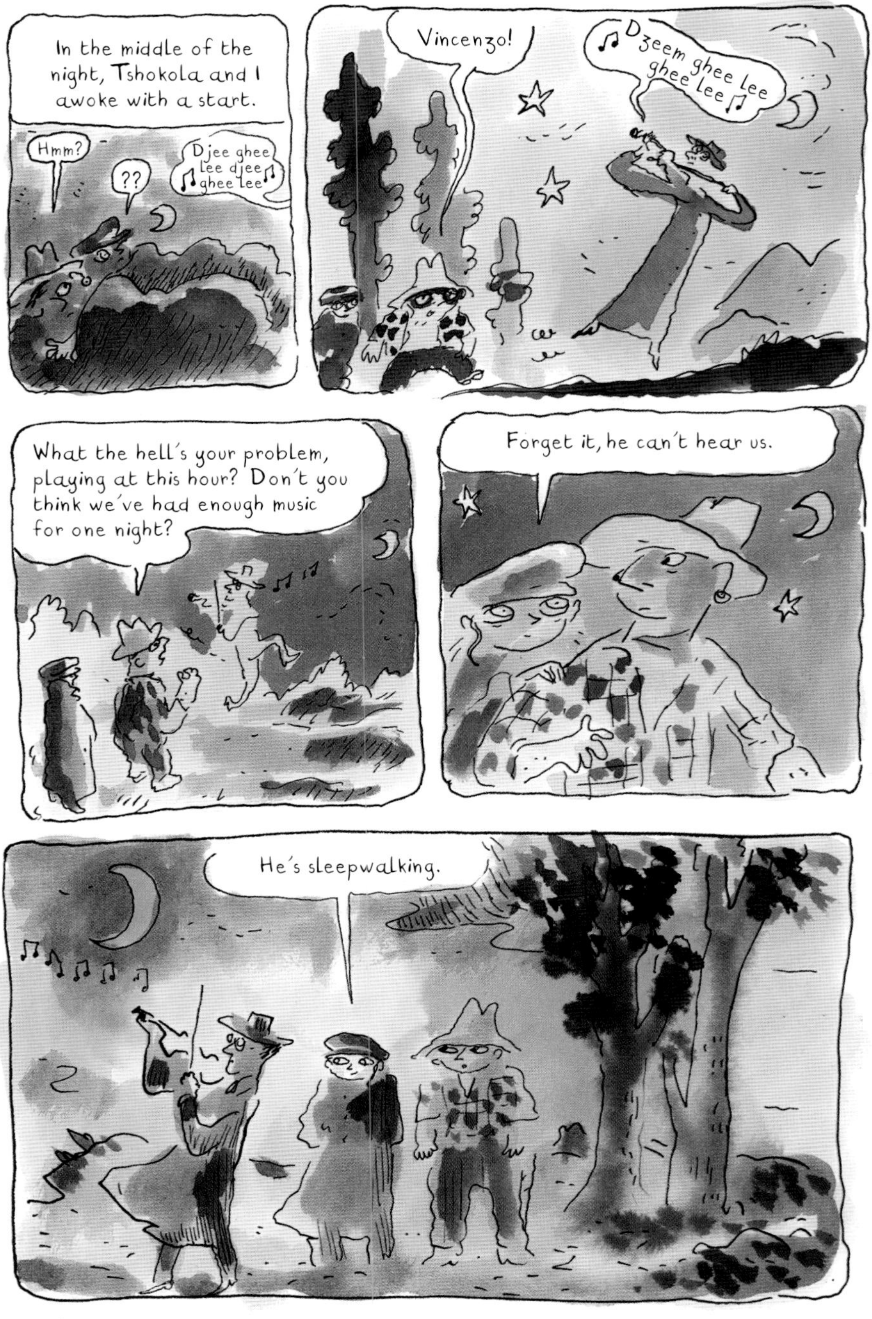
In the middle of the night, Tshokola and I awoke with a start.
Hmm?
??
Djee ghee lee djee ghee lee
Vincenzo!
Dzeem ghee lee ghee lee
What the hell's your problem, playing at this hour? Don't you think we've had enough music for one night?
Forget it, he can't hear us.
He's sleepwalking.

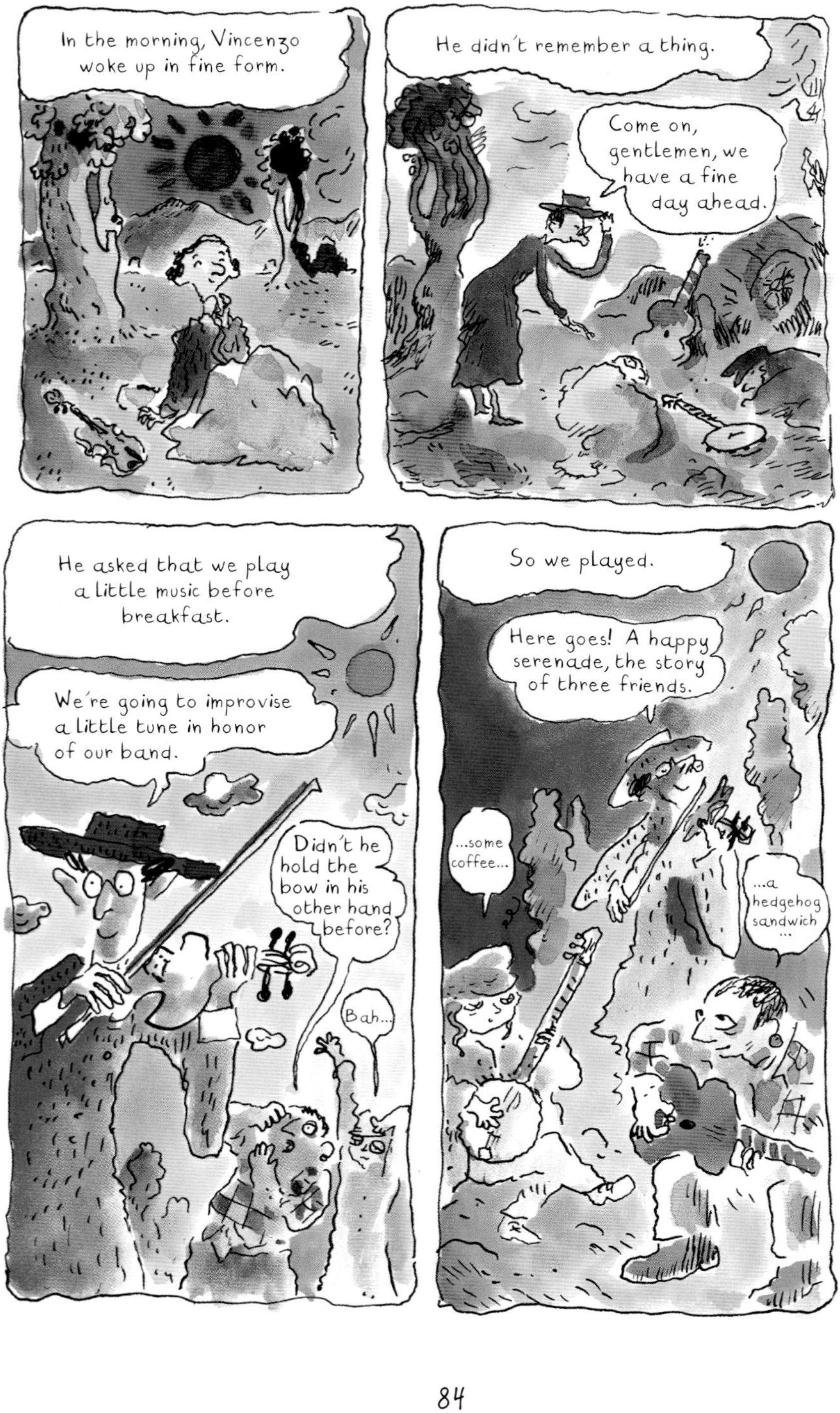
In the morning, Vincenzo woke up in fine form.
He didn't remember a thing.
Come on, gentlemen, we have a fine day ahead.
He asked that we play a little music before breakfast.
We're going to improvise a little tune in honor of our band.
Didn't he hold the bow in his other hand before?
Bah...
So we played.
Here goes! A happy serenade, the story of three friends.
...some coffee...
...a hedgehog sandwich...

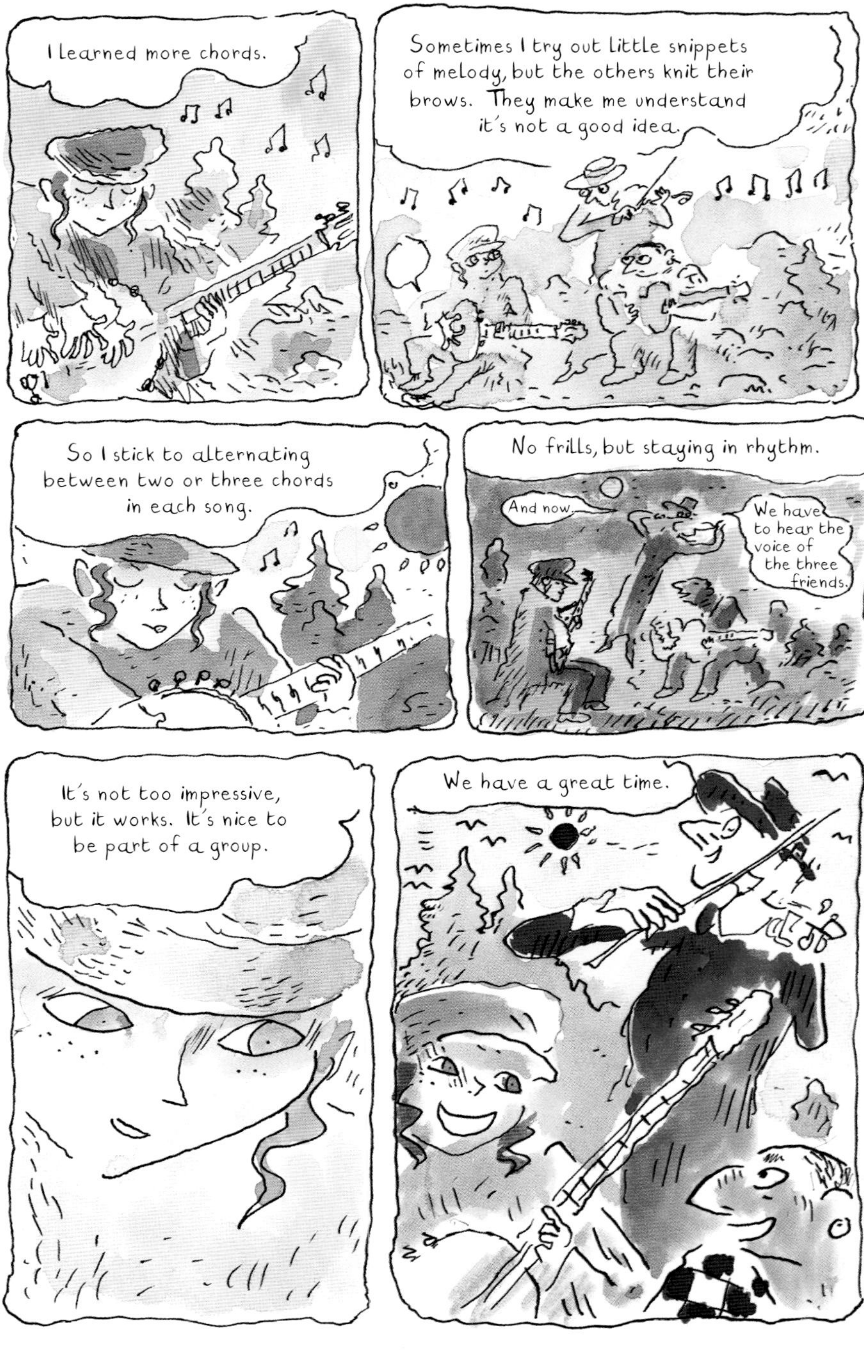
I learned more chords.
Sometimes I try out little snippets of melody, but the others knit their brows. They make me understand it's not a good idea.
So I stick to alternating between two or three chords in each song.
No frills, but staying in rhythm.
And now...
We have to hear the voice of the three friends.
It's not too impressive, but it works. It's nice to be part of a group.
We have a great time.

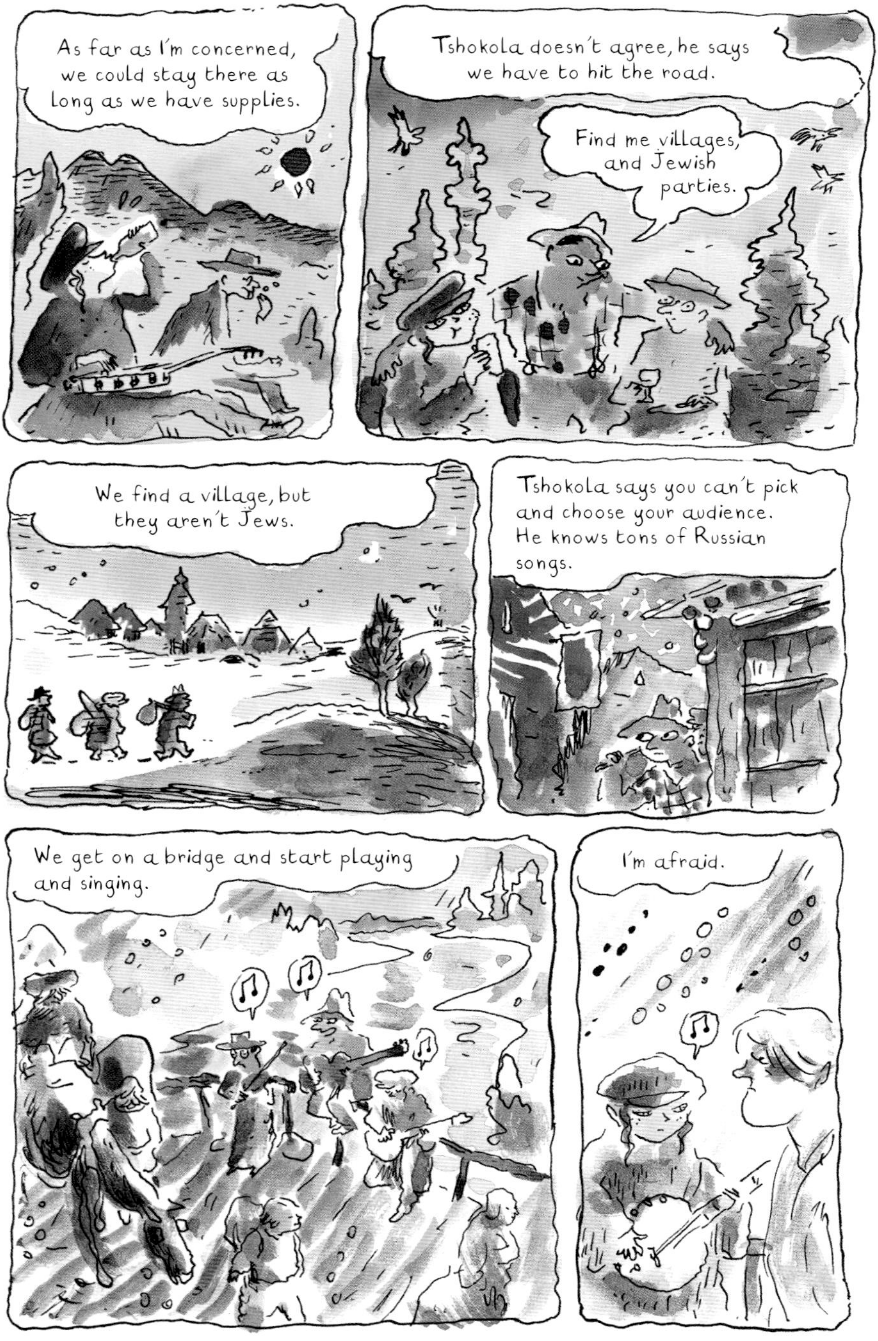

As far as I'm concerned, we could stay there as long as we have supplies.
Tshokola doesn't agree, he says we have to hit the road.
Find me villages, and Jewish parties.
We find a village, but they aren't Jews.
Tshokola says you can't pick and choose your audience. He knows tons of Russian songs.
We get on a bridge and start playing and singing.
I'm afraid.

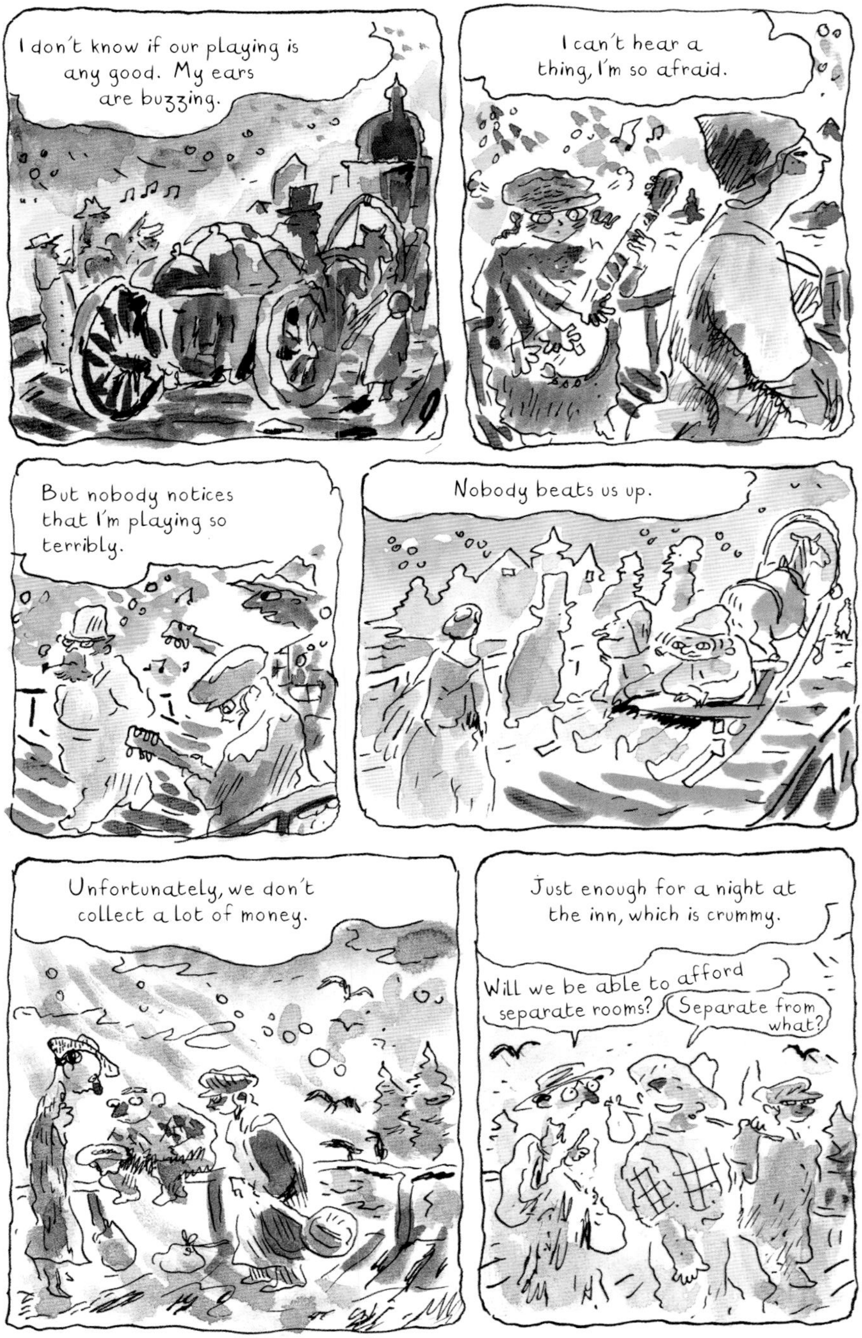
I don't know if our playing is any good. My ears are buzzing.
I can't hear a thing, I'm so afraid.
But nobody notices that I'm playing so terribly.
Nobody beats us up.
Unfortunately, we don't collect a lot of money.
Just enough for a night at the inn, which is crummy.
Will we be able to afford separate rooms?
Separate from what?

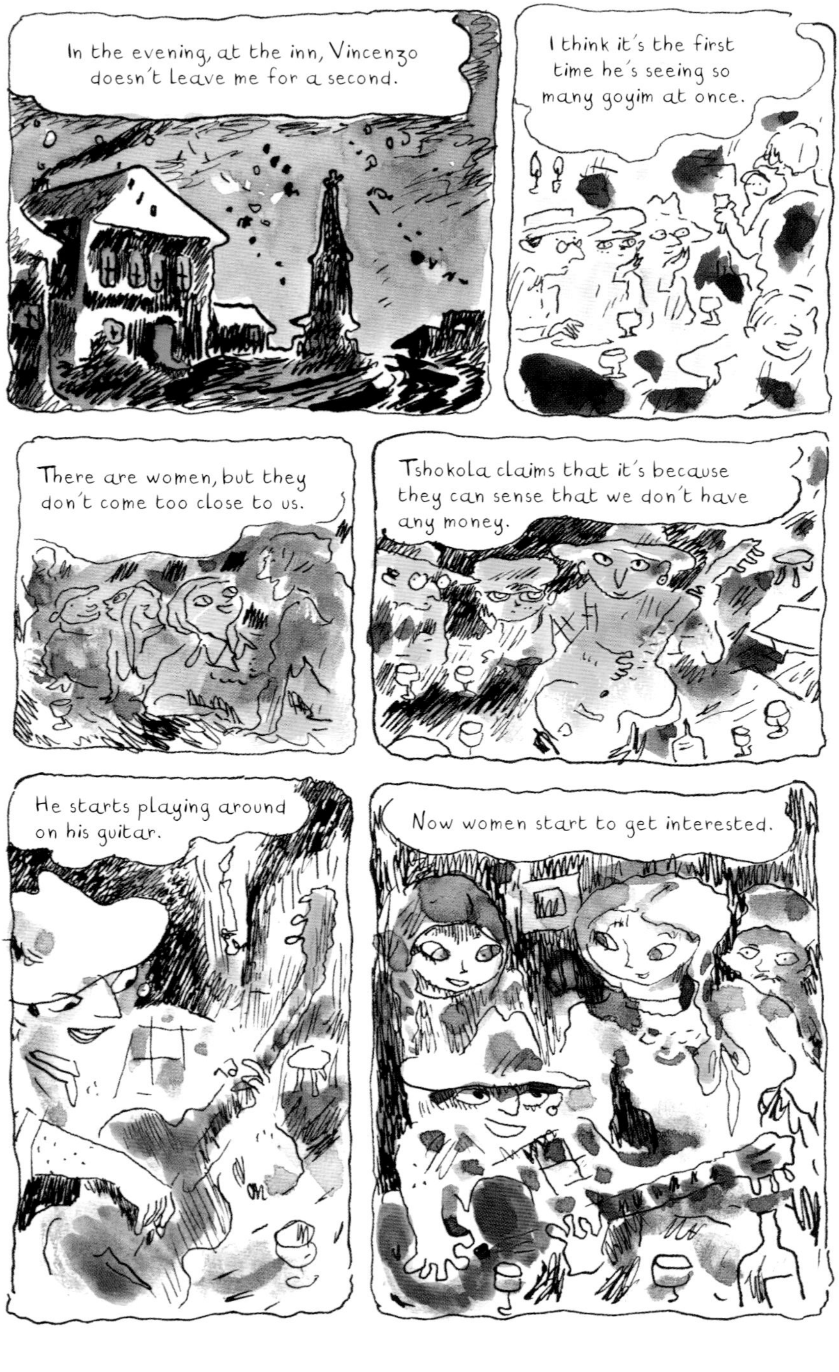
In the evening, at the inn, Vincenzo doesn't leave me for a second.
I think it's the first time he's seeing so many goyim at once.
There are women, but they don't come too close to us.
Tshokola claims that it's because they can sense that we don't have any money.
He starts playing around on his guitar.
Now women start to get interested.

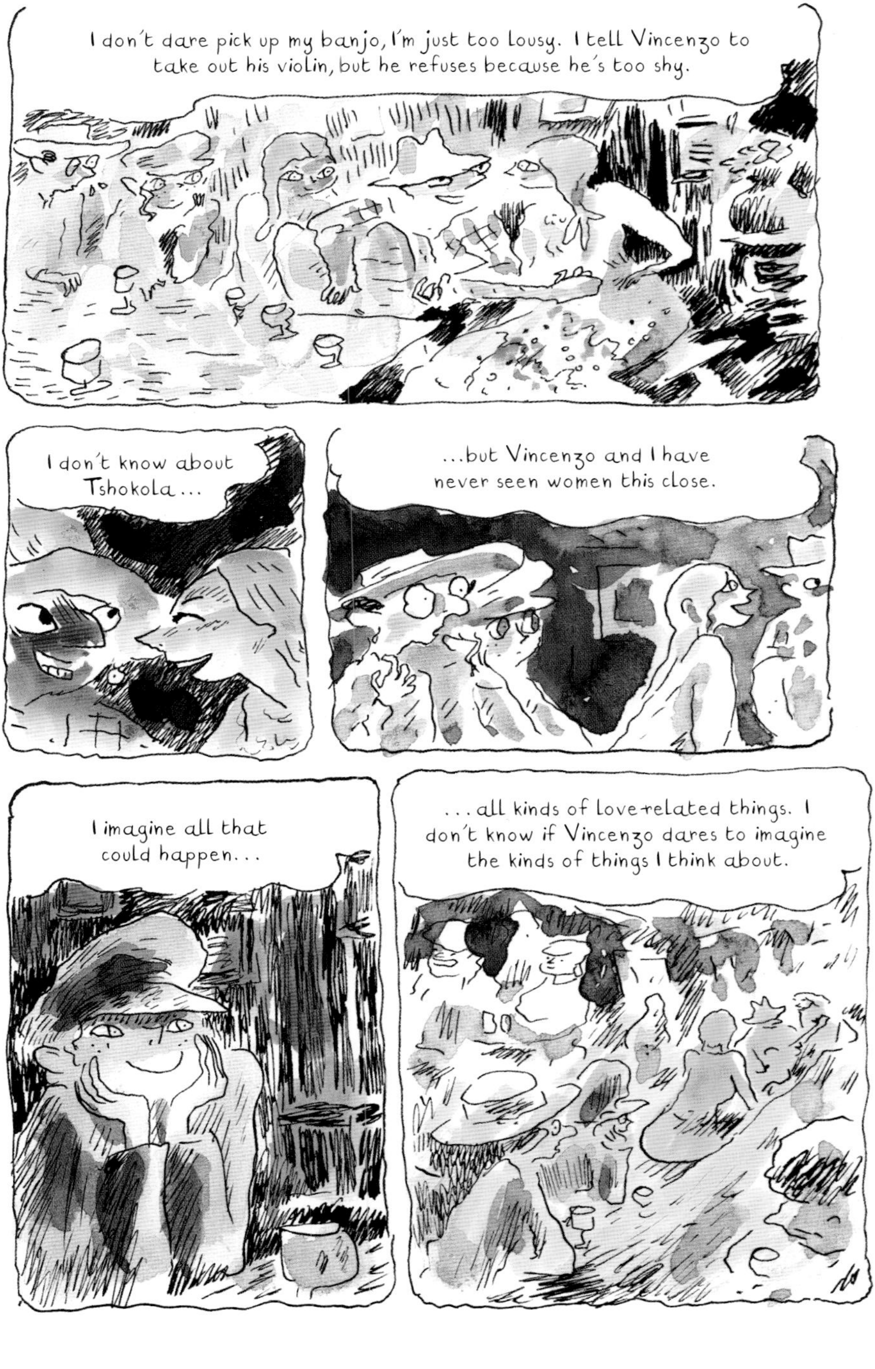
I don't dare pick up my banjo, I'm just too lousy. I tell Vincenzo to take out his violin, but he refuses because he's too shy.
I don't know about Tshokola...
...but Vincenzo and I have never seen women this close.
I imagine all that could happen...
...all kinds of love-related things. I don't know if Vincenzo dares to imagine the kinds of things I think about.

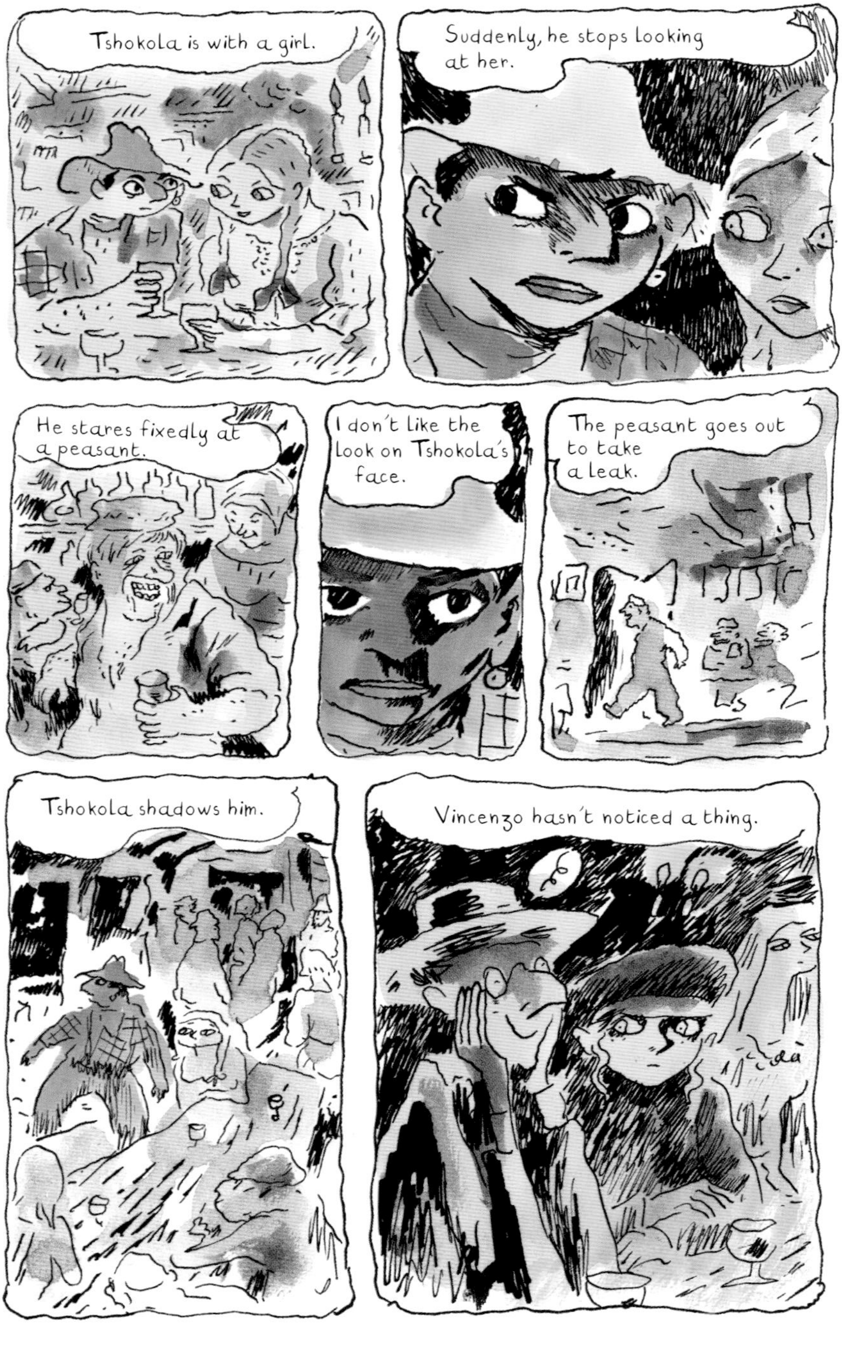
Tshokola is with a girl.
Suddenly, he stops looking at her.
He stares fixedly at a peasant.
I don't like the look on Tshokola's face.
The peasant goes out to take a leak.
Tshokola shadows him.
Vincenzo hasn't noticed a thing.

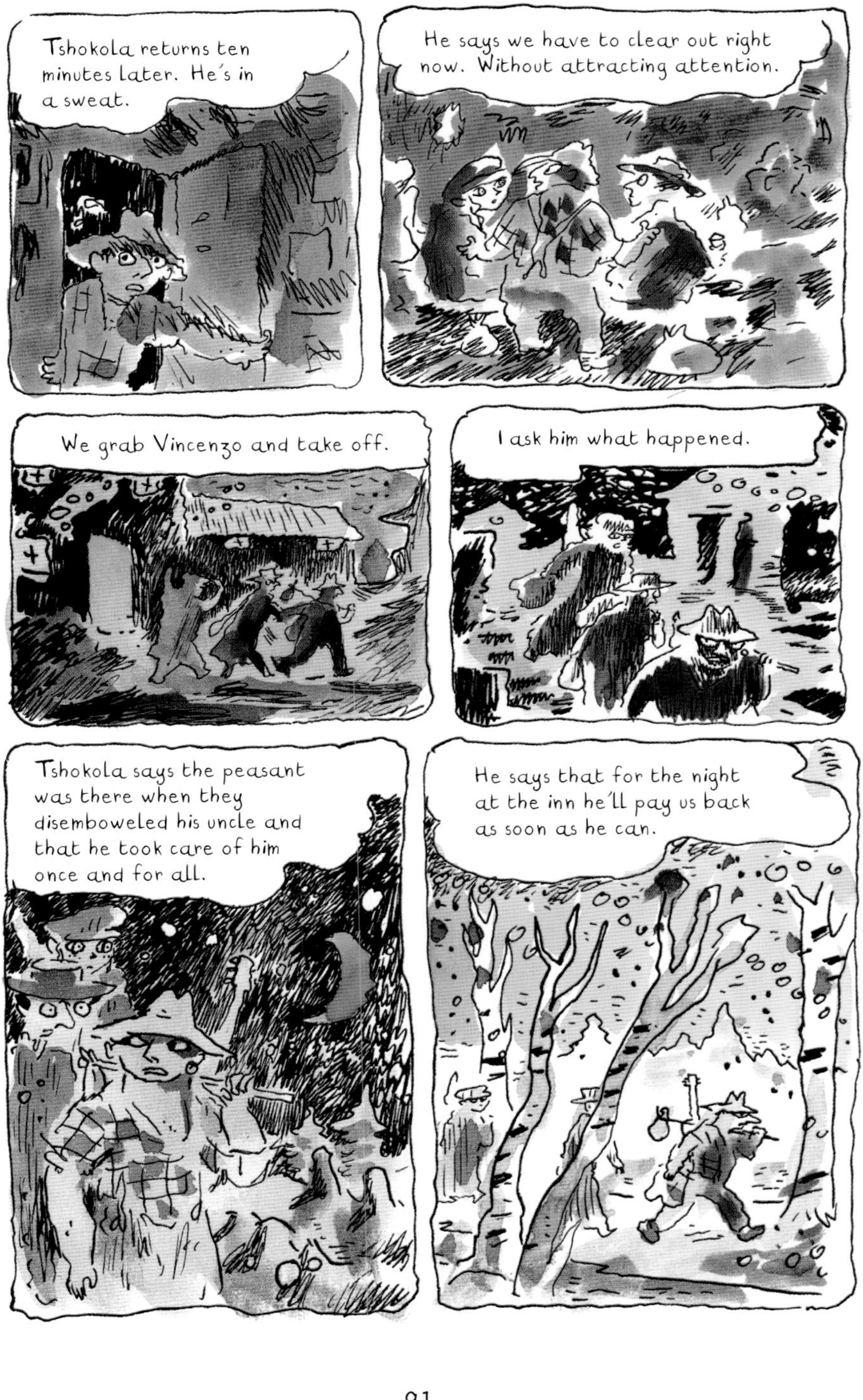
Tshokola returns ten minutes later. He's in a sweat.
He says we have to clear out right now. Without attracting attention.
We grab Vincenzo and take off.
I ask him what happened.
Tshokola says the peasant was there when they disemboweled his uncle and that he took care of him once and for all.
He says that for the night at the inn he'll pay us back as soon as he can.

We make a fine gang of criminals. I watch Tshokola walk ahead with big strides, jaw clenched. I try to convince myself he didn't assassinate anyone. After all, he's a liar and nothing proves that the muzhik is dead.

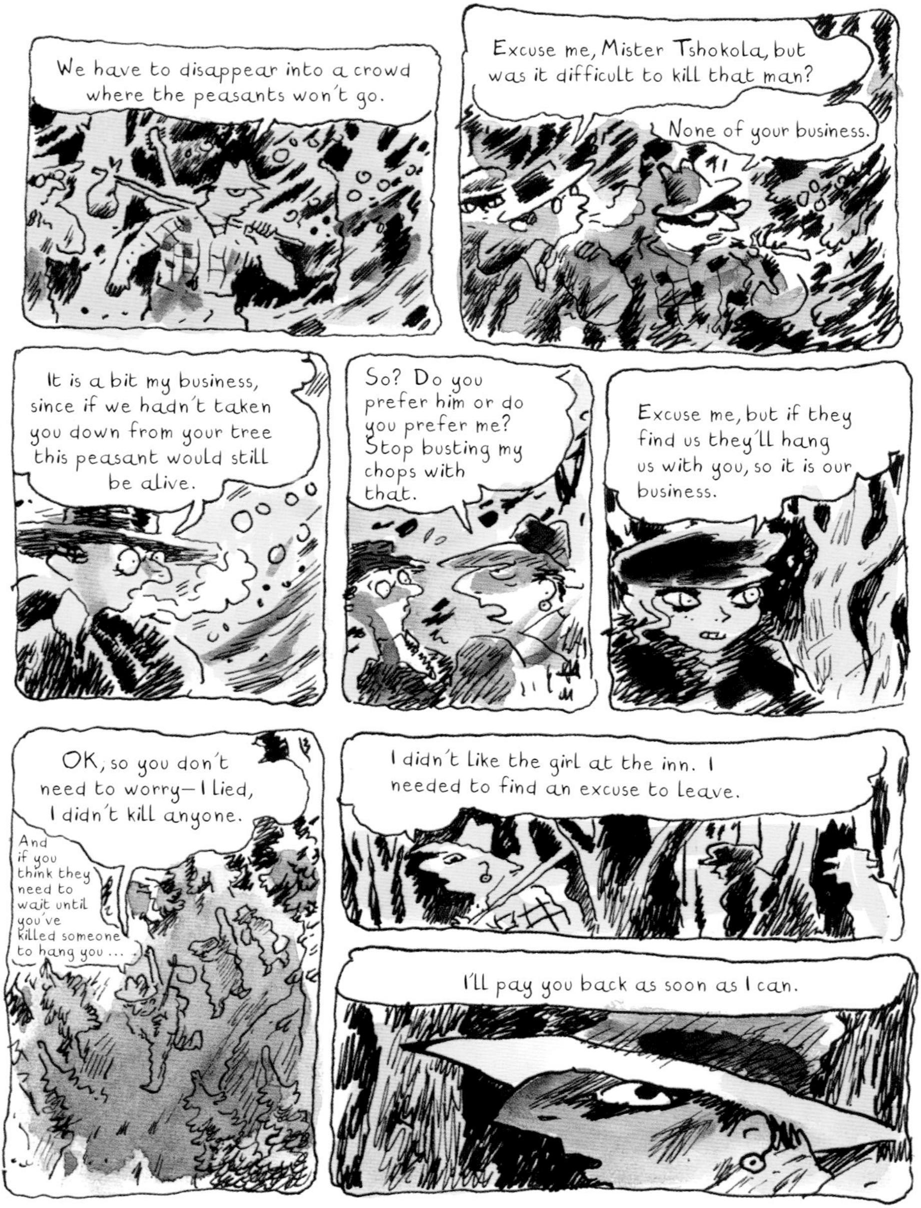
We have to disappear into a crowd where the peasants won't go.
Excuse me, Mister Tshokola, but was it difficult to kill that man?
None of your business.
It is a bit my business, since if we hadn't taken you down from your tree this peasant would still be alive.
So? Do you prefer him or do you prefer me? Stop busting my chops with that.
Excuse me, but if they find us they'll hang us with you, so it is our business.
OK, so you don't need to worry—I lied, I didn't kill anyone.
And if you think they need to wait until you've killed someone to hang you . . .
I didn't like the girl at the inn. I needed to find an excuse to leave.
I'll pay you back as soon as I can.

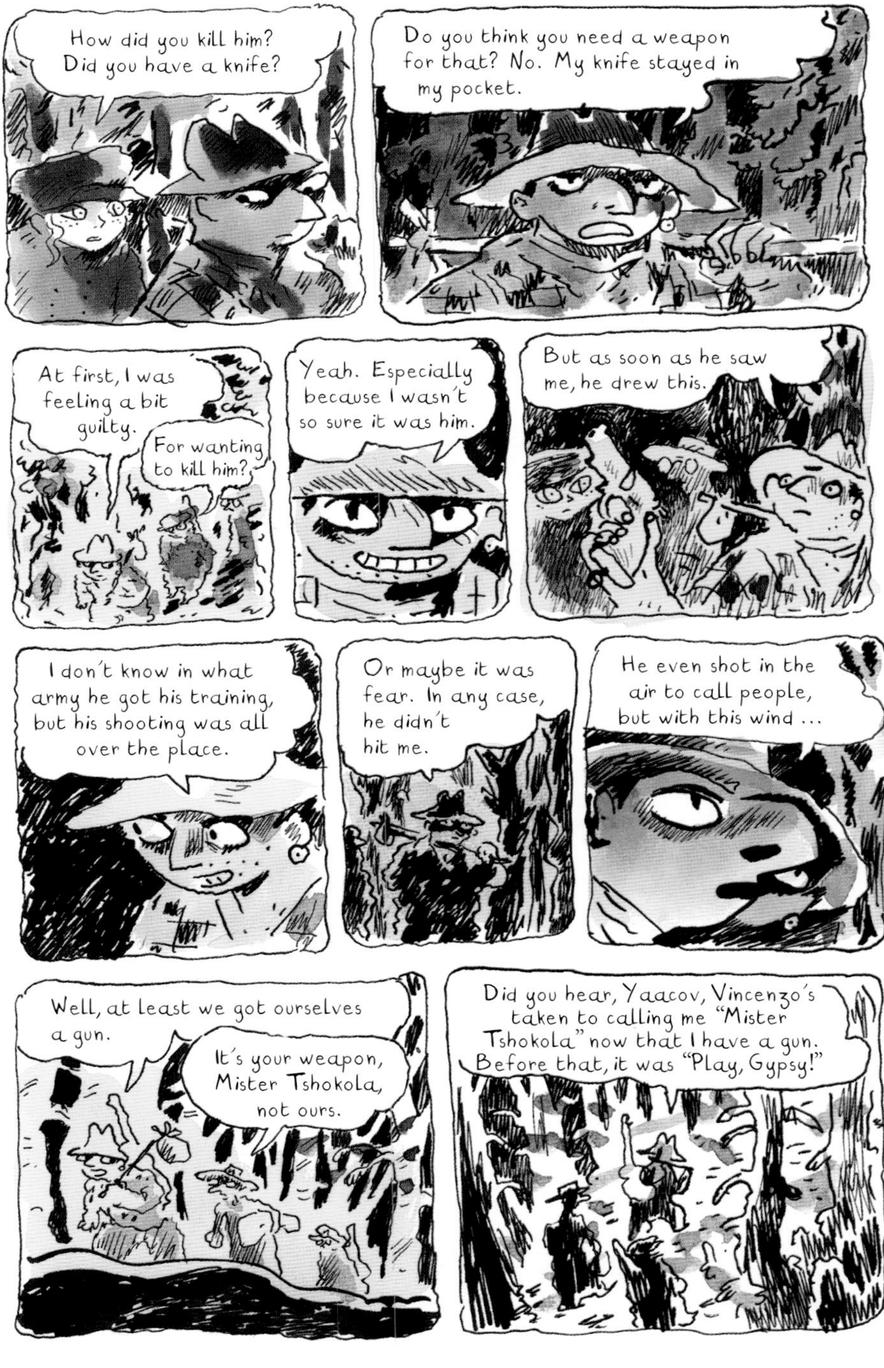
How did you kill him? Did you have a knife?
Do you think you need a weapon for that? No. My knife stayed in my pocket.
At first, I was feeling a bit guilty.
For wanting to kill him?
Yeah. Especially because I wasn't so sure it was him.
But as soon as he saw me, he drew this.
I don't know in what army he got his training, but his shooting was all over the place.
Or maybe it was fear. In any case, he didn't hit me.
He even shot in the air to call people, but with this wind ...
Well, at least we got ourselves a gun.
It's your weapon, Mister Tshokola, not ours.
Did you hear, Yaacov, Vincenzo's taken to calling me "Mister Tshokola" now that I have a gun. Before that, it was "Play, Gypsy!"

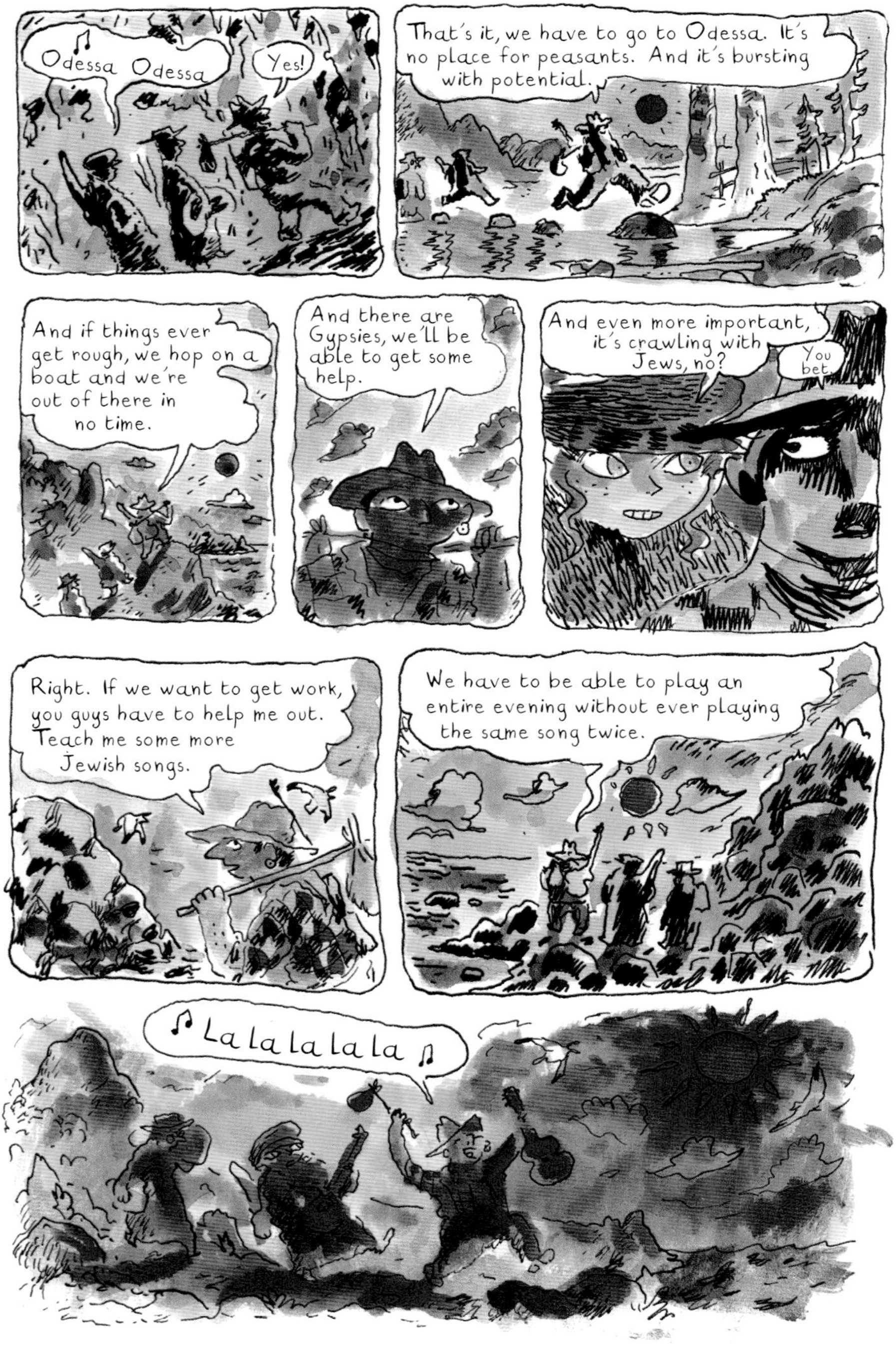
Odessa Odessa
Yes!
That's it, we have to go to Odessa. It's no place for peasants. And it's bursting with potential.
And if things ever get rough, we hop on a boat and we're out of there in no time.
And there are Gypsies, we'll be able to get some help.
And even more important, it's crawling with Jews, no?
You bet.
Right. If we want to get work, you guys have to help me out. Teach me some more Jewish songs.
We have to be able to play an entire evening without ever playing the same song twice.
La la la la la la

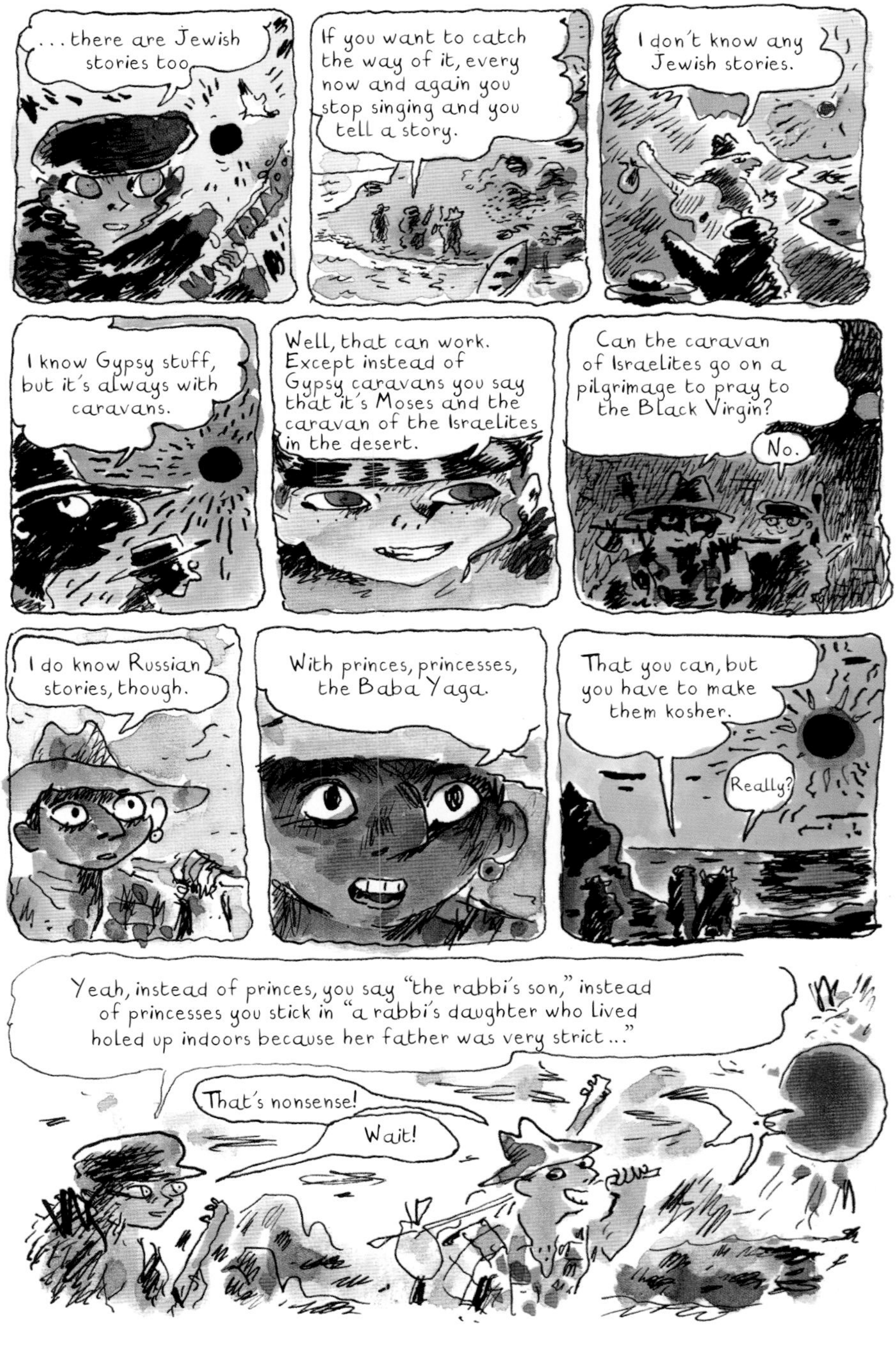

...there are Jewish stories too.
If you want to catch the way of it, every now and again you stop singing and you tell a story.
I don't know any Jewish stories.
I know Gypsy stuff, but it's always with caravans.
Well, that can work. Except instead of Gypsy caravans you say that it's Moses and the caravan of the Israelites in the desert.
Can the caravan of Israelites go on a pilgrimage to pray to the Black Virgin?
No.
I do know Russian stories, though.
With princes, princesses, the Baba Yaga.
That you can, but you have to make them kosher.
Really?
Yeah, instead of princes, you say "the rabbi's son," instead of princesses you stick in "a rabbi's daughter who lived holed up indoors because her father was very strict..."
That's nonsense!
Wait!

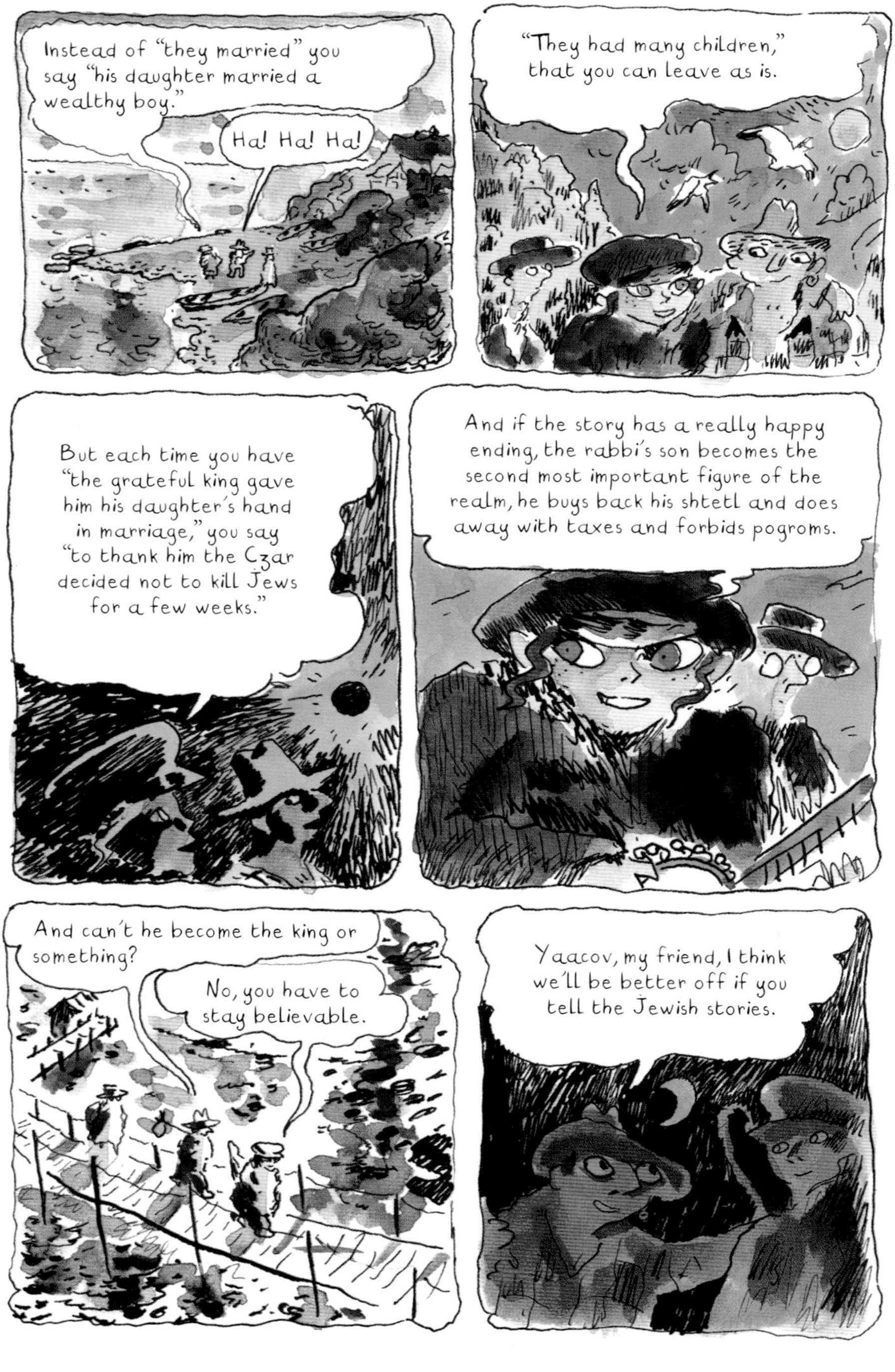
Instead of "they married" you say "his daughter married a wealthy boy."
Ha! Ha! Ha!
"They had many children," that you can leave as is.
But each time you have "the grateful king gave him his daughter's hand in marriage," you say "to thank him the Czar decided not to kill Jews for a few weeks."
And if the story has a really happy ending, the rabbi's son becomes the second most important figure of the realm, he buys back his shtetl and does away with taxes and forbids pogroms.
And can't he become the king or something?
No, you have to stay believable.
Yaacov, my friend, I think we'll be better off if you tell the Jewish stories.

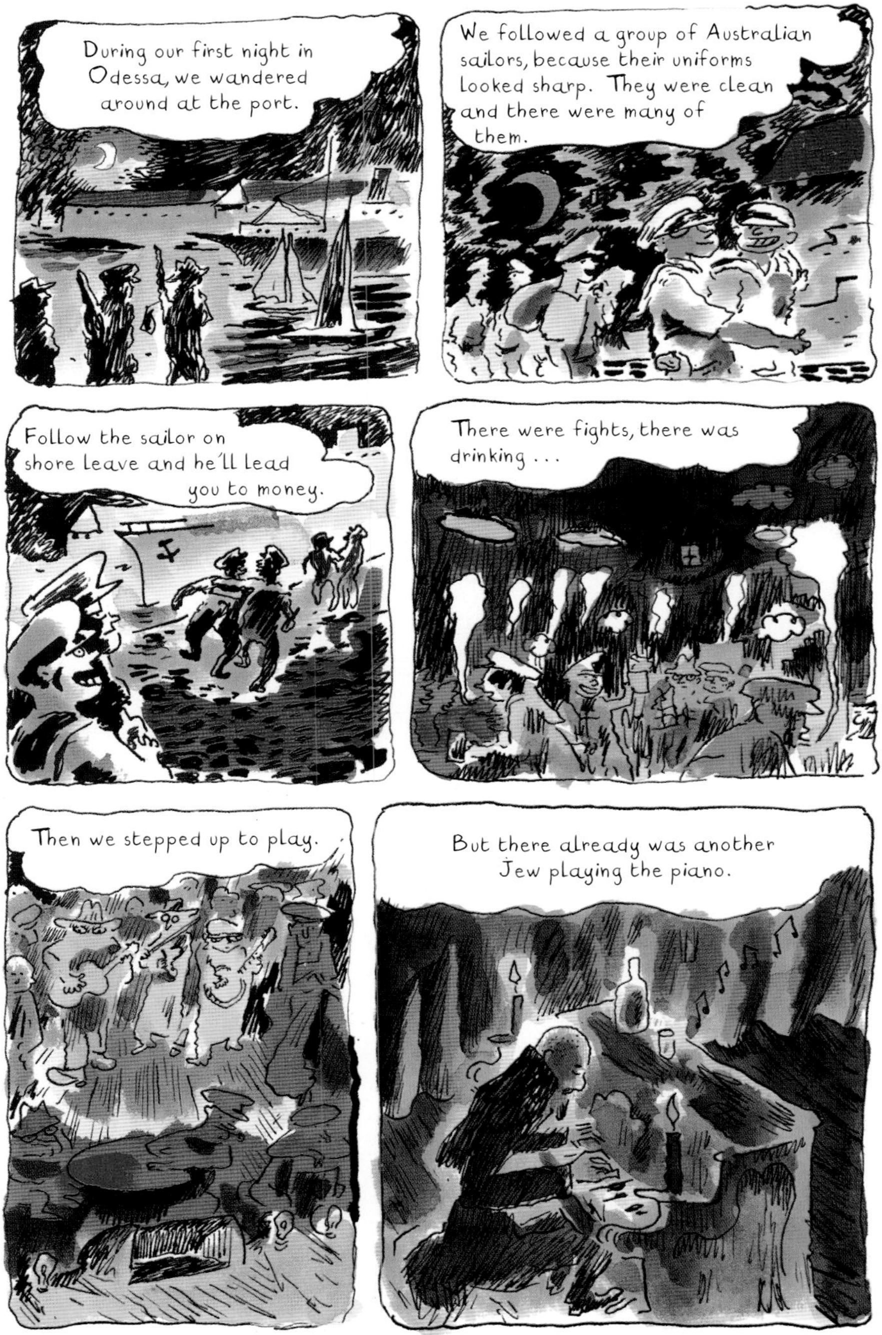
During our first night in Odessa, we wandered around at the port.
We followed a group of Australian sailors, because their uniforms looked sharp. They were clean and there were many of them.
Follow the sailor on shore leave and he'll lead you to money.
There were fights, there was drinking . . .
Then we stepped up to play.
But there already was another Jew playing the piano.

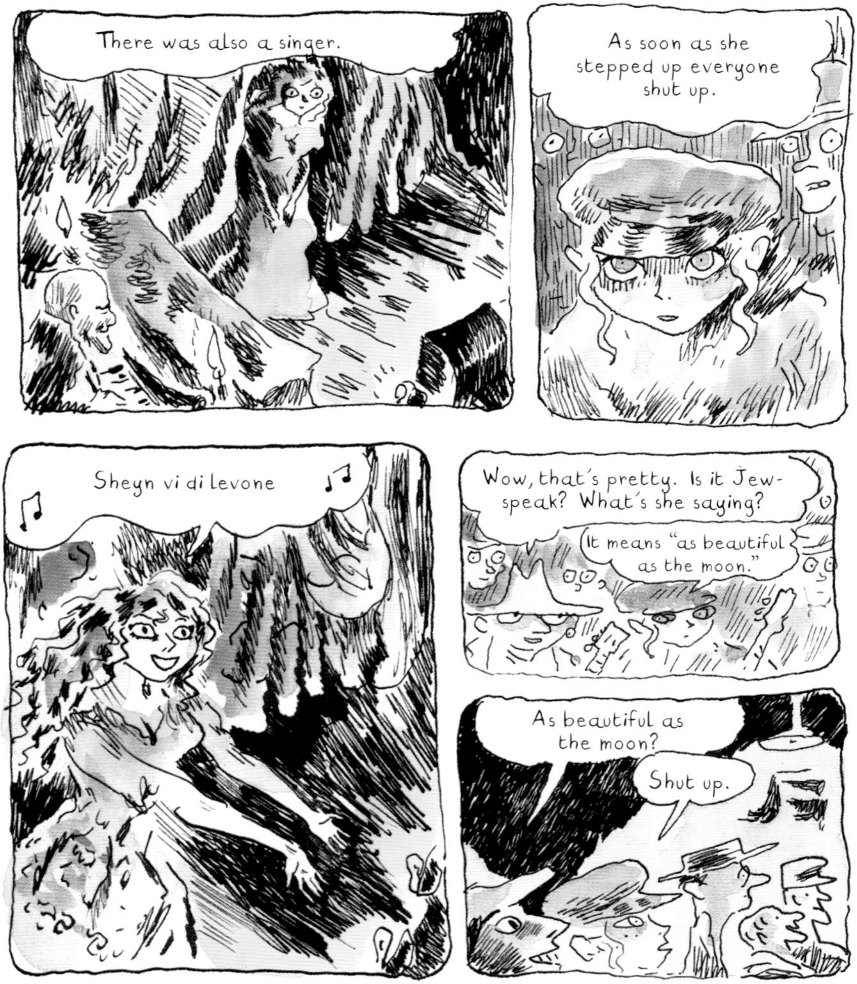
There was also a singer.
As soon as she stepped up everyone shut up.
Sheyn vi di levone
Wow, that's pretty. Is it Jew-speak? What's she saying?
It means "as beautiful as the moon."
As beautiful as the moon?
Shut up.

Coming from Vincenzo or anyone else, "as beautiful as the moon" would sound really dumb.

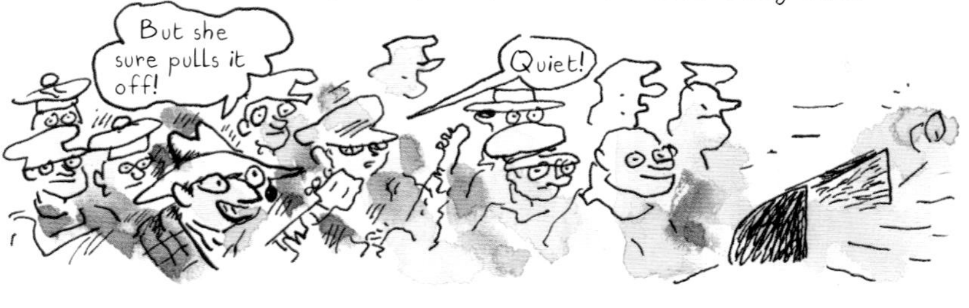
But she sure pulls it off!
Quiet!

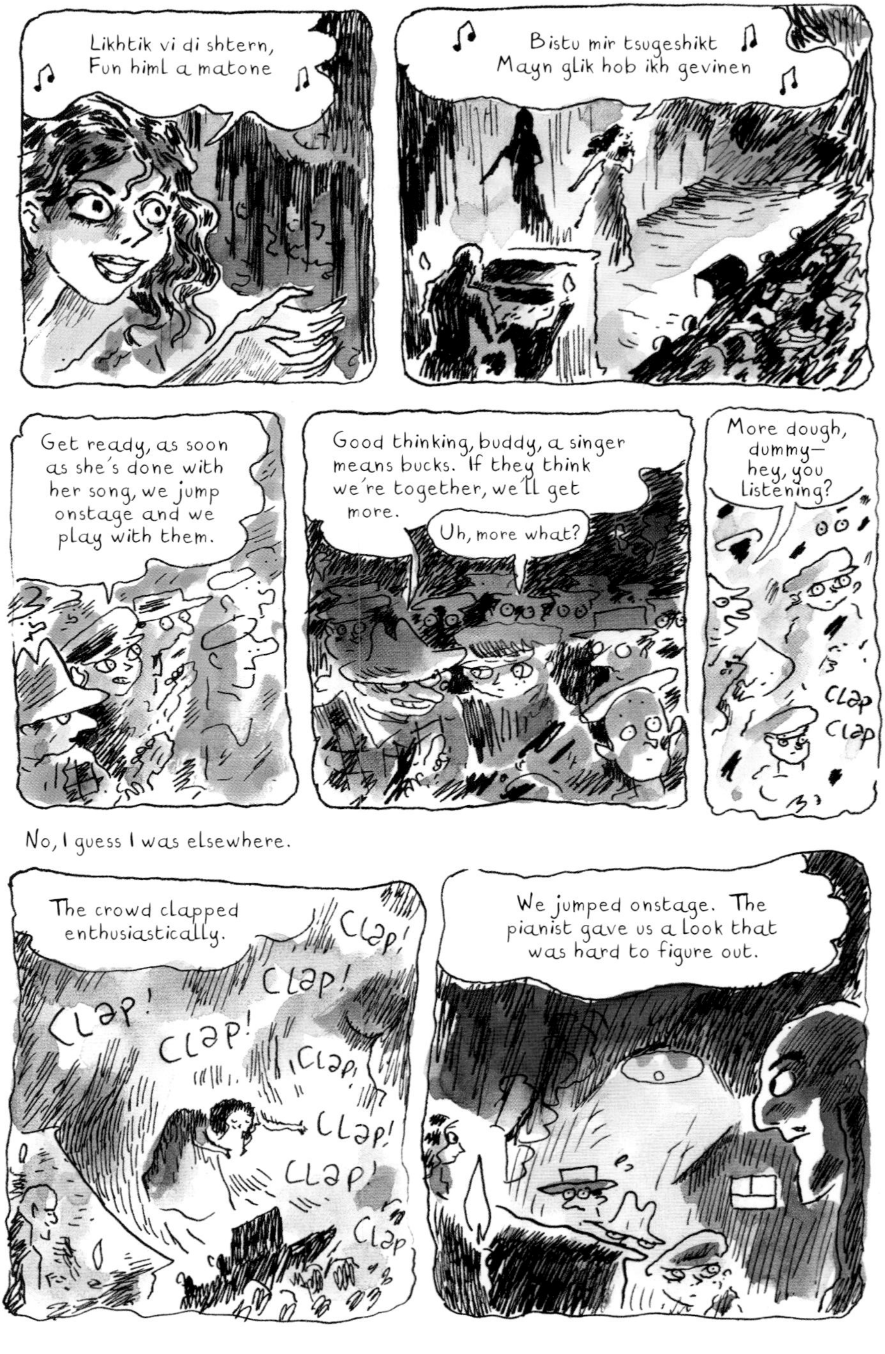
Likhtik vi di shtern,
Fun himl a matone
Bistu mir tsugeshikt
Mayn glik hob ikh gevinen
Get ready, as soon as she's done with her song, we jump onstage and we play with them.
Good thinking, buddy, a singer means bucks. If they think we're together, we'll get more.
Uh, more what?
More dough, dummy— hey, you listening?
Clap
Clap
No, I guess I was elsewhere.
The crowd clapped enthusiastically.
Clap!
Clap!
Clap!
Clap!
Clap!
Clap!
Clap
Clap
We jumped onstage. The pianist gave us a look that was hard to figure out.

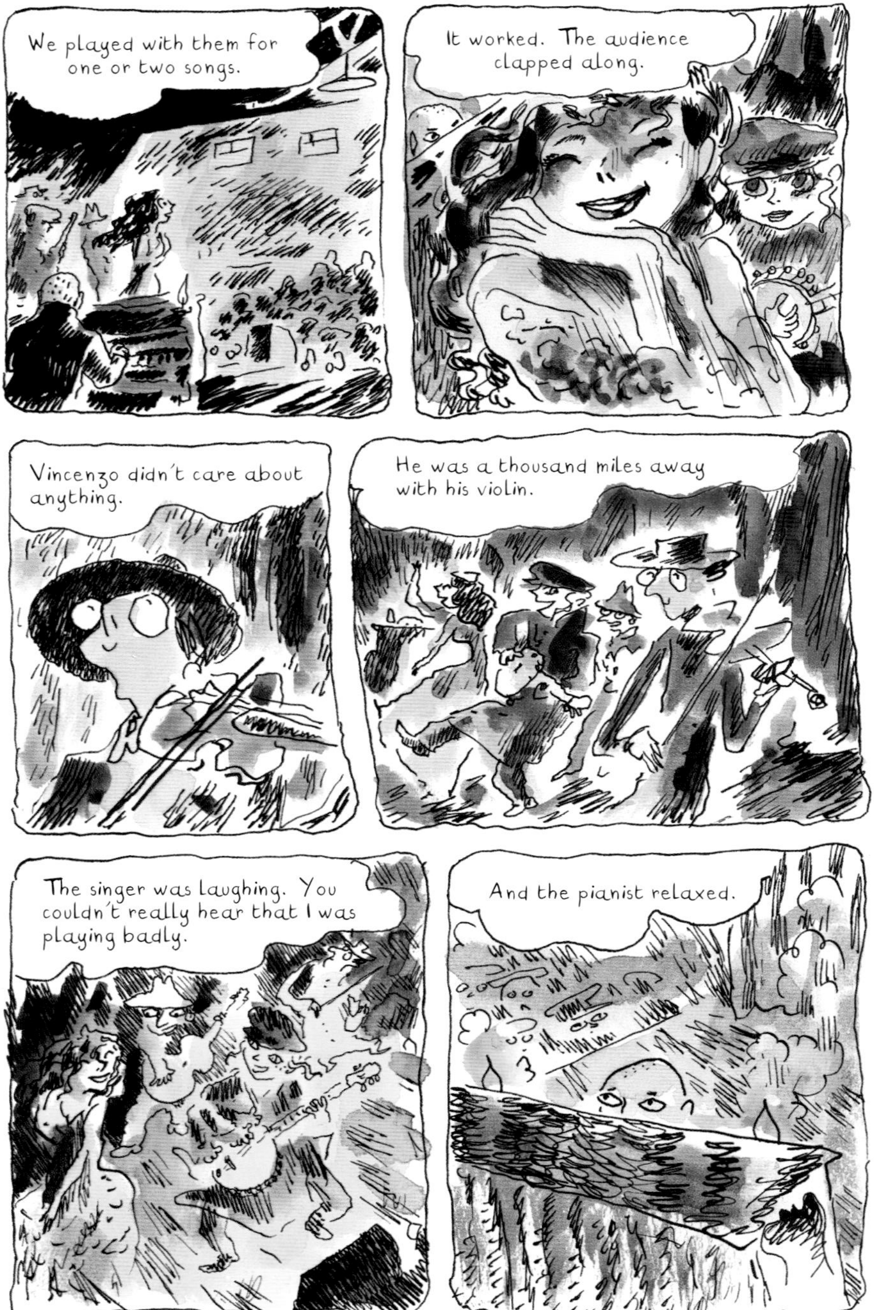
We played with them for one or two songs.
It worked. The audience clapped along.
Vincenzo didn't care about anything.
He was a thousand miles away with his violin.
The singer was laughing. You couldn't really hear that I was playing badly.
And the pianist relaxed.

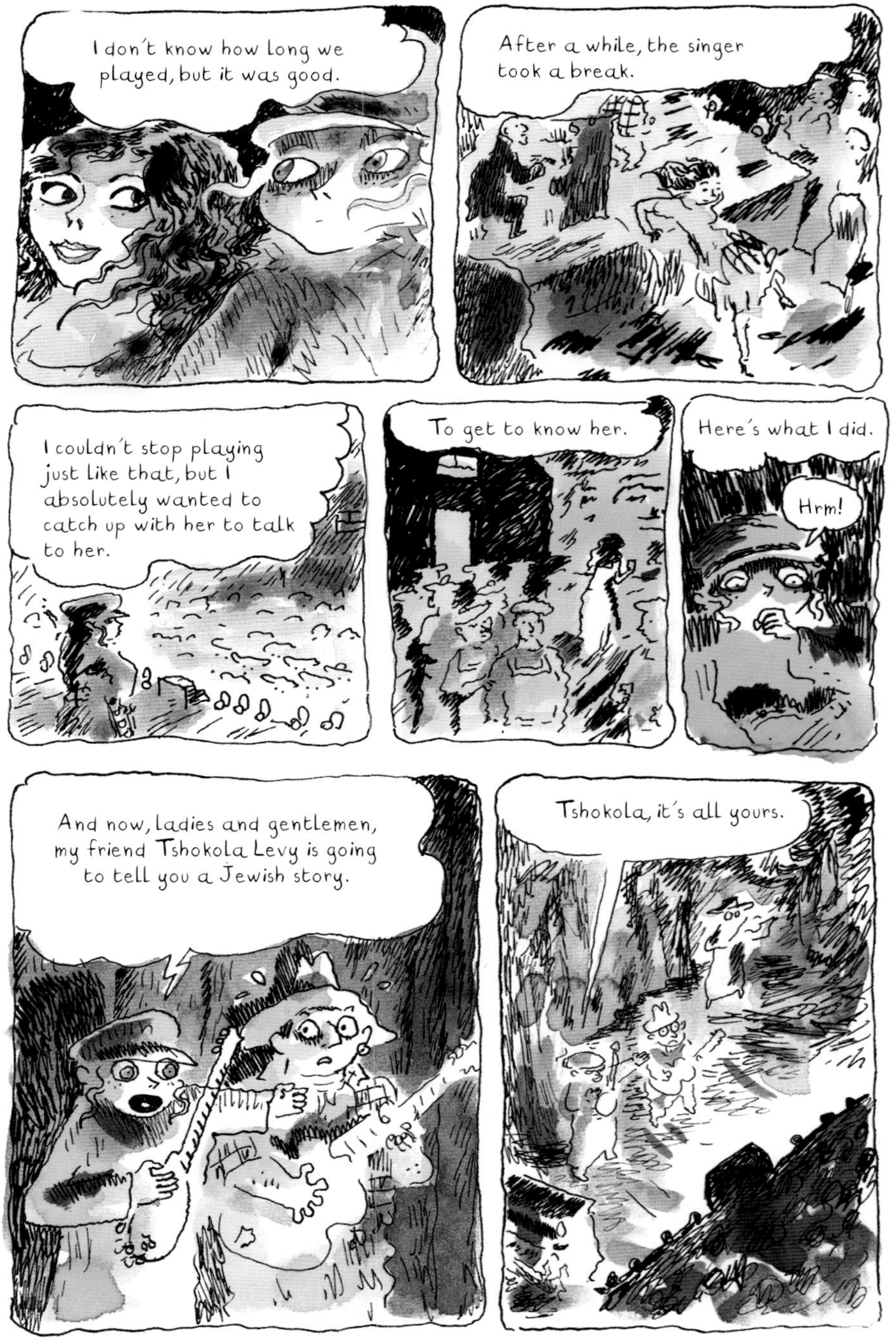

I don't know how long we played, but it was good.
After a while, the singer took a break.
I couldn't stop playing just like that, but I absolutely wanted to catch up with her to talk to her.
To get to know her.
Here's what I did.
Hrm!
And now, ladies and gentlemen, my friend Tshokola Levy is going to tell you a Jewish story.
Tshokola, it's all yours.

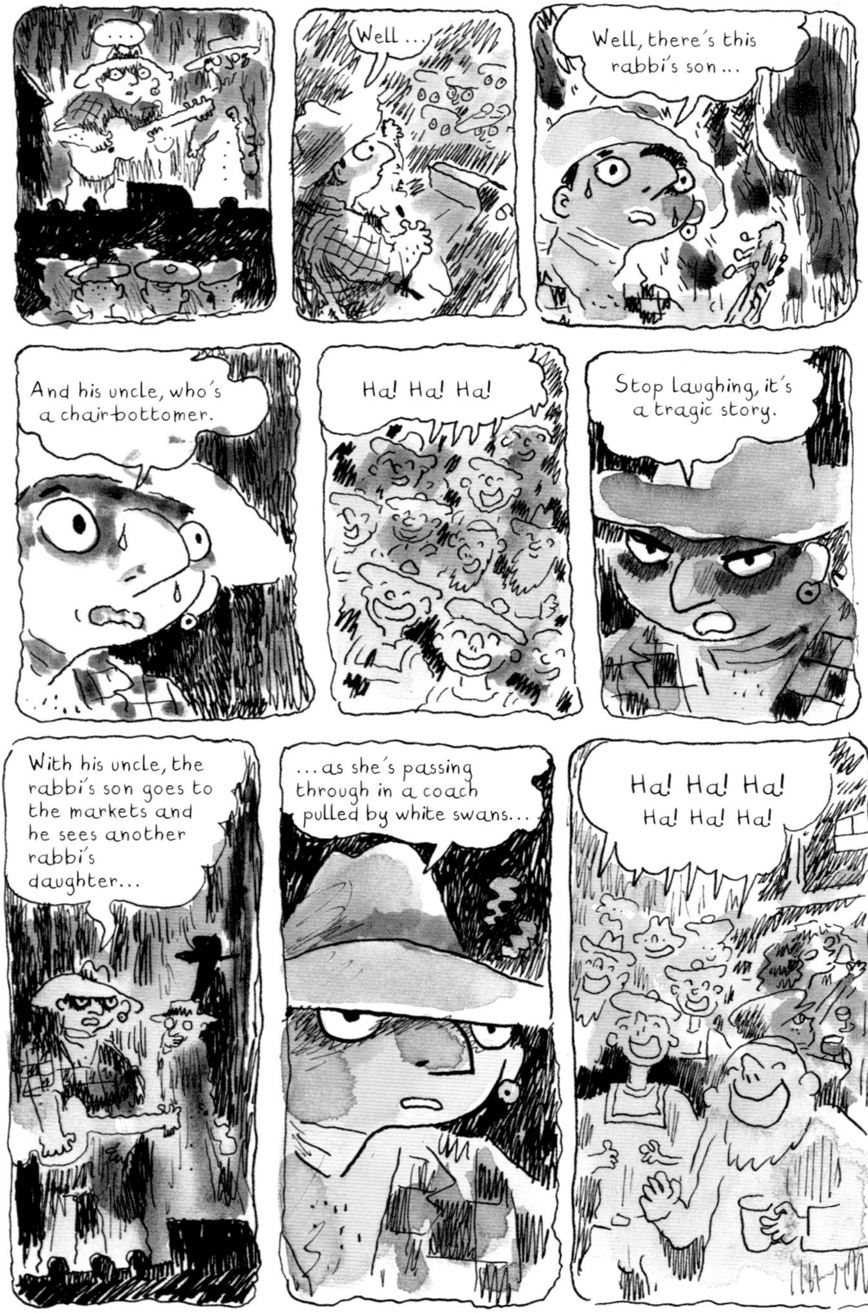

...
Well...
Well, there's this rabbi's son...
And his uncle, who's a chairbottomer.
Ha! Ha! Ha!
Stop laughing, it's a tragic story.
With his uncle, the rabbi's son goes to the markets and he sees another rabbi's daughter...
...as she's passing through in a coach pulled by white swans...
Ha! Ha! Ha! Ha! Ha! Ha!

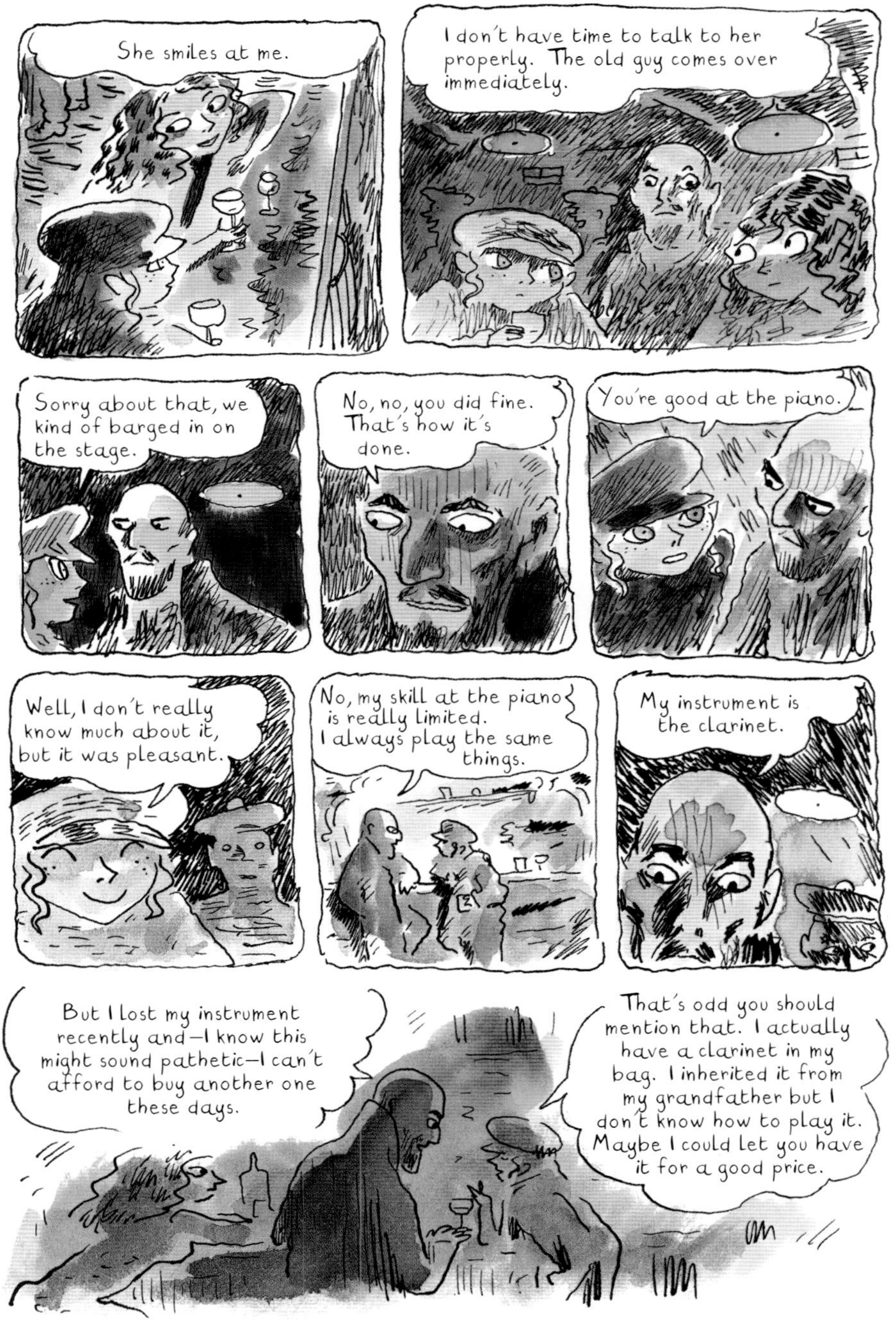
She smiles at me.
I don't have time to talk to her properly. The old guy comes over immediately.
Sorry about that, we kind of barged in on the stage.
No, no, you did fine. That's how it's done.
You're good at the piano.
Well, I don't really know much about it, but it was pleasant.
No, my skill at the piano is really limited. I always play the same things.
My instrument is the clarinet.
But I lost my instrument recently and—I know this might sound pathetic—I can't afford to buy another one these days.
That's odd you should mention that. I actually have a clarinet in my bag. I inherited it from my grandfather but I don't know how to play it. Maybe I could let you have it for a good price.

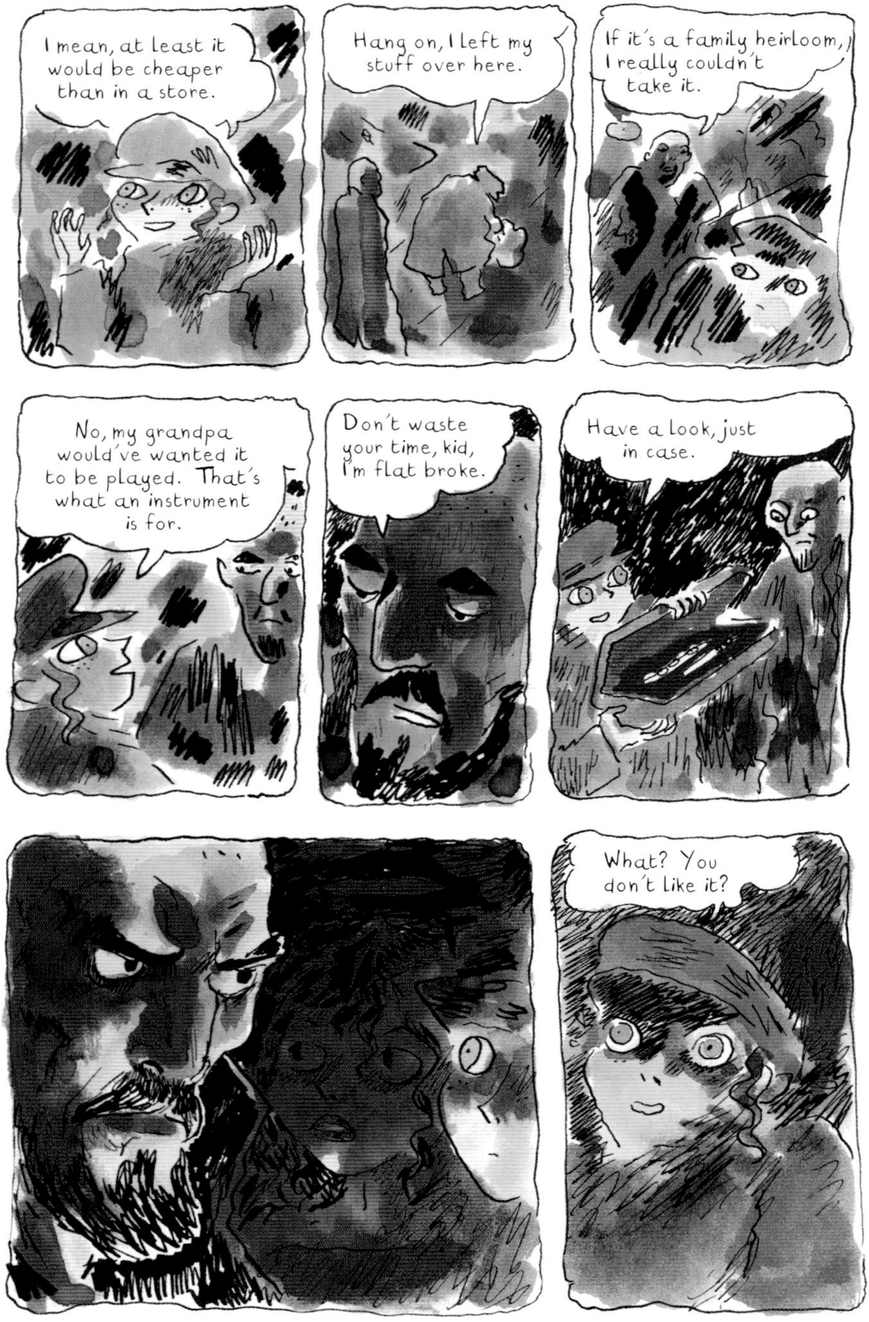
I mean, at least it would be cheaper than in a store.
Hang on, I left my stuff over here.
If it's a family heirloom, I really couldn't take it.
No, my grandpa would've wanted it to be played. That's what an instrument is for.
Don't waste your time, kid, I'm flat broke.
Have a look, just in case.
What? You don't like it?

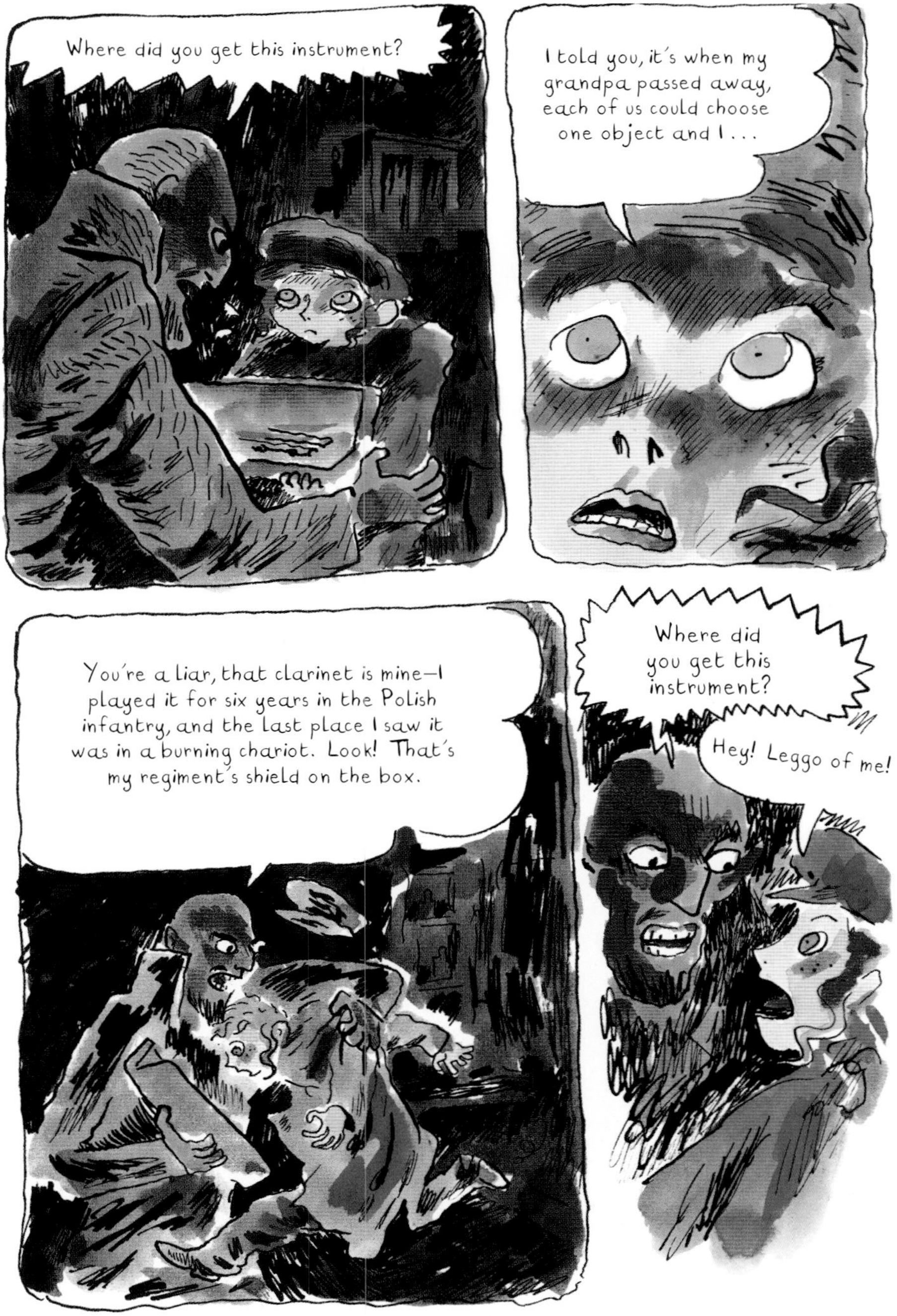
Where did you get this instrument?
I told you, it's when my grandpa passed away, each of us could choose one object and I . . .
You're a liar, that clarinet is mine—I played it for six years in the Polish infantry, and the last place I saw it was in a burning chariot. Look! That's my regiment's shield on the box.
Where did you get this instrument?
Hey! Leggo of me!

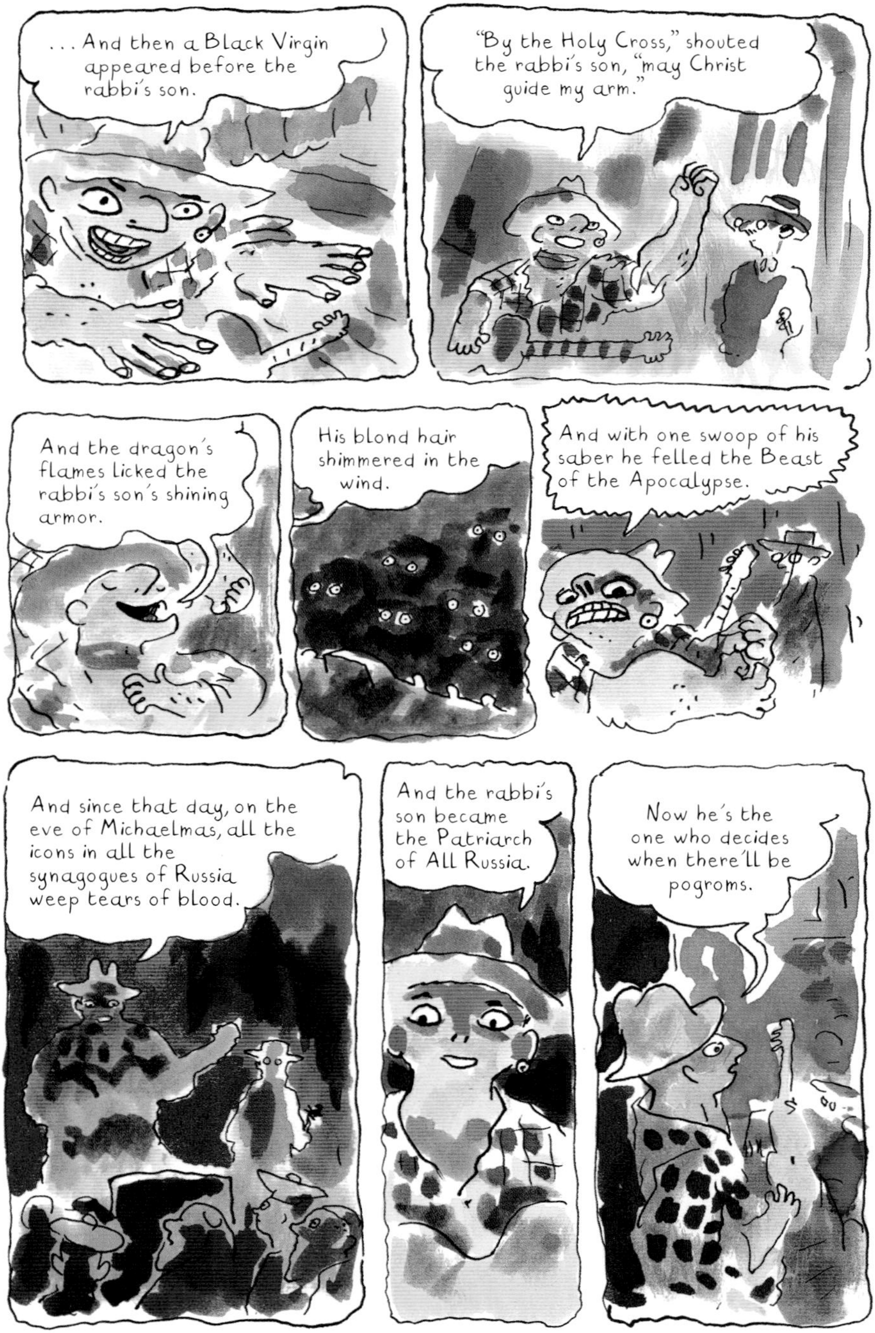
...And then a Black Virgin appeared before the rabbi's son.
"By the Holy Cross," shouted the rabbi's son, "may Christ guide my arm."
And the dragon's flames licked the rabbi's son's shining armor.
His blond hair shimmered in the wind.
And with one swoop of his saber he felled the Beast of the Apocalypse.
And since that day, on the eve of Michaelmas, all the icons in all the synagogues of Russia weep tears of blood.
And the rabbi's son became the Patriarch of All Russia.
Now he's the one who decides when there'll be pogroms.

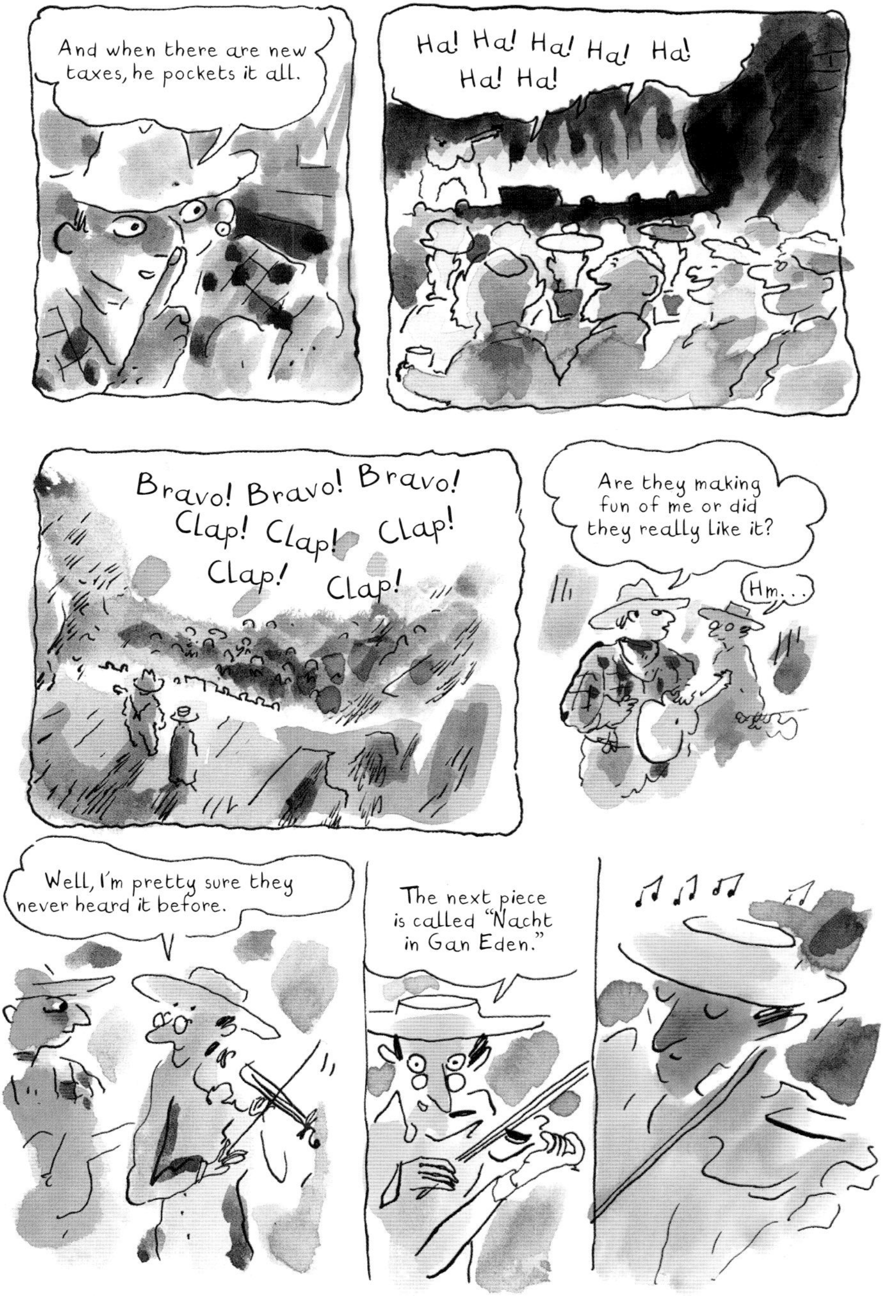
And when there are new taxes, he pockets it all.
Ha! Ha! Ha! Ha! Ha! Ha! Ha!
Bravo! Bravo! Bravo!
Clap! Clap! Clap! Clap! Clap!
Are they making fun of me or did they really like it?
Hm...
Well, I'm pretty sure they never heard it before.
The next piece is called "Nacht in Gan Eden."

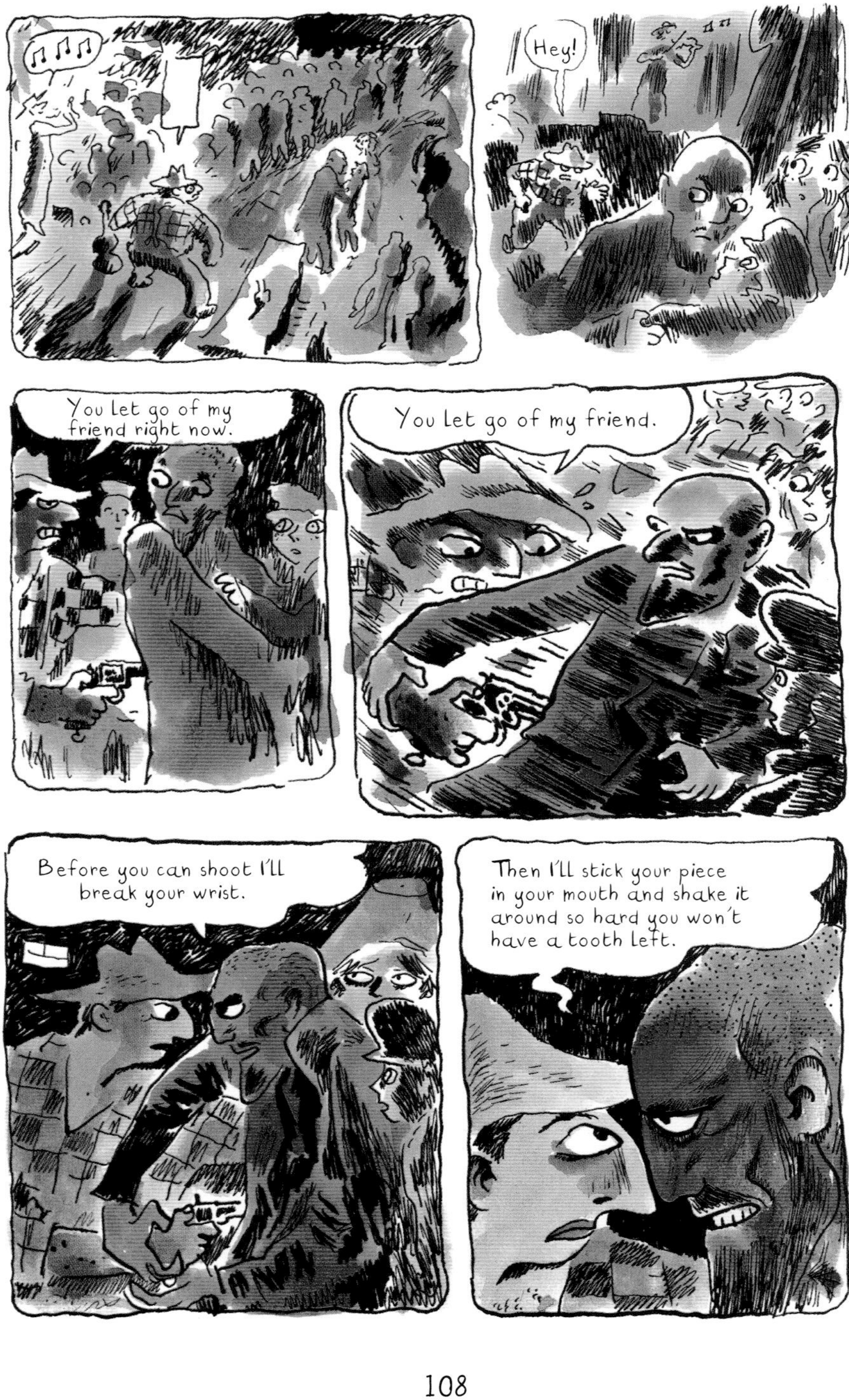
♫♫♫
Hey!
You let go of my friend right now.
You let go of my friend.
Before you can shoot I'll break your wrist.
Then I'll stick your piece in your mouth and shake it around so hard you won't have a tooth left.

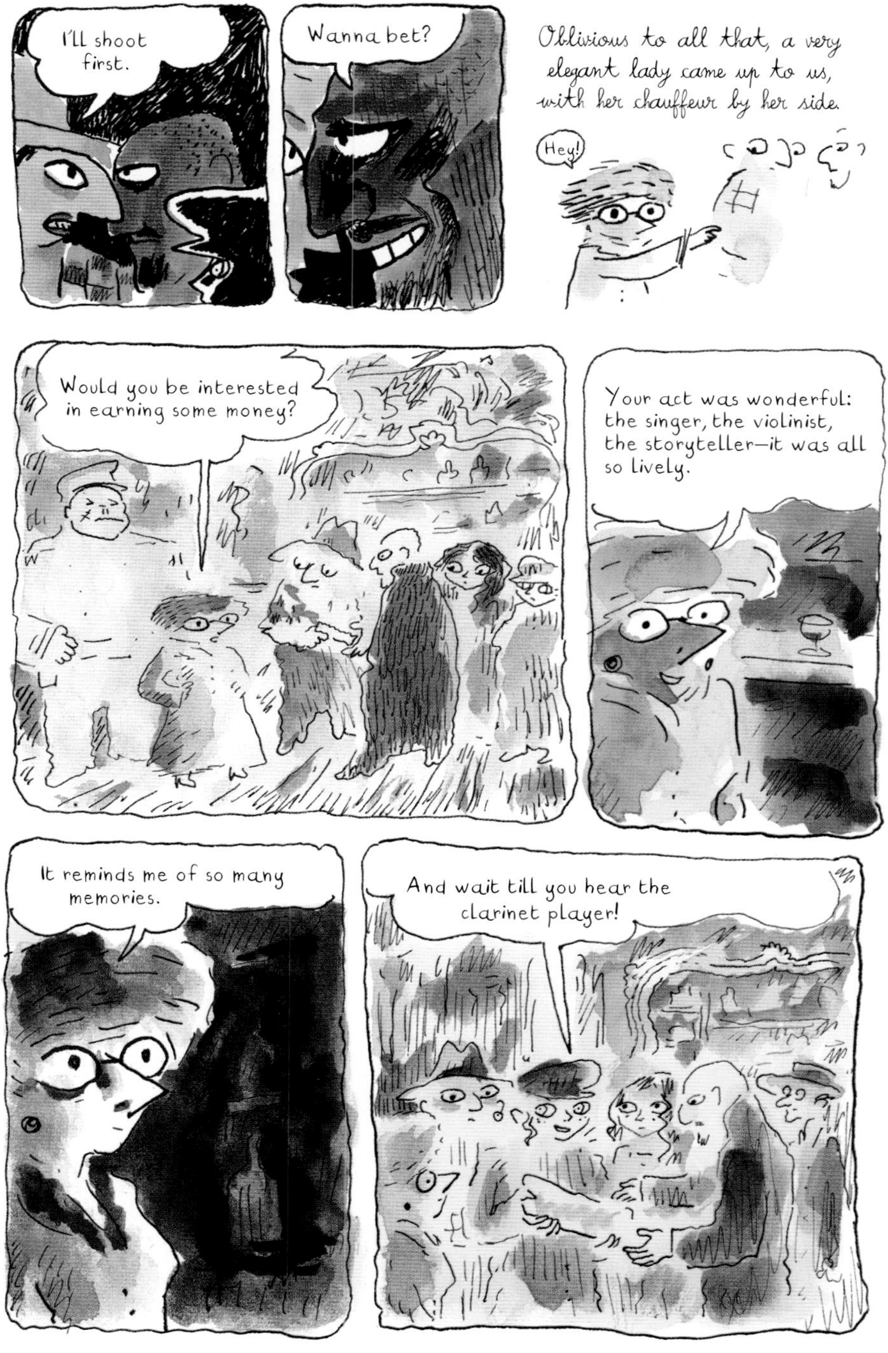
I'll shoot first.
Wanna bet?
Oblivious to all that, a very elegant lady came up to us, with her chauffeur by her side.
Hey!
Would you be interested in earning some money?
Your act was wonderful: the singer, the violinist, the storyteller—it was all so lively.
It reminds me of so many memories.
And wait till you hear the clarinet player!

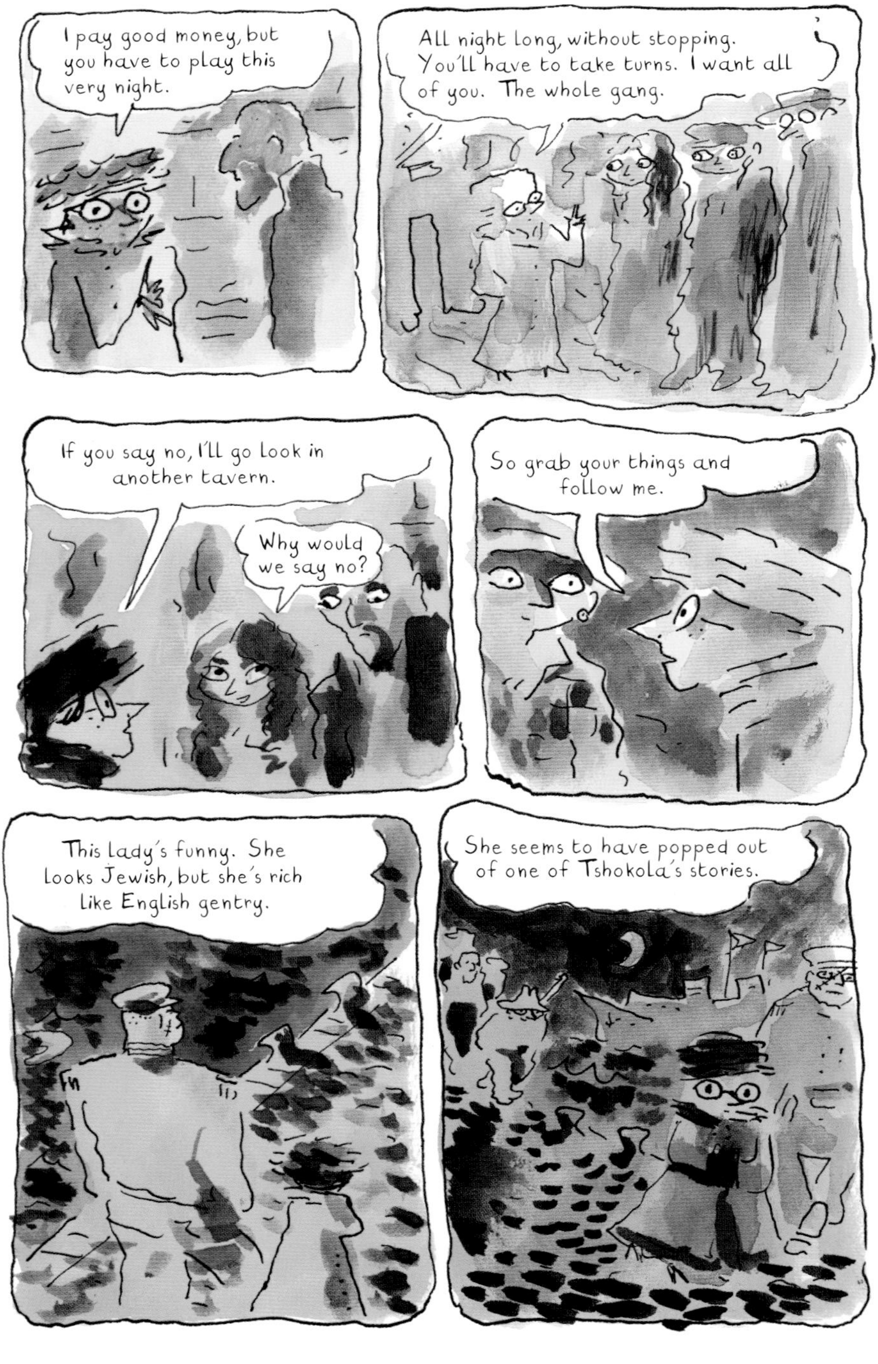

I pay good money, but you have to play this very night.
All night long, without stopping. You'll have to take turns. I want all of you. The whole gang.
If you say no, I'll go look in another tavern.
Why would we say no?
So grab your things and follow me.
This lady's funny. She looks Jewish, but she's rich like English gentry.
She seems to have popped out of one of Tshokola's stories.

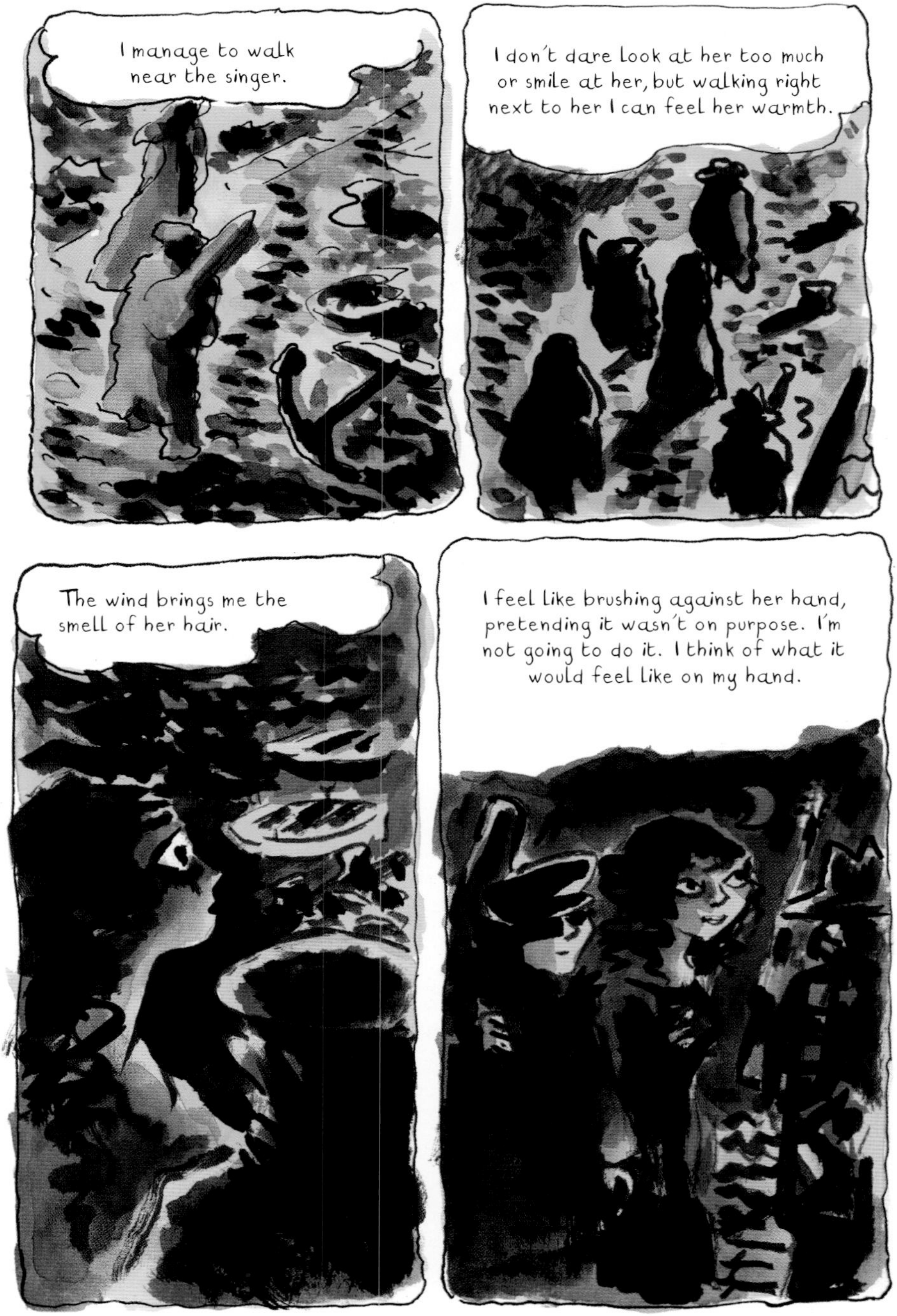
I manage to walk near the singer.
I don't dare look at her too much or smile at her, but walking right next to her I can feel her warmth.
The wind brings me the smell of her hair.
I feel like brushing against her hand, pretending it wasn't on purpose. I'm not going to do it. I think of what it would feel like on my hand.

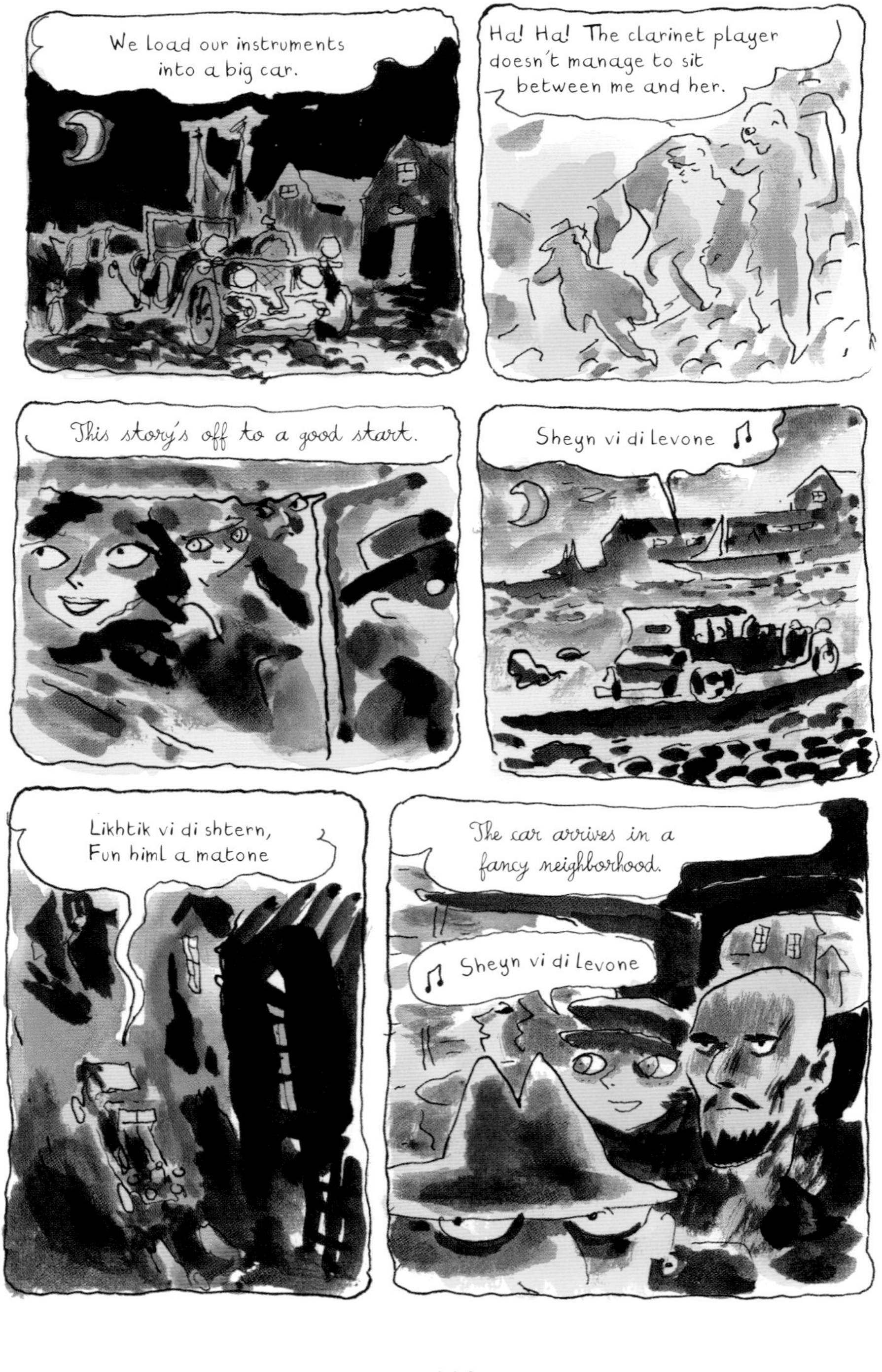
We load our instruments into a big car.
Ha! Ha! The clarinet player doesn't manage to sit between me and her.
This story's off to a good start.
Sheyn vi di levone ♫
Likhtik vi di shtern, Fun himl a matone
The car arrives in a fancy neighborhood.
♫ Sheyn vi di levone

We stop in front of a town house. A butler opens the door.
I wonder what it is we're about to land in.

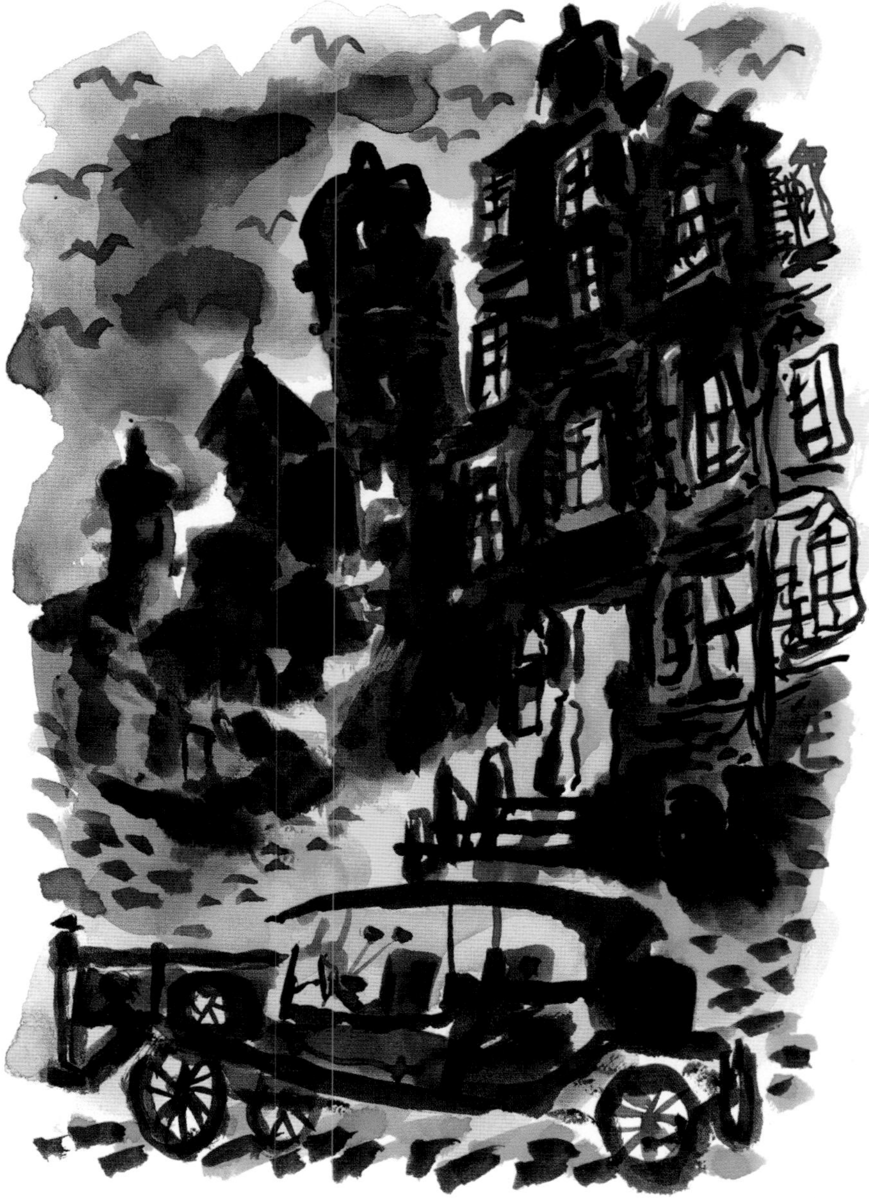

I wonder whose place it is we're going to play in . . .

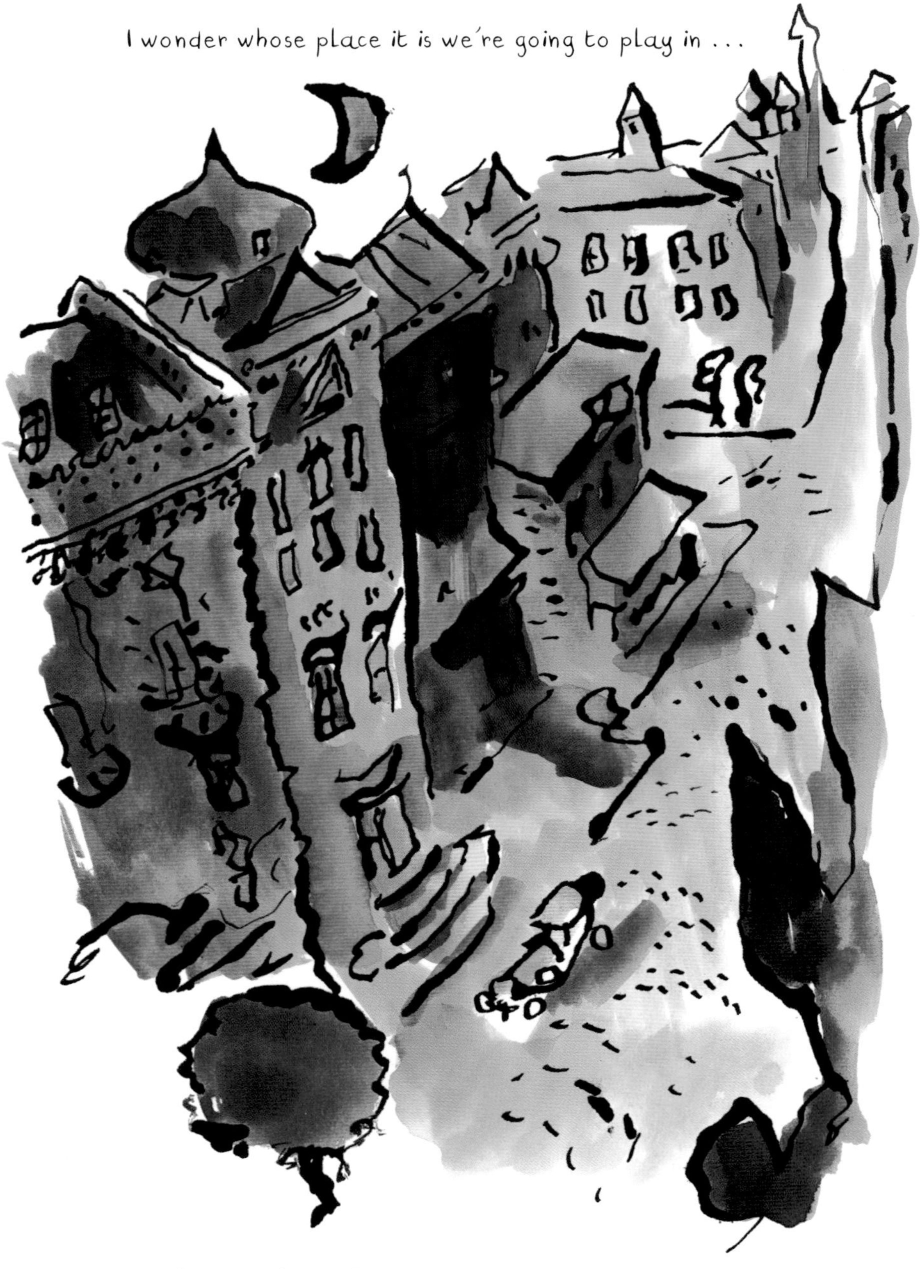

Joann Sfar, April 29, 2005 (to be continued)

All the musicians will be back
in "Happy Birthday, Scylla"

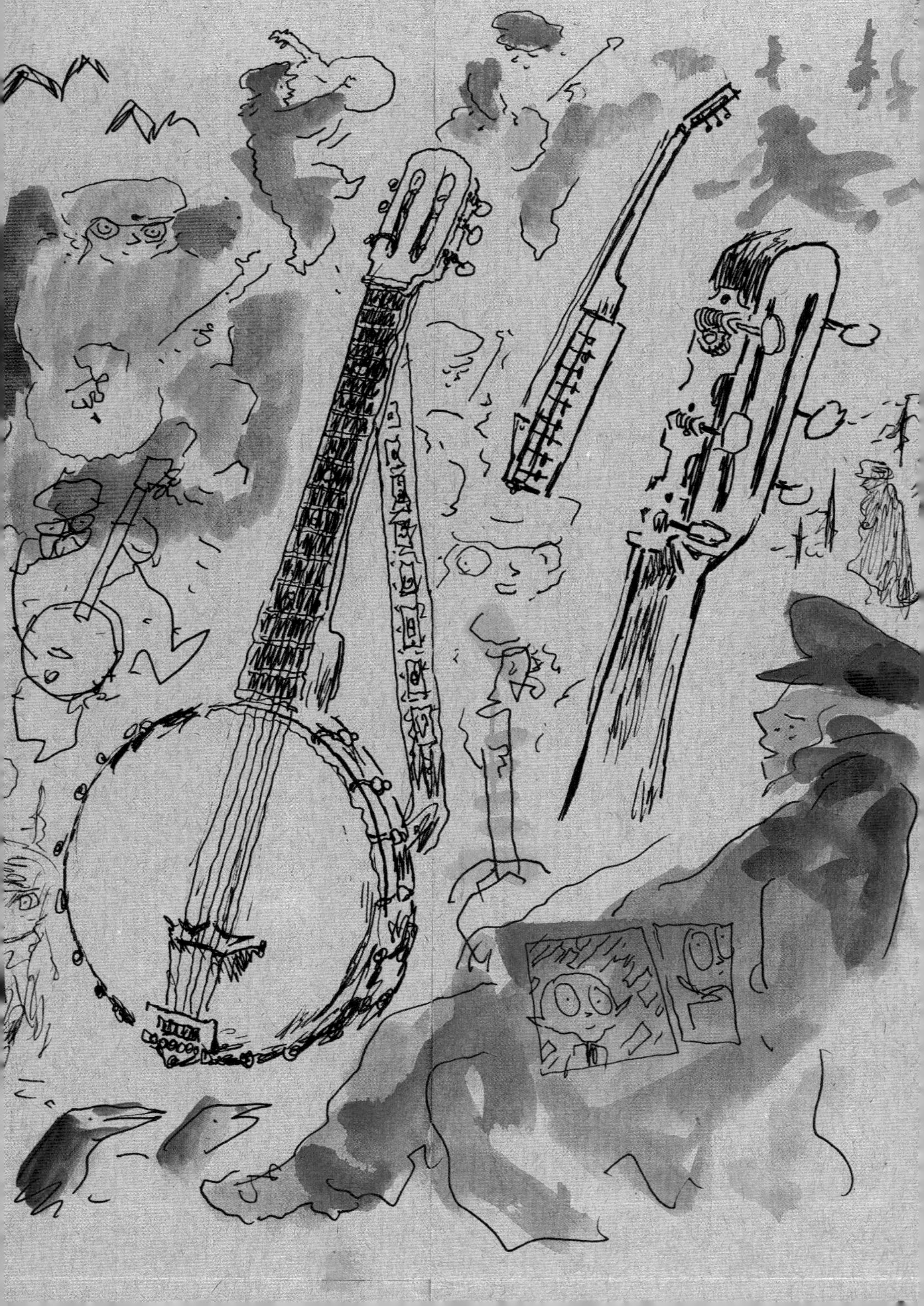

Notes for KLEZMER, Volume 1

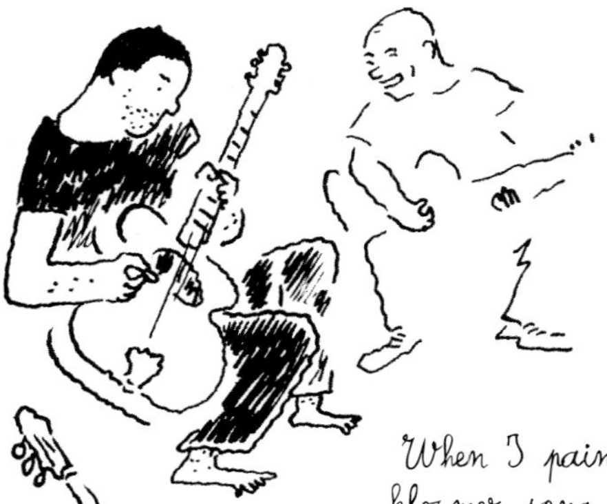

"This song flows within man's ephemeral shell like the waters of eternity. It washes away everything, it gives birth to everything."

Isaac Babel

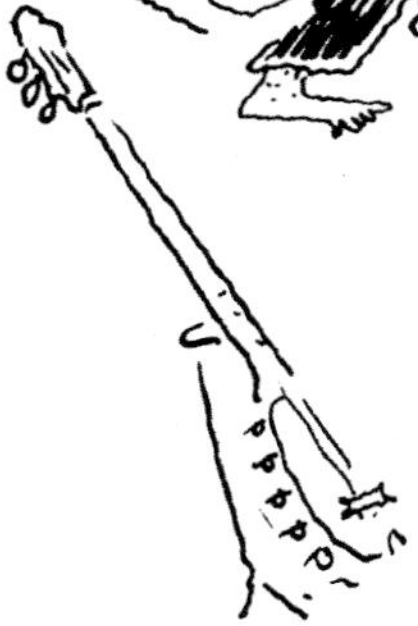

When I painstakingly try to learn a new klezmer song, I feel as if I'm rekindling a fire.

I watch the fingers of my teacher,* I imitate him, I retain in my mind the path my fingers have to follow on my German guitar to bring these Jewish tunes back to life.

That gives me the feeling of nestling in my hands a few nearly cold embers and carefully blowing on them to try to make them burn once again.

And when the song gets off to a good start, I tell myself that something about it is still alive.

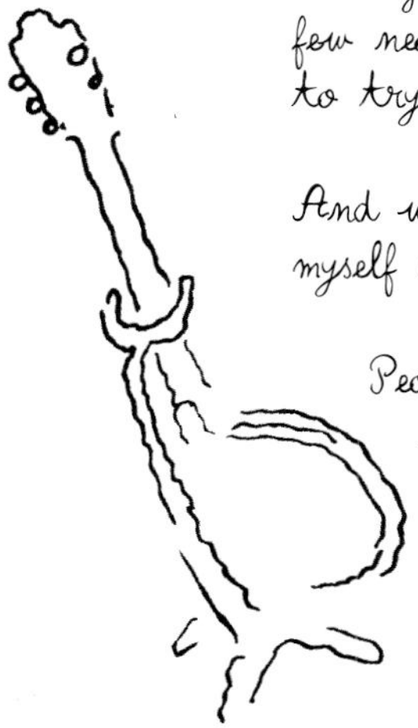

People have been explaining the Jewish people to me since I've been able to speak and I still don't know for sure what it is we're talking about. What I do know, though, is that those from "Poyln," from the land of "Ashkenaz," they no longer exist at all.

*My klezmer teacher, Fred Vandebeer

It's true that in Israel they still have Jews, and in America too, and probably in my home country of France as well. Maybe those are descendants of the people who shivered in Russia, but I don't know if you can say that it's the same people.

No, no, it's definitely dead. The Czar won. And the Cossacks and Hitler and Stalin. The only Jews they left us think the Jewish soul is to be found in compliance with dietary rules.

The secularizing of Judaism is the idea that people are more Jewish in Israel than in the Diaspora. I love Israel, because it's a beautiful country and I have family there, but give me a break! Israel is the opportunity to transform my fellow Jews into ordinary people: Jewish farmers with a fence around their field, with an army — regular people, in fact. From a quality of life standpoint that's a good thing, but I don't see what I have in common with them. They are far less Jewish than I am.

A Jew who has nothing else to do but protect his land, that's a bit too much like a Pole. Not that I mean to detract in any way from the merits of Poland. Everyone should be entitled to be in an old country, to own one's land, to place one's trust in priests, to want to live in peace within secure and recognized borders. Humanly and politically, that's a beautiful project. It so happens that it's the opposite of what my ancestors have been doing since the destruction of the Temple of Jerusalem.

II

People who don't like Jews

never asked them to do anything else: go home! And live like everyone else. And forget your dreams and your ecstasies and your wanderings.

When my grandfather had to leave Ukraine, in the 1930s, to come study medicine in France, his rabbi summoned him. I tell this story because it's the only anecdote he used to repeat concerning his rabbi. This took place in Bolekhov, near Lvov:

He was my master from childhood, you understand; I was his Talmud prodigy, his favorite student.

Before we found out I'd be able to study in France, my entire community expected me to become a rabbi.

And on the eve of my departure, the Rav summoned me and closed the door to his office and made me sit next to him.

I expected a present or a blessing.

Instead of that, he looked me straight in the eyes and said: "You know, Arthur, eating kosher, wearing the talith and the yarmulke, all that was good while you were in Poland. Now, you're going to France, to a civilized country, so over there you have to behave like the French." And he insisted a lot that I observe this commandment.

III

And the more my grandfather studied medicine, the less he wanted to be a rabbi. One day he said to me:

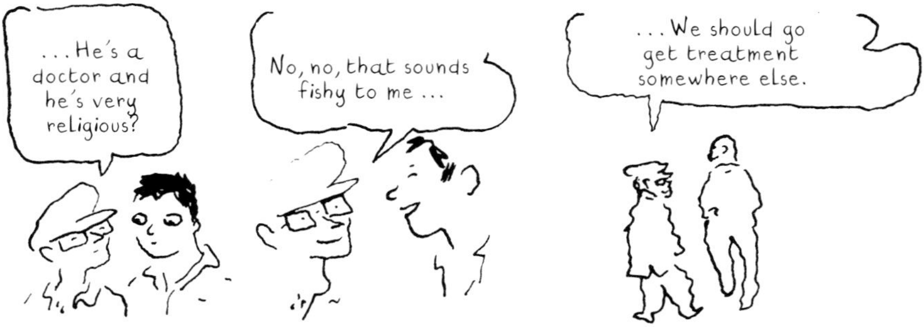
...He's a doctor and he's very religious?
No, no, that sounds fishy to me...
...We should go get treatment somewhere else.

But my grandfather died speaking Hebrew, repeating endless psalms that he knew by heart. My Aunt Saby and I listened to all that, and to this sentence in French he repeated over and over, because breathing was so difficult:

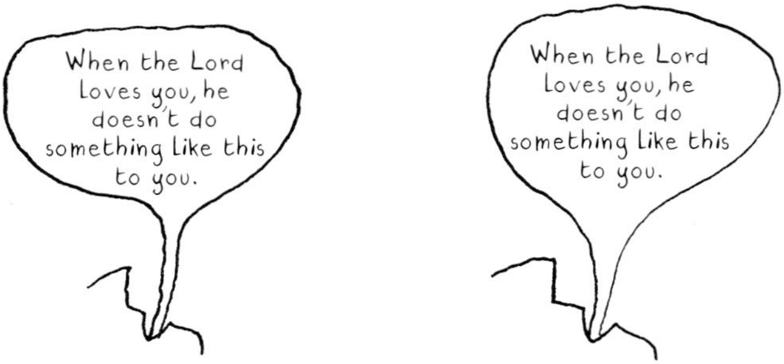
When the Lord loves you, he doesn't do something like this to you.
When the Lord loves you, he doesn't do something like this to you.

If Judaism can be found somewhere it's in those paradoxes.

If I'm my grandfather's student, I can't join the camp of those who try to make Judaism sensible. Finding a place for Jews, explaining how to be a good Jew, that's not Jewish at all. Believing that the Bible will solve men's problems, that's good for the Vatican.

saying that you've been in mourning since the destruction of the Temple and that life doesn't last long and it's sad but that perhaps one day the Messiah will come, and all the while implying that he won't but that you should still await him expectantly, that's more to my liking.

And watching over the dead. I'd want to take the Jews from my village and bring them to safety inside my paintings, Chagall used to say.

* Can you sing the lore of a place that no longer exists (without seeming like an archaeologist)?

* "How can you give klezmer a street credibility?"

— as the Amsterdam Klezmer Band put it.

For example, if somebody today once again did oil paintings describing life in the shtetls, it wouldn't be worth much. We'd think, and rightly so, that all that has already been done. It would be like those painters who sell their work at Jewish community events: they think what they're doing is Chagall-quality, but the truth is their pictures aren't worth much more than those Nativity-scene figurines they make in Provence. The reason is that painters who do that behave as though nothing had happened. They behave as though they still lived in a shtetl, as if Hungary, Poland, Lithuania, Russia, Germany, Austria, Ukraine, still had violin-playing and pickle-eating Jewish communities.

If you realize that that world is dead, you can probably give klezmer songs a value that goes beyond folklore.

V

There are musicians inside a broken-down caravan. They are dead and the snow covers their corpses. I shiver and risk a hand inside their caravan. I borrow a banjo from them and start to play their songs. Because it's too cold and I can't bury them I sing their song instead of saying the prayer for the dead. I'm sure they'd prefer to see their instruments survive.

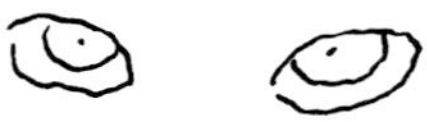

Young Yaacov looks like the animal I draw in "The Rabbi's Cat."

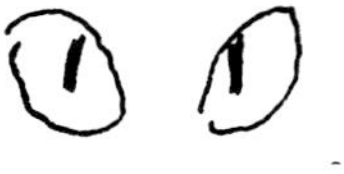

They have the same way of looking at people and things. When I make them talk, it's the same voice that I hear. It's as if the cat had become a human boy. And he makes use of those privileges of being a man: he talks without concealing his private intentions any longer. The simple reason being that everything becomes tougher when the weather's colder. Yaacov is a bit like the cat would be if he was no longer afraid of hurting the people he loves.

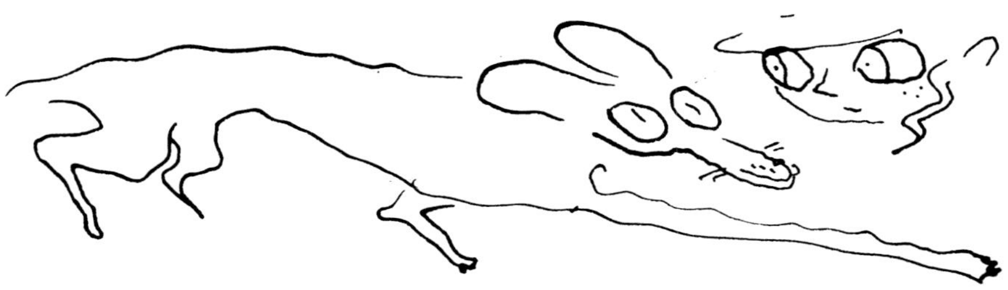

*And the girl — is she the same one as in "The Rabbi's Cat?"

Oh no, Zlabya's a woman of her day and age, she obeys her dad, she's no revolutionary; whereas Chava is a snow leopard.

*Oh yeah? They look exactly alike and you didn't do it on purpose?

Yes, it's on purpose. It's as though the same person had been born in two different places and that had given rise to a different individual. For the same reason that I mentioned earlier: in a colder environment, you develop more of a fighting spirit.

I think North African Judaism was fairly tolerant and enlightened. In my impression of it at least, you find less misogynistic ways and less rigor than in Eastern communities. Zlabya has fewer reasons to run away from her home than Chava does.

Those two girls aren't the same character, but they share the same soul. They're the same actress in two different roles.

Maybe it makes sense to read "Klezmer" and "The Rabbi's Cat" together. Klezmer is the flip side of the story. The Cat was for my dad's family.

My mother's family is a snow-covered desert. My grandpa and grandma told me lots of stories, but never about their ancestors. I don't know anything about Poland or Ukraine. I stick all that in the same drawer as "it's a big secret but I don't remember much about my Mommy."

Today I know that it's very fortunate, if you want to tell stories, to have memory lapses.

VII

* <u>In "Klezmer," the heroes are not religious.</u>

If you take Jews and remove the Jewish religion from them, are they still Jews?

In "The Rabbi's Cat," they are constantly going on about God. Not so here. Yaacov tries his best to be a bad Jew, Vincenzo lives with the terror of his yeshiva experience, Chava hates the backward traditions of her shtetl, and the Baron of My Backside tries hard to forget his dead. They make a fine gang of freethinkers! They know you have to make your way in life alone.

I believe God loves those moments when we do without him. He thinks, "At last, they're going to stop walking around with their nose up in the air awaiting some supernatural magic; they're going to watch the snow and the trees and start to think a bit. They're doing the job without me, inventing utopias that don't have me as their essence; they are finding within themselves the reason for all things. In fact, without realizing it, they are understanding my Law, for it is the Law of the world."

They are behaving like the student learning the guitar who discovers that you improve more by looking at your instrument than by burying your head in a music textbook.

We always feel a certain sadness when the kids grow up, but it seems to me that the Lord still finds it reassuring when his creatures stop giving credence to pipe dreams. Good parents are glad to see their children become adults.

In the end, what makes those characters Jewish in spite of everything is this awareness of their frailty: nobody's there for them. And this isn't talking only about the absence of God, but also of their social and political vulnerability. They are at the mercy of aggression from all sides. At the time of my story the Jews have no country, no police, no army, and slim chances that any non-Jewish court will rule in their favor about anything. Even their shtetls offer only illusory protection, since they are only tenants in the villages where they live. Russian peasants were able to put up with serfdom because they knew that there was another social category below them: the Jews. It goes without saying that the Gypsies were subject to the same treatment and that even within the European Union today it is not clear that their status has improved radically.

In the major cities of Western Europe, in the shadow of the ideals born of the French Revolution, things were far better. Except for the occasional Dreyfus Affair, the Jews of Paris, London, Vienna could pretty often forget that they were Jewish and dream of blending into the social melting pot. The reason why I find myself drawing "Klezmer" today is probably that I was born after Auschwitz and that I grew up with this worrisome thought: that humanist ideals and utopias of equality for all citizens are revocable at any time.

* <u>What branch will I grab on to if it starts up again?</u>

Some will answer: "I'll take off to Israel." Others, and I'm one of them, prefer to brandish the shield of the French Republic, even to the point of absurdity. Still, in Israel you have tanks on every street corner and in the Diaspora you have a police car in front of each synagogue. We've been trained to accept the idea that going to pray in a Jewish temple today still depends on police goodwill. And as for the Jewish state, it has only survived thanks to the omnipresent influence of its implacable army. And it's not always easy to forget that you're the grandson of someone who was born in a shtetl.

IX

So even if we didn't ask for these memories, they resurface. It's like the black person whose ancestors were slaves a very long time ago and who still feels the chains from time to time. Not out of paranoia. Not always for valid reasons. He hears the sound of chains rattling because some wounds take centuries to heal. The pain gets passed on through the social body, through the blood and the muscles too; we carry the anguish of the dead.

<u>But those who try to make a tool out of this terror inherited from our ancestors, may they be damned.</u>

When Jewish community leaders organize ceremonies to honor the memory of the dead, they fulfill a key educational responsibility. But when fools who have no conscience start a sentence with Auschwitz and end it by lashing out against Arab terrorism, that's an insult to the victims of the death camps. Because no matter how horrific it is, indiscriminate terrorism should never be compared to Auschwitz. When I was growing up, I attended a Hebrew class where we were told that the two greatest enemies of the Jews were Hitler and Arafat. Do those who make those kinds of comparisons dare to look in the mirror? Raising a child in the painful knowledge of his ancestors' history is certainly desirable. But whipping up fierce rage by talking about the death camps and then channeling this rage into contemporary political issues to use it as a tool, that amounts to trampling the memory of the dead.

May the Lord turn away from those who use people's history for their own ends, on <u>whatever side.</u>

☒

At the time of the ceremonies marking the 60th anniversary of the end of World War II on May 8, 1945, France agreed for the first time to speak officially about the Sétif insurrection in Algeria.

My dad, who is from Sétif, called me to say that he was pleased to finally hear people talking on TV about the "massacres" of Sétif. Before that, they were either not talked about or referred to euphemistically as the "events," to describe the fact that the French army indiscriminately massacred 40,000 people as retribution for the murder of about one hundred colonists and for independence-minded yearnings. Honor to France, which at last dares to look its history in the eye.

But as was to be expected, Tariq Ramadan and his buddies took advantage of this to fuel their own agenda and call themselves "the indigenous peoples of the Republic." And to claim everywhere that France today still behaves like a colonial power.

Have they no respect for the countless victims of colonial contempt and brutality?

France today is not the land of equal opportunity for all and racism is a cruel fact of life, just like everywhere else in the world. But to go around squealing that the country hasn't changed since its colonial days amounts to spitting on the memory of those who truly experienced the yoke of colonial imperialism.

The purpose of memory is not to claim victimhood, demand special treatment, or ask for reparations. Knowledge is an end in itself. Those who want it to serve some purpose have no conscience and despise their dead. But maybe it's OK to sing old songs.

XI

True to the idea that you're better off practicing useless activities than doing harm, I put my memories into klezmer songs. They're better off there than elsewhere. Those are Jewish voices, but they don't speak only to Jews. I think back about Shostakovich, who for years carried around in his suitcase his Opus 79, "On Jewish Folk Poetry." And each time Stalin or the others would forbid him to present it. I think about Isaac Babel, whose short stories on Odessa were scattered, banned, lost. I love that mad project they had, of getting people to like the Jews.

I think human populations need friendship. When men sense that they are not liked, they invent the blues or Gypsy music or klezmer.

That's how they make their condition understandable to others. Their language then reaches out to everyone and from within the most self-contained communities rises a universal song. Extending a hand to your neighbor is a momentous thing, in fact.

The fact that klezmer is still played today, and with such gusto, and with so many non-Jews on stage and in the audience—which is great—says that plenty of people are willing to carry a bit of Jewish memory on behalf of the Jews. And as a result, klezmer is no longer music that is played by Jews for Jews.

That gets us out of the realm of folklore; we all dance together while drinking up a storm, we have fun. From a personal standpoint, I ask for nothing more.

XII

The idea of doing a musical graphic novel

appeals to me hugely, because the graphic novel is a world of silence. Cartoonists like Pratt or Blutch or Sempé who have tried to stage music push the reader into the ropes. They convey an order that the reader must reawaken his poetic imagination and manufacture silent music while reading, as though their drawings provided a kind of musical score.

Like theater with its audience, the graphic novel asks a lot of the reader. To read a comic, not only do you need an active imagination, but you must also accept a whole array of conventions that are inherent to the genre. Whereas a spectator at the movies is a lazy creature that is only asked to plop its buttocks down in a seat and consume what is served. Those who prefer graphic novels or the theater are harder workers. These people accept that one actor can do all the voices, pretend not to see the backstage area, believe in the masks that are waved in front of them, enter into a succession of events governed by a clock that is not the timing of our world. They truly are good customers.

But leaving aside these thoughts on the silent melody of drawing, I must now list my sources: the songs mentioned in this book are among the most frequently played tunes of the klez-mer repertory. Below, I provide references to records in which they can be heard. Of course, there are tons of other versions. The forthcoming volumes in this series will probably provide an opportunity to mention other records.

* At the beginning of the book, I'm not too sure what tune the Baron of My Backside plays with his harmonica. But I imagine that when it heats up it must sound like some pieces from the album entitled "Limonchiki," by the Amsterdam Klezmer Band. They're my favorite group. They know what it's like to play in bars. They sound like a klezmer version of The Pogues.

* "In Odessa," the song that Yaacov butchers throughout the story, was composed by Aaron Lebedeff. You can find an outstanding version of it on the album "Krasbek, Klezmer à la Prusse." This album includes 18 incredible songs or melodies. The musicians put in plenty of balalaikas instead of the instruments you hear usually. I'm no musicologist, but if you can listen to that without feeling hungry for herring and thirsting after a vodka then you definitely don't have a Slavic heart!

* "Beltz," the first song that the Baron teaches Chava, can be heard on the record called "Yankele," by Moshe Leiser, Avi Flammer, and Gérard Barreaux. That album makes you realize how much the guitar and accordion can enhance Yiddish songs. It's a beautiful album but very sad.

* "Tumbalalaika" is the story of a guy who figures that when you marry a girl you make many others unhappy and that he'd be better off listening to music than doing anything irreversible. You can hear that song everywhere, but when I make Chava sing it I'm thinking of the stunningly beautiful voice of the singer in the Maxwell Street Klezmer Band. On their album "You Should Be So Lucky," you can also hear a haunting version of "Shayn Vi Di Levone," the song in the cabaret with the sailors. Be careful, that's a tune that makes you fall in love.

XIV

To musicians who wish to add klezmer tunes to their repertoire,
I must point out some good news: this music is not reserved for
virtuosos. For anyone who is willing to adapt to the off-beat
rhythm, accompaniment seems to me as easy as in the blues. The
melodies often consist of recurrent passages that are fairly short and
easy to memorize; you repeat them to the point of dizziness, changing
the tempo as inspiration dictates. Then all you need to do is
purchase a clarinet player or violinist and let them do all the work.
(I can't blame purists who might find this summary incomplete, so
I'd advise them to buy, immediately if not sooner, Henry Sapoznik's
method called *The Compleat Klezmer*, published by Tara—all the pieces
on the accompanying CD are period recordings. You can hear the
incredible clarinetist Naftule Brandwein.)

Listen, Fabien, it couldn't be easier: I do umpa-umpa with my guitar and you play the piece.

KLEZMER

STUDIES

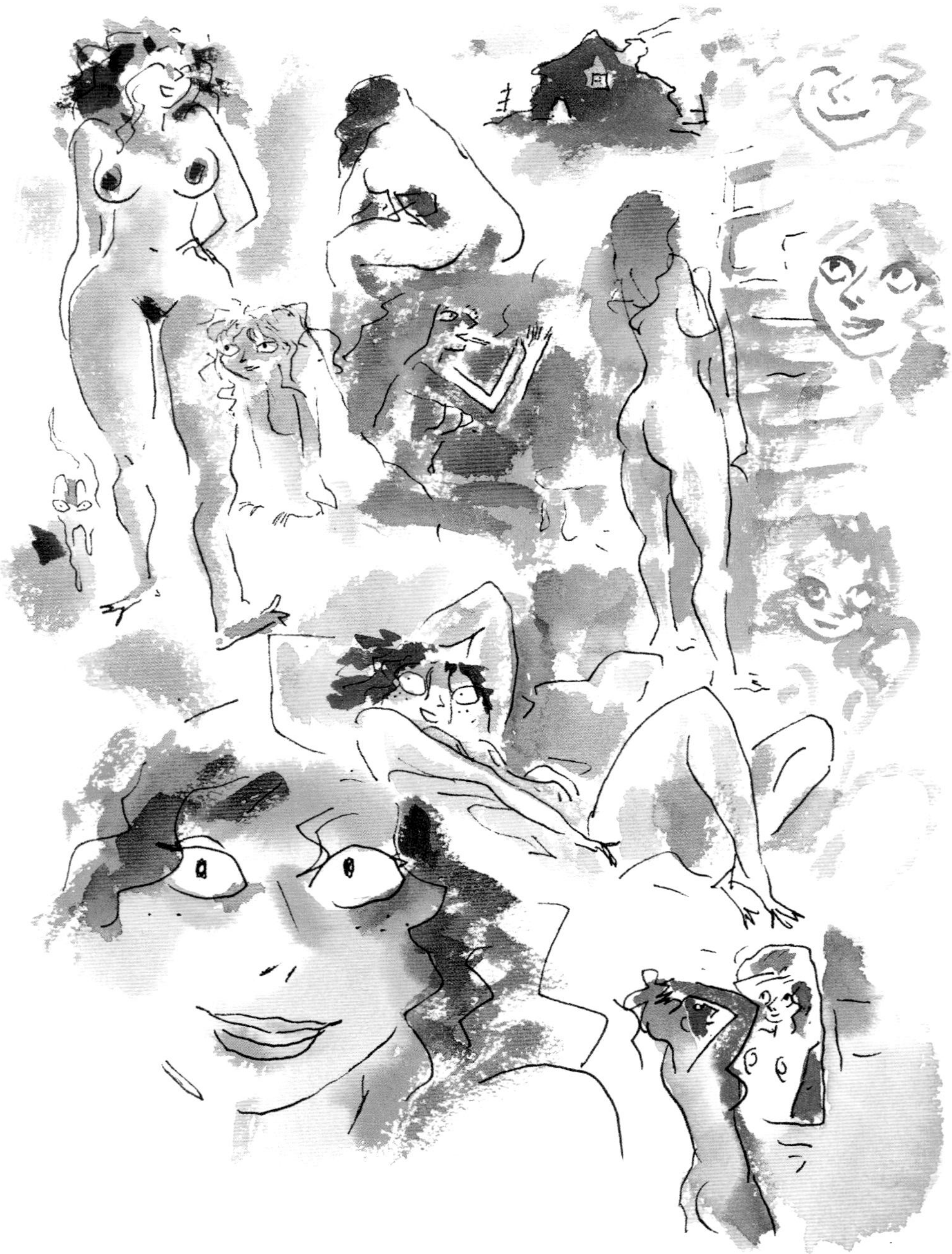

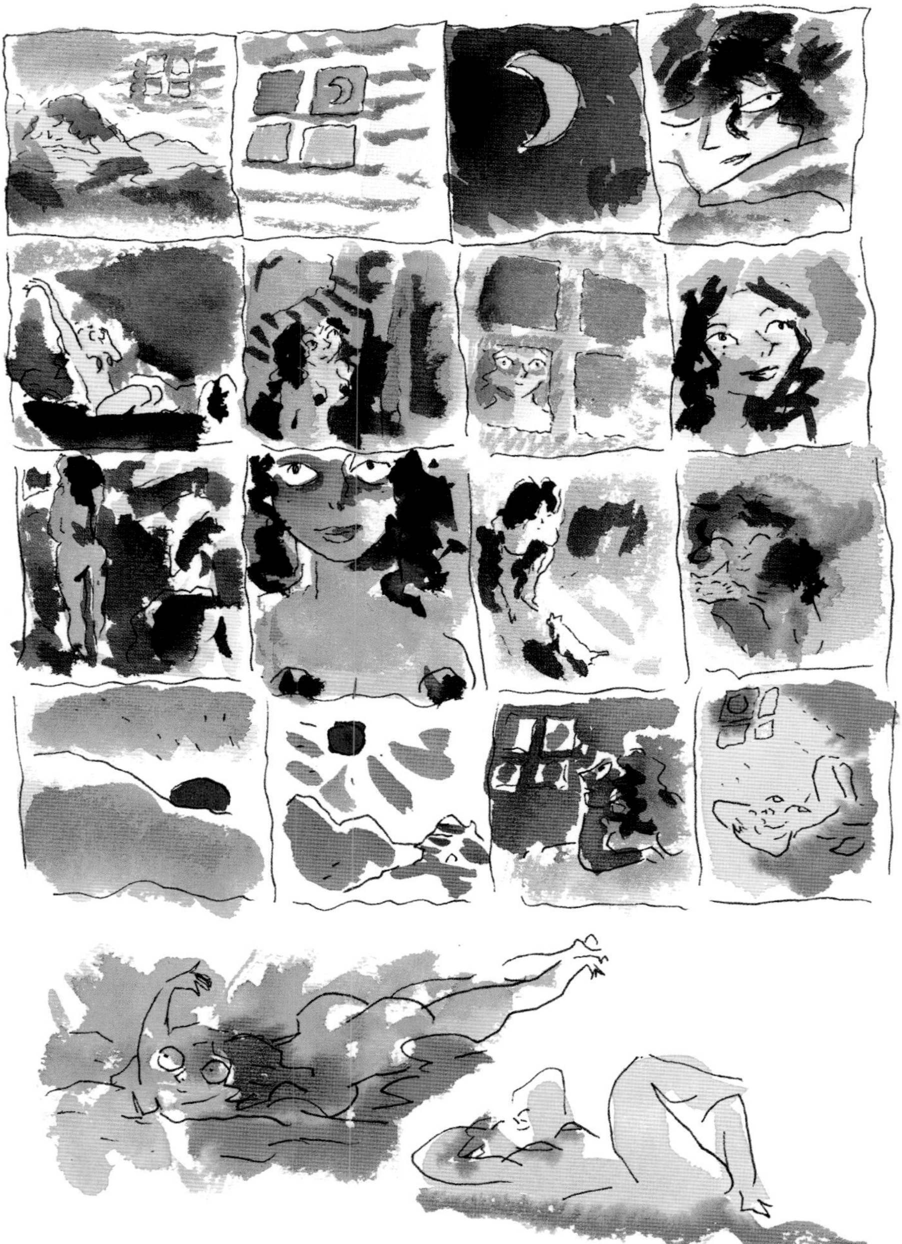

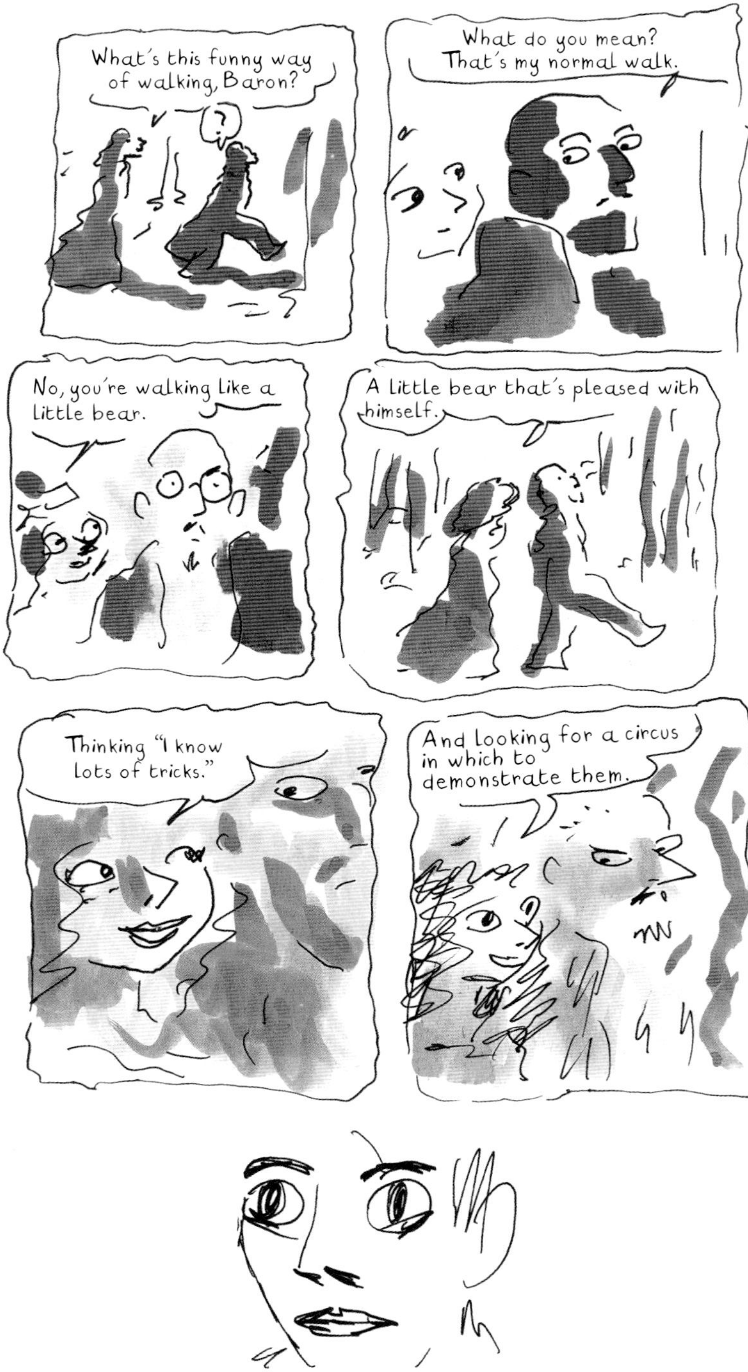
What's this funny way of walking, Baron?
?
What do you mean? That's my normal walk.
No, you're walking like a little bear.
A little bear that's pleased with himself.
Thinking "I know lots of tricks."
And looking for a circus in which to demonstrate them.

It's only very recently that I've learned to draw suns.
Before, it was always moons that I drew.

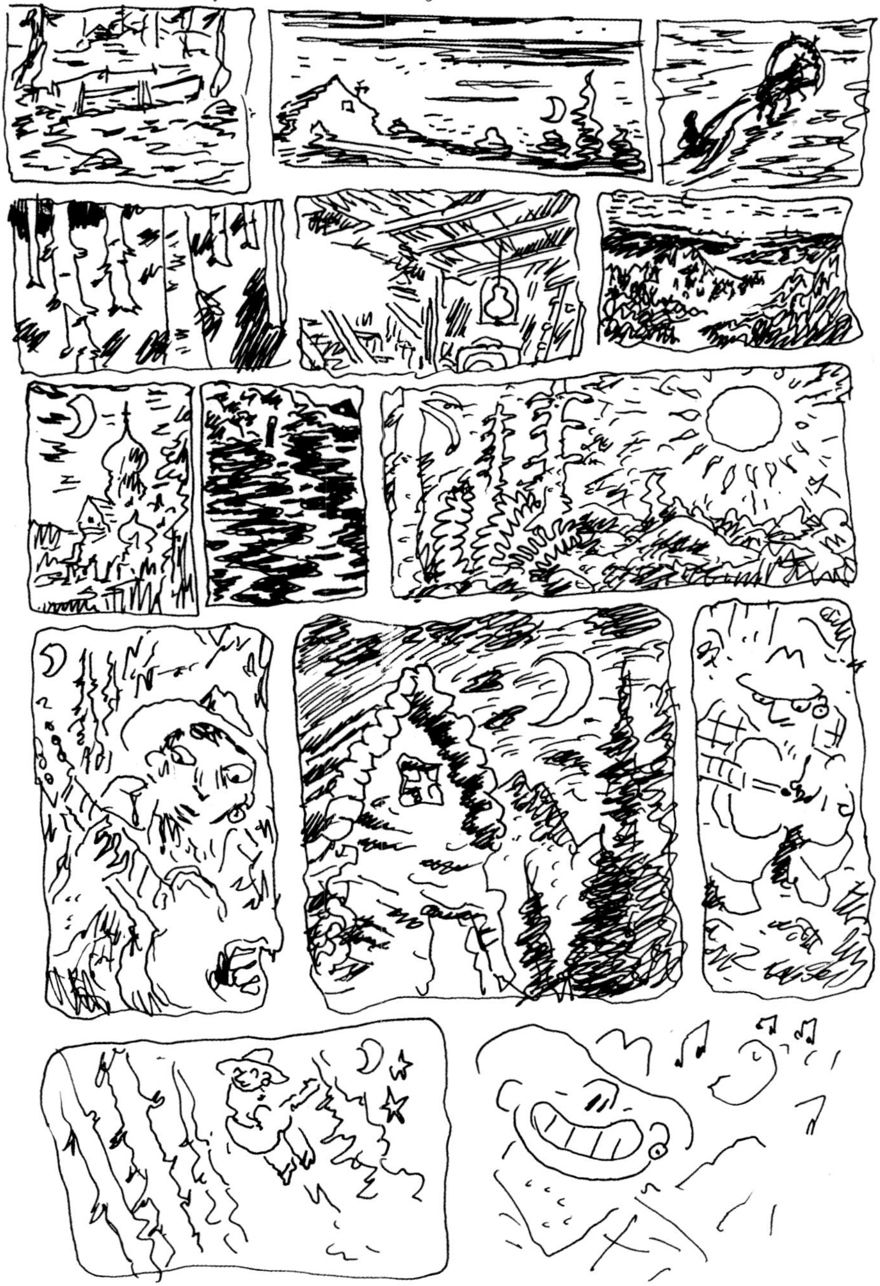

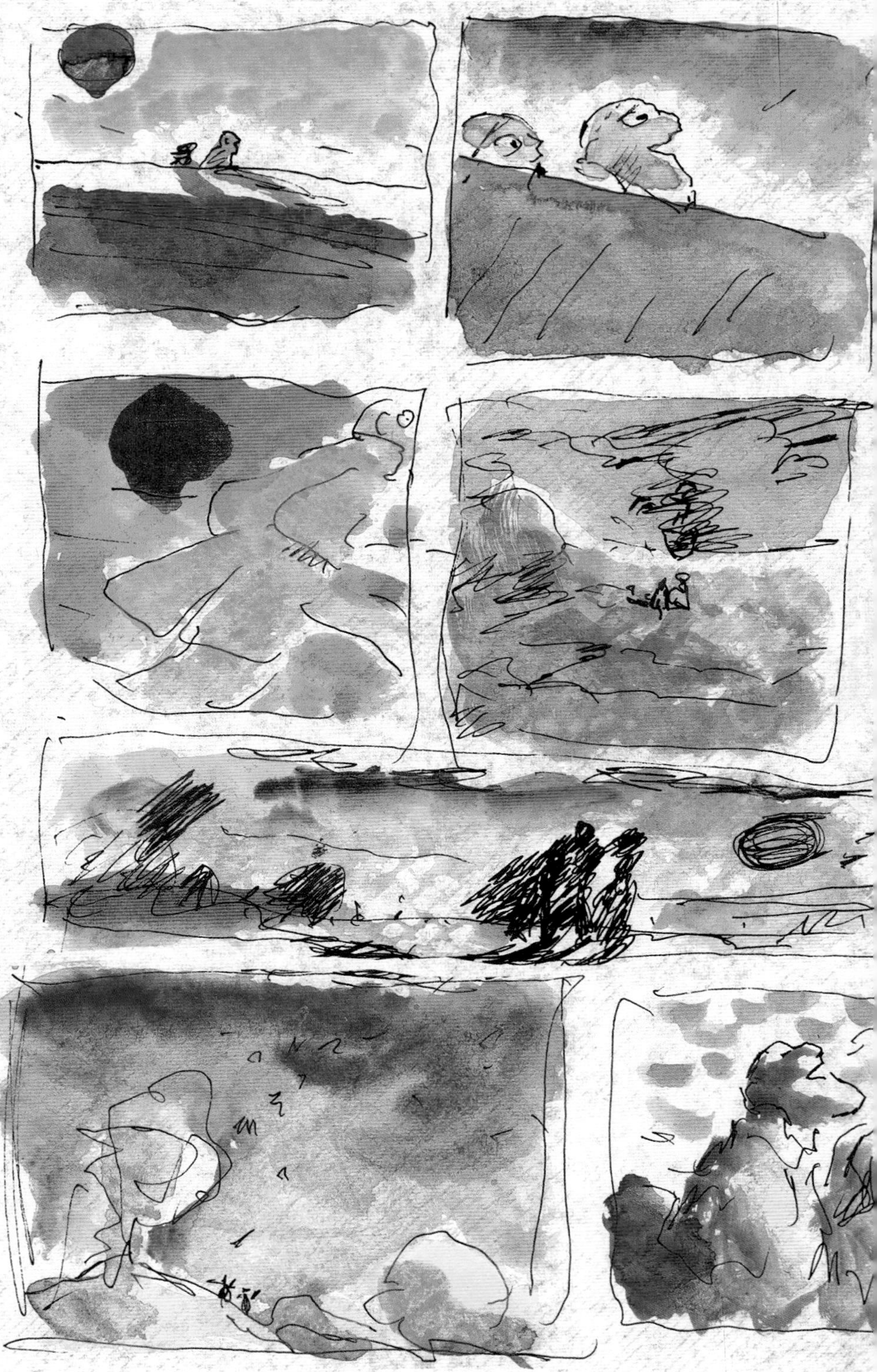

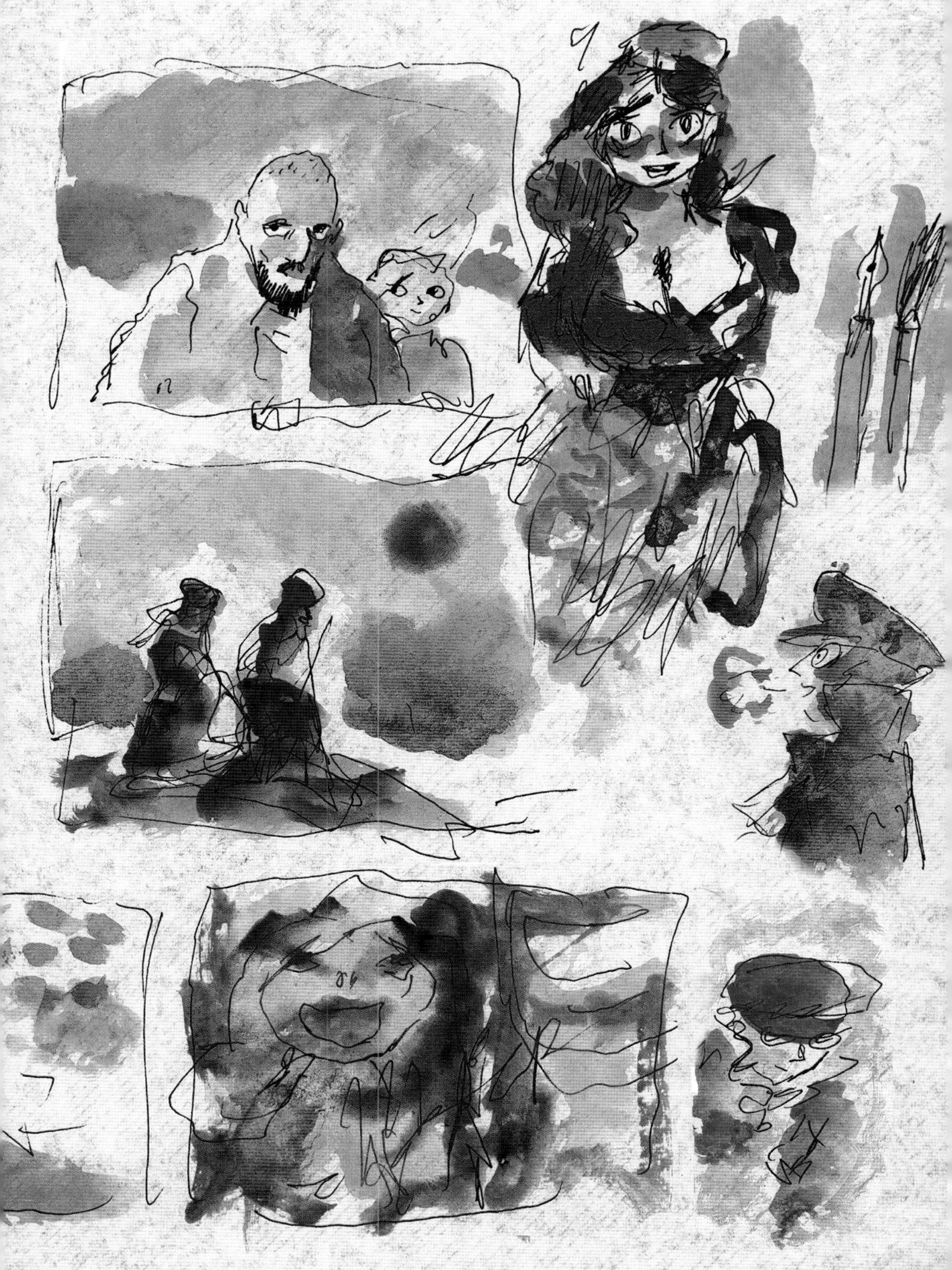

:01
Fïrst Second

New York & London

Copyright © 2005 Gallimard Jeunesse
English translation copyright © 2006 by First Second

Published by First Second
First Second is an imprint of Roaring Brook Press, a division of Holtzbrinck Publishing Holdings Limited Partnership
175 Fifth Avenue, New York, NY 10010

Distributed in Canada by H. B. Fenn and Company Ltd.
Distributed in the United Kingdom by Macmillan Children's Books, a division of Pan Macmillan.

Originally published in France in 2005 under the title *Klezmer* by Gallimard Jeunesse, Paris.

Design by Danica Novgorodoff

Library of Congress Cataloging-in-Publication Data

Sfar, Joann.
Klezmer : tales from the wild East / by Joann Sfar ; translated by Alexis Siegel.-- 1st American ed.
p. cm.
"Graphic novel in which nomadic Jewish musicians meet, clash, fall in love
and make music at the birth of klezmer" -- Data view.

ISBN-13: 978-1-59643-198-0
ISBN-10: 1-59643-198-9

COLLECTOR'S EDITION
ISBN-13: 978-1-59643-210-9
ISBN-10: 1-59643-210-1

I. Siegel, Alexis. II. Title.
PN6747.S48K54 2005
741.5'944--dc22

2005034660

First Second books are available for special promotions and premiums.
For details, contact: Director of Special Markets, Holtzbrinck Publishers.

First Edition September 2006

Printed in China

10 9 8 7 6 5 4 3 2 1